Spirit of Place

The Petroglyphs of Hawai'i

Every continent has its own great spirit of place . . . . Different places on the face of the earth have different vital effluence, different vibration, different chemical exhalation, different polarity with different stars: call it what you like. But the spirit of place is a great reality.

—D. H. Lawrence

Georgia Lee and Edward Stasack

Spirit of Place: The Petroglyphs of Hawai'i

Georgia Lee and Edward Stasack

To Cynthia + John with best wishes — Aloha nui!

Georgia Lee

EASTER ISLAND FOUNDATION
LOS OSOS, CALIFORNIA

Georgia Lee and Edward Stasack

Spirit of Place: The Petroglyphs of Hawai'i

Published by the Easter Island Foundation

First printing 1999, second printing 2000.
Copyright © 2000 Easter Island Foundation

ISBN: 1-880636-14-X

Front cover photograph of Puakō: Wally MacGalliard

 BEARSVILLE PRESS
PO BOX 6774
LOS OSOS, CALIFORNIA 93412-6774
FAX (805) 534-9301;
EMAIL: rapanui@compuserve.com

To the memory of J. Halley Cox, and to all Hawaiians—past and present. We acknowledge the example set by Protect Kahoʻolawe ʻOhana, and others who recognize the spirit of place embodied in the sites and born in the expanses of pāhoehoe: a gift of the 400,000 gods, the 40,000 gods, the 4,000 gods.

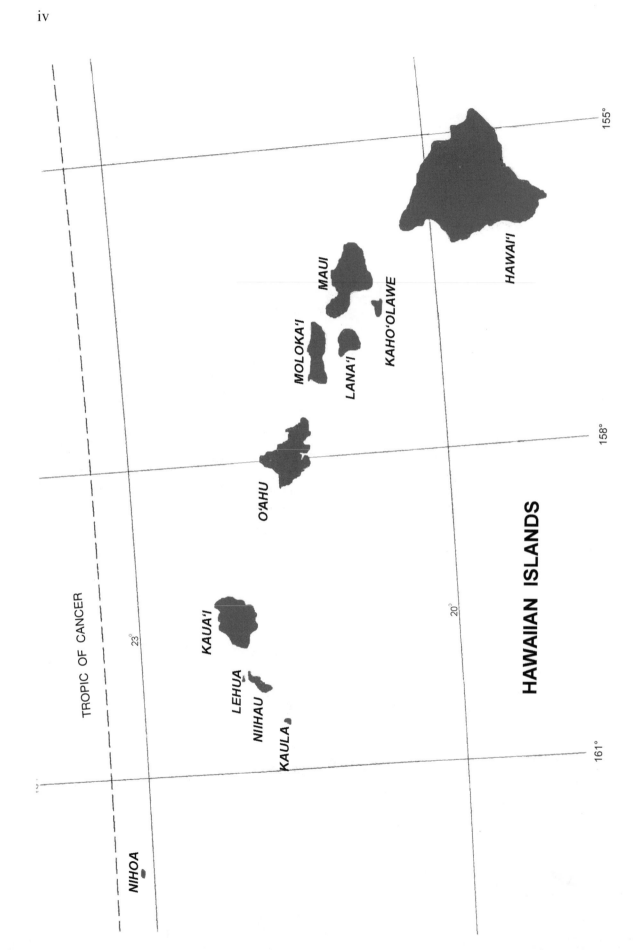

HAWAIIAN ISLANDS

CONTENTS

ACKNOWLEDGEMENTS

Halley Cox and I [E.S.] were thinking of and talking about this book even as we were working on *Hawaiian Petroglyphs* (1970) which we considered as an introduction or a primer. It thus seems appropriate to begin these acknowledgments with a statement of my debt to Halley, who opened my eyes to the wonder of the petroglyphs. Next, to Dr Georgia Lee whom, before we had met, Halley and I had constructed in imagination in order to satisfy the need for an archaeologist with the appropriate skills of the discipline, and two more major attributes: an unconditional love of petroglyphs and statistical facility. These Georgia has.

Over the years, support for the preservation and proper appreciation of the petroglyphs came from diverse sources: Dr William Bonk, O. A. Bushnell, Jean Charlot, Alika Cooper, Roger Dell, Sam Elbert, Bob Goodman, Dr Paul Faulstich, Joe Feher, High Chief Apelu Galea'i, Hui O Petroglyph, Rocky Jensen, Dr William Kikuchi, Tom Klobe, Iolani Luahine, Joanne and Gordon Morse, Greg Owen, Dwight Hamilton, Alfred Preis, Rowland Reeve, Alan Saunders, John Slivon, Juanita Vitousek, Herb Warner, Jeanne Wiig and, realistically, too many others to mention. My heart and gratitude go out to the above and to the unnamed—who know who they are—and to Dr Diane Miura Stasack, the best friend and observer imaginable.

The authors are grateful to the editors of the Easter Island Foundation as well as those who read and commented on various versions of the manuscript. These include Gordon Morse, Antoinette Padgett, and Dr Alan Watchman. We thank Dr Terence Barrow, Mark Blackburn and Wally MacGalliard for their contributions. Of course, friends and associates have no responsibility for the interpretations and syntheses of their input which appear in this book.

We wish to express our particular appreciation to those who helped directly in the rock art projects covered in this book and/or to the many whose indirect help was almost as necessary. Among these are Rubellite Kawena Johnson and Dr John Charlot, who provided information on Hawaiian culture; Dr Ronald Dorn, who headed the dating of the Kaho'olawe petroglyphs; Nancy Morris, of the Hamilton Library, University of Hawai'i; the Bishop Museum Archives for permission to reproduce two of Kenneth Emory's early photographs; Dr Rita Knipe; Leilani Hino, and the late Francine Duncan of Mauna Lani Resort; Fred Duerr, Nancy Ginter-Miller, Leina'ala Lighter, and Lani Opunui-Ancheta of the Kona Village Resort; Dr Gary Somers; Dr Yoshihiko Sinoto of the Bishop Museum; the late Dr Kenneth Emory, who launched most of the ships in Hawaiian archaeological and cultural research; Drs Ross Cordy and Pat McCoy of Historic Sites, Department of Land and Natural Resources, State of Hawai'i.

We are grateful to those who assisted and facilitated our documentation project on Kaho'olawe: the Kaho'olawe Island Reserve Commission;

Kahoʻolawe Island Conveyance Commission; Rowland Reeve, for invaluable help and good company; Frank Morin, for mapping our sites; Lt Vern Young, Lt Michael Nahoopii, and Captain Milton Roth, USN for assistance with logistics; and to Hardy Spoehr and the Spoehr Foundation for providing support for the enterprise. Thanks also to the University of Hawaiʻi Committee for the Preservation and Study of Hawaiian Language, Art and Culture, and to Mikilani Ho for her help with the recording of petroglyphs during our first season on Kahoʻolawe, as well as on Lānaʻi and at Puakō, and to Rubellite Kawena Johnson, whose interest in the petroglyphs of Kahoʻolawe helped identify the need for a scientific documentation project. We would like to express our gratitude to the United States Navy for providing access to Kahoʻolawe Island and allowing us the use of their facilities at Hana Kanaia; and to the Protect Kahoʻolawe ʻOhana for sharing their hospitality and their knowledge during our time at Hakioawa. Without the assistance of these groups, the Kahoʻolawe Island survey would not have been possible.

The authors acknowledge the National Park Service, Hawaiʻi Volcanoes National Park, for permitting us to document the Puʻuloa petroglyph site and other sites within the Park. Our thanks to Dr Gary Somers, Jim Martin, Dan Taylor, Jan Keswick, Laura Carter Schuster, Jennifer Waipa, Bobby Camara, and all of those who facilitated our projects.

Georgia Lee wishes, in addition, to thank the University Research Expeditions Program (UREP), University of California, Berkeley, and the program's director, Jean Colvin, for generously supporting many years of field research; Joann and Gordon Morse of Volcano, for their assistance, hospitality, and friendship; Sidsel Millerstrom for sharing her Marquesan petroglyph data; Antoinette Padgett for data entry, and Frank Morin, petroglyph-finder extraordinaire, for his field assistance, editorial comment, computer expertise, constant support and good company.

A debt of gratitude is owed to all the participants in the UREP projects who worked so diligently under difficult conditions and a blazing hot sun: George and Ana Berry; Bettie Bowman; Linda Hotslander-Burton; Helen Callbeck; Milley de Caprariis; Ann Cullen; Joan Dean; Alan Drake; Don and Elaine Dvorak; Terry Eleftheriou; Dr Paul Freitas; Joan Hanor; Mikilani Ho; Bette Hurlbut; Brent Javaine; Curtis Joe; Blanche Lindmark; Ligee Logan; Sue Loy; Jonathan Marget; Calvin and Delores Malone; Mary Martinez Nielubowski; Mary Kaye Mennet-Martin; William Mele; W. B. Mitchell; Anne Moore; Ted Nagel; Frank C. Neal, Jr.; Joellyn Pollock; J. B. Rechen; Robert Rogner; Marion Rozger; Esther and Jack Schwartz; Jill Shimasaki; Sue Ann Sinay; Sandra Snow; Philip Stack; Hal Starratt; Marilyn Garrett Stearns; Dr Ralph and Patricia Stewart; Susana Vapnek; Dr M. R. Vrtilek; Kristi Wessenberg; Dr Eva Weiler; Christopher Windle; Marianna Wolfe; and Barbara Zeff.

PROLOGUE

The authors of this landmark book, *Spirit of Place: Petroglyphs of Hawai'i*, are both established authorities who have, by dint of arduous field work and academic pursuit, produced the best and one might say 'only' area books on the subject. In the corpus of literature on Polynesian petroglyphs their two books stand alone: I refer to Georgia Lee's *The Rock Art of Easter Island: Symbols of Power, Prayers to the Gods*, published by the Institute of Archaeology, University of California, Los Angeles, 1992; and Edward Stasack's *Hawaiian Petroglyphs* (with J. Halley Cox), published by the Bishop Museum Press, Honolulu, Hawai'i, 1970. Both of these publications are models of what can be done in the realm of describing and commenting on the rock art of Polynesian islands.

It is fortuitous that these two experts, Georgia Lee and Edward Stasack, teamed up to produce the current book *Spirit of Place: The Petroglyphs of Hawai'i*. I know both authors as friends and am personally aware of their having the kind of persistence and hardiness vital to petroglyph fieldwork in the Hawaiian Islands. Also, both are sensitive to the art aspect of petroglyphs, which is a necessary qualification of writers on this subject. Academics are often somewhat blind to the aesthetical side of the subject, including some who write on Polynesian art. Ed Stasack was a professor of art at the University of Hawaii from 1956 to 1988 and is a painter and graphic artist of considerable repute, and Georgia Lee also comes from an art background.

When I speak of the need for persistence and hardiness in rock art fieldwork, I am thinking of my own experiences from the 1960s when I would set out over some barren lava field armed with water bottle, sun hat, art equipment, and camera—intrepid and foolhardy in the face of dehydration and heat exhaustion. The realms of petroglyphs are usually arid regions where rays of the high Hawaiian sun beat down on the lava to radiate like an oven. Most people imagine Hawai'i as a lush green paradise of shady trees and flowers, which is true for many parts, but bone-dry smooth lava fields of pāhoehoe type were the most inviting to petroglyph artists.

Spirit of Place: The Petroglyphs of Hawai'i is in all respects a welcome monograph destined to become a standard reference book. The sites included are described in clear language, while the commentaries are rich in historical details. Congratulations to Georgia Lee and Ed Stasack on a job well done.

— *Terence Barrow, Honolulu, Hawai'i*

x

HOW THE GODS MADE PEOPLE

The great gods came to Hawaii *nei*.
They surfed in the waves.
They rested on the beach.
They climbed the gulches and drank from bubbling springs.
They saw fish playing in the sea.
They saw birds swooping from the rocks.
They saw lizards catching insects.
"This earth is good," they said.
But one thing more was needed.
Kāne took his staff and drew the figure of a man.
He drew it in the red earth of the mountain.
It was a good figure. It looked like a god.
Kanaloa drew a figure too.
The figures of two men lay side by side.
"Change your figure into a living man," Kāne said to his brother.
But Kanaloa could not.
Kū and Lono had stood quiet, watching.
Now Kāne turned to them for help.
"Will you say the word that I say?" he asked.
"Live!" said Kāne.
"Live!" answered Kū and Lono.
Slowly Kāne's figure woke to life.
But Kanaloa's was only a figure of rock.
It was seen for many years—a stone picture,
on the mountain above Mokapu.

—Mary Kawena Pukui
Water of Kāne

Figure 1.1 The oasis at Ka'ūpūlehu with its fine beach and fish ponds was a prime locale in ancient times. It still is today.

Figure 1.2. Wahi pani, legendary places, often are sites where the ancient Hawaiians made petroglyphs. This evocative locale is Ka'ūpūlehu, Hawai'i Island; it contains some elegant designs such as this finely-pecked triangle torso figure.

1

INTRODUCTION

The Hawaiian's sense of place . . . indicates that he endowed the earth with a quality that made it alive.

~Ku Kanaka, George Huʻeu Sanford Kanahele

Hawaiʻi is an archipelago (see map, page iv) which includes an amazing range of climate and landscape. It is best known for its seductive beaches, exotic *wahines* in hula skirts, and lush resorts (Figure 1.1). Many visitors to the islands tend to be unaware of the archaeological heritage that often is represented by a formless pile of stones marking the site of an ancient *heiau* or seemingly random carvings on rocks. Some of the islands' most extraordinary petroglyph sites are given a quick glance; a few photos are taken and then the visitor is off to view something more understandable and less enigmatic, like a volcano. Despite the proliferation of petroglyph motifs on tee-shirts and other tourist objects, the interested observer who desires further information has few sources to consult.

The Hawaiian Islands are the tips of volcanoes, and are graded in age. The oldest is at the northwest end of the chain; the youngest—and still growing—is at the southeast end. Age is reflected in the degree of weathering that created valleys and coastal plains of the main high islands: Kauaʻi and Oʻahu are the oldest and the most eroded. That Hawaiians recognized the age factor is revealed in their legends. Māui used his magic fishhook to pull up the islands—beginning with Kauaʻi. Age and weathering was an important factor for the colonizing Hawaiians who were drawn to areas of deep soils (Kirch 1985:24-26) and age also affected the likely surfaces for petroglyph locations. One reason for the stunning numbers of motifs found on the Big Island of Hawaiʻi surely can be found in the acres of available *pāhoehoe*.

The islands of Hawaiʻi are rich in rock art[1] sites. A few are protected inside the grounds of luxury hotels (Figure 1.2); others are open to the public and receive an inordinate amount of vandalism. Erosion has affected some sites, and several have been lost to developments—bulldozed to make way for resorts or parking lots. Nature itself, in the form of lava flows, has eliminated many.

Hawaiian petroglyphs typically are found in clusters along trails (Figure 1.3), at *wahi pana* (storied places), and in caves. One of the important facts about petroglyphs in ancient Hawaiʻi is that they had a place in the transfer of information. Long distance runners, *kūkini*, carried the news orally, along with proclamations, military orders, and so forth (Figure 1.4). Hawaiians had no literal transfer of information, ". . . but some attempt at glyphic representation and symbolic communication of meaning may be seen in certain petroglyphs which were, perhaps, the closest thing to communication, a beginning toward pictographic representation." (Johnson 1983:1-2).

Figure 1.3. A few sites have trails that lead through the petroglyph areas. This pathway is at ʻAnaehoʻomalu, Hawaiʻi island. Foot traffic over the centuries has worn down the *pāhoehoe*, eliminating some designs.

Hawaiian Petroglyphs by J. Halley Cox and Edward Stasack (1970) introduced the rock art of Hawai'i to the general public. At that time, some sincerely discounted the importance of petroglyphs, believing them to have been created as idle activities without religious overtones. Archaeologists generally gave them slight notice for they were considered to be impossible to date and thus of questionable scientific value.

One of the key persons in Hawaiian studies in earlier days was Kenneth Emory, former chairman of anthropology of the Bishop Museum. Although Emory conducted research in the 1920s, photographing and sketching the petroglyphs on Lāna'i, he considered them as childish scrawls and stated that "The most that can be said for picture writing among the Hawaiians is that it was in an experimental stage . . . . No special significance need be attached to the location of the petroglyph centers . . . ." (Emory 1924:120). This latter statement is at variance with the sites he recorded, for virtually all of them are associated with either heiau or *koa* (shrines). Emory's view of Hawaiian rock art has resulted in another author's description of petroglyphs as 'native doodles' (McBride 1969:46). In fairness, as time passed, Emory modified his views and encouraged Cox and Stasack to write their book, *Hawaiian Petroglyphs*. He also recommended that petroglyph sites on the Big Island (Figure 1.5) should be recorded before their loss or damage from lava flows, earthquakes or tsunami.

In the few other books that exist about Hawaiian rock art, petroglyphs are described as discrete objects and little effort is made to associate them with their physical and archaeological contexts or to postulate how they functioned in the ancient society. Sites have not been compared on an island-wide basis nor island-to-island; rather, there is a tendency to describe the outstanding motif while leaving out the universe of design types at any given site. This has resulted in a misreading of the evidence and has fostered the idea that the petroglyphs have limited meaning and vari-

Figure 1.4. A runner from the Puakō site, Hawai'i island.

Figure 1.5. The great site at Puakō. The pāhoehoe is literally covered with petroglyphs. The area today is surrounded by exotic kiawe trees imported in historic times.

ety, and that the sites themselves are of minor importance.

Times have changed, and the field of study for petroglyphs has grown in recent years: further information is now available about ancient Hawai'i as well as Hawaiian petroglyphs. It is suggested that belief systems—inseparable from the culture—permeate the petroglyphs. The two are mutually intertwined.

The studies upon which this book is based are unique for Hawai'i in that we have complete inventories of the sites recorded, in which all units have been scientifically documented in their context and placed into a computerized data base. The Kaho'olawe project and work at Puakō (Figure 1.6) and Pu'uloa has provided provisional dates for Hawaiian petroglyphs and, if substantiated, this technology will be an important new tool for rock art research in the Hawaiian Islands.

Scientific inquiries aside, the petroglyphs themselves speak to us from the past. They tell us unique things about the ancient culture, for the values of the person who made these images are inevitably embodied in the work. Consequently, so are the values of the culture that engendered them.

The petroglyphs of Hawai'i are to be treasured and appreciated—and protected. Walk softly amongst them. Listen to the *'āina* (land).

Figure 1.6. A fine example of a triangle-torso anthropomorph from Puakō, Hawai'i island. Human figures with triangle torsos are a later development in the rock art. Note the exaggerated leg muscles. The petroglyph in the upper right part of the picture is a deeply pecked "stick" figure.

EARLY HAWAI'I: A BRIEF OUTLINE

The people who first came to the islands of Hawai'i apparently sailed from the Marquesas, but the time of that initial landing is still in question, and odds are against finding hard evidence of that 'first' settlement. Many of the most inviting sites for a settlement are still attractive today, so evidence of early occupation likely has been destroyed by successive layers of occupation. According to Kirch (1985:298), the earliest settlement probably occurred around AD 300. But Hawai'i may have been in contact with the Society Islands or the Marquesas after that time, for oral traditions tell about multiple voyages back and forth. There is some support for this idea from linguistics as well as the two-way experimental voyages made in recent years (Finney 1977). If this second 'wave' happened, it likely was between AD 1100 and AD 1300. As archaeological studies continue, these questions may be answered. But, as Kirch (1985:66) points out, to understand the development of Hawaiian culture we must look to internal processes of change.

When Captain James Cook sailed into the islands of Hawai'i in 1778, he considered them to be his greatest discovery. He felt that in all of the Pacific region the Hawaiians showed the greatest potential for becoming 'civilized,' their leaders being on an equal footing with him and his officers. Cook respected and admired the chief, Kalani'opu'u, and was impressed by the social organization and the control and power of the *ali'i* (chiefs).

Some believe that Cook was not the first to land in these islands. It is possible that the Spanish made landfall during one of their annual voyages from Mexico to Manila—voyages that were made for 223 years before Cook's arrival in the Pacific. Although Spanish sea routes theoretically took them north or south of the Hawaiian islands, vessels could have been blown off course. A Spanish navigator, Juan de Gaetano, who sailed from Chile to the Moluccas on an expedition in 1542, reported "*las islas del Rey*" about 900 leagues from the coast of Mexico (Ward 1967, vol.3:187-195). Cook is said to have observed a piece of a wide sword on Hawai'i for which he had no explanation. Some claim it is of Spanish origin (Taylor 1926:72-73). Stories exist that describe foreigners arriving to the islands, possibly from shipwrecks as early as AD 1555 (ibid.:79).

Twenty-two years before Cook's ships came to Hawai'i, a book was published by George Anson. In it is a chart showing the track of Anson's ship, *Centurion*, around the world in which a group of islands is shown at the approximate position of the Hawaiian Islands. This chart was prepared from the records of the Anson expedition and the islands of Hawai'i were placed from a Spanish map captured by Lord Anson from a Spanish galleon in 1745. William Ellis, the early missionary, noted some traditions that describe visits of Europeans prior to that of Cook, and in 1926 Taylor wrote:

> There is no uncertainty among Hawaiians as to the truth of their tradition that centuries before Captain James Cook, the British explorer, sailed his ships into Hawaiian waters, that fair-haired and light-skinned people were cast upon the shores of the island of Hawaii from a strange-looking craft, and that these people continued to dwell among the Islanders, married among them and became the progenitors of a type of people whose descendants today are of light complexion among the Hawaiians, their hair even slightly reddish in hue (Taylor 1926:68).

Metal was found in a burial dating from the end of the 17th century; cloth similar to sailcloth also was contained in the burial along with a shard of Chinese porcelain and a fragment of a painted fan. These were associated with other traditional Hawaiian items in a burial cave on Hawai'i Island. The non-Hawaiian items may have arrived after Cook's time or may have washed ashore from a wreck but, until they are scientifically studied, the question remains unanswered (Brigham 1906; Taylor 1926; Whitney 1994). If earlier contact occurred, it may explain the appearance in Hawai'i of grand cloaks, helmet-like headdresses, and daggers—items not found in other Polynesian groups.

Aside from such earlier problematical contacts, what we know about the "first" impact with Hawai'i comes to us from the famous navigator and explorer, Captain James Cook. Cook arrived at Kealakakua, Hawai'i, at the time of the great celebration for the god Lono and was immediately taken to be his reincarnation. Every year Lono returned symbolically to preside over a festival, *makahiki*, in which tribute (annual taxes in the form of produce) was collected and the fruitfulness of the earth was celebrated. Lono was supposed to arrive from the sea and thus Cook's circling the island of Hawai'i followed the route of the Makahiki procession. Although delighted by the expansive and tumultuous welcome they received, the significance of it was not clearly understood by Cook and his men. After saying their farewells and leaving for the north, they were forced to turn back when a gale cracked the foremast on the *Resolution*. But it was not the expected time for the return of Lono. Cook's welcome had been exhausted, and subsequent events led to the death of the great explorer (Daws 1974:11-28).

At the time of Cook's arrival, the islands had a population that probably did not exceed 500,000. But the people were not neatly assimilated into a unified and singular tradition: various local chiefs had divided the islands into mini-nations, ruled by four to six rival and competing chiefdoms centered in Kaua'i, O'ahu, Maui and Hawai'i. Moloka'i was at times subject to O'ahu or Maui; Kaho'olawe and Lāna'i were usually under the control of Maui.

At that point in time, Hawaiian society resembled a conical clan of chiefs superimposed over a truncated class of commoners (*maka'āinana*). The latter worked the land and paid tribute to their lords (Kirch 1984:257); in turn, chiefs were expected to take care of the people through rituals and provide subsistence during shortages. However, the burden placed upon the commoners was often oppressive and there were revolts led by junior members of the status groups.

Ali'i and *kahuna* (priests) dominated and controlled everything. *Mana* (supernatural or divine power) was the source of mastery for the ali'i who were believed to be descended directly from the gods. The primary god was Kū, god of war, who represented the male generating power and required sacrifices and impressive rituals to insure success in war. Kanaloa was the lord of the ocean and companion of Kāne, the leading god among the great gods, while Lono was a god of thunder, rain, agriculture and fertility.[2] Commoners in general relied upon lateral kin relationships and concerned themselves with numerous ancestral deities and spirits. They also participated in the makahiki agricultural rituals connected to Lono.

The makahiki had its origins in the first fruits rites of ancestral Polynesian society (Handy and Handy 1972:351) and it was a political means to reward the supporters of the paramount chief.

Ali'i themselves were divided into ranks. A considerable body of priests and other retainers formed a court of the paramount chief; a group of stewards, often lower ranked chiefs, were in charge of administering land segments. An elaborate system of *kapu* (taboo) decreed that commoners had to prostrate themselves before the high chiefs; prohibited women from eating pork, coconuts, or bananas; and prohibited men and women from consuming food cooked in the same oven. Kapu directed daily life and caste relationships and was not to be taken lightly: a common penalty for kapu violation was execution.

Thus the kapu system affected every aspect of life in Hawai'i, from birth to death. Some kapu were instigated by priests who used their power to oppress the lower classes.

The family, the *'ohana*, was preeminent—and yet subordinate to the power of the ali'i. The belief system, in all its aspects and dimensions, was the dominating factor in the life of every individual. The myths lived and legends of demi-gods were a determining part of the culture, providing models for both men and women. Images of these models were carved in wood and preserved in stone as petroglyphs (Figure 1.7). Material goods were few, fine craftsmanship was prized.

Shortly after Cook's visit, a power struggle over dominion began. The political heir to Kalani'opu'u was Kiwala'o, but a nephew named Kamehameha had been given the great feathered image of the war god Kūkā'ilimoku. The stage was set for a battle over inheritance. Years of conflict culminated in the unification of all the islands under Kamehameha I.

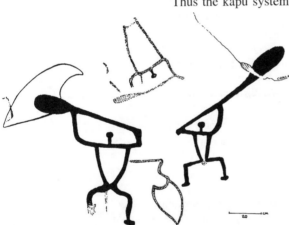

Figure 1.7. Two active triangle-torso figures with raised paddles, from Ka'ūpūlehu, Hawai'i Island, are superimposed over other, fainter motifs.

Hawai'i's political history is complex, with cycles of conquest, expansion to take over neighboring districts, collapse and retrenchment. A critical role was played by high ranking women who transmitted more sanctity in their chiefly lines than their male counterparts (Kirch 1984:254). In the midst of such power struggles, the need for concealment and secrecy is heightened. Hawai'i was no stranger to either: at every level of society there were secrets: of initiation, of ritual, of the men from the women, of the fishermen of one *ahupua'a* from another, and so on.

Thus we see that old Hawai'i was highly stratified, sophisticated and intricate, with ali'i who were themselves ranked and graded from the paramount chief downward. Chiefs had access to status goods; craft specialists turned out a variety of artistic and useful items, some of which are among the most exquisite artworks in Polynesia.

Hawaiian domestic and ritual sites were temporary or permanent, simple or elaborate. A bewildering variety of structures existed; these ranged from simple C-shaped shelters of piled up stones in the form of a half-circle, to thatched dwellings, cookhouses, canoe sheds and massive heiau (temples) (Figure 1.8). More to our interest are the trails which formed an important part of the landscape, providing a link between communities. Many can still be seen today, and at least two play an important role in our petroglyph study (see Figure 1.3). Some trails coincided with boundaries between land divisions, as we will see.

Figure 1.8. The massive heiau wall at Puʻuhonua. This is an excellent example of Hawaiian stonework.

Kamehameha I ceded the island of Hawaiʻi to Great Britain in 1794, receiving help and supplies to build a ship, although he later claimed that he had been promised an armed vessel from the king of England (Daws 1968:38). In 1802 Kamehameha left Hawaiʻi to make war on Kauaʻi, stopping off with his large fleet at Oʻahu. There they encountered an epidemic, perhaps cholera or typhoid fever. It decimated the army and aborted plans for war.

Kamehameha I died in 1819, leaving a soundly-based Hawaiian society. He had managed to take what he wanted from the *haole* (foreigner) and leave the rest. But six months after his death, his favorite wife, Kaʻahumanu, created a new post for herself, that of *kuhina nui*. She persuaded the heir to the throne, Liholiho (Kamehameha II), to abandon the kapu system. By so doing, the ancient religion was ended. Messengers were sent to all the districts of Hawaiʻi and to the leeward islands, ordering heiau to be desecrated and the images destroyed. Liholiho had created a spiritual vacuum (ibid:55).

A new culture moved in assuming the authority of supremacy over the Hawaiians—and proceeded to remake Hawaiʻi *nei*[3] in its own image. The story of the missionaries and the early days of the government has been told many times (for example, see Daws 1968); it is akin to a vast quilt comprised of many actors and actions, a period of Hawaiian history that goes beyond the scope of this book.

Today Hawaiians seek the path to understanding and a rekindling of Hawaiian values, meanings and lifestyle. Without a written history the task of securing a base for this social change is prodigious. There is little on record that is not repeatedly reinterpreted, including the petroglyphs—although these are among the few sign-posts and sources of insight into the culture and that still embody its values, history, and 'story' .

---

[1] Not all rock art in Hawaiʻi is in the form of petroglyphs. Paintings in red have been noted on the island of Kauaʻi; one site is known on the island of Hawaiʻi and the others are found on Maui.

[2] In Hawaiʻi, the four major gods, Kū, Kāne, Kanaloa, and Lono, enveloped the majority of the many other gods. Four (the basis of the principle numerical system) connotes totality: ". . . four is assumed as the lowest class or collection of numbers and the classes proceed in a regular scale upwards, from four to four hundred thousand . . . . " Before praying, the following words were often spoken: *"I kini o ke akua, ka lehu o ke akua, ka mano o ke akua"* [the 400,000 deities, the 40,000 deities, the 4,000 deities] (Valeri 1985:13).

[3] Hawaiʻi *nei*: literally, "this beloved Hawaiʻi").

2

THE PETROGLYPHS

Figure 2.1. Kamoʻoaliʻi: This nearly inaccessible site is said to be a hula heiau. The petroglyph on the wall of the heiau is in an active pose. Note *puʻulo* bundle on the left; such offerings are still made today at many sacred Hawaiian sites.

Figure 2.2. Cave near Kalaoa, Hawaiʻi Island. A long frieze of dancing or fighting figures disappears into the gloom of this deep lava tube.

It is vital that Hawaiʻi's petroglyphs be studied in their contexts, for they are intimately related to their natural settings. The most satisfying examples of petroglyphs are in harmony with their environment and placed aesthetically in relation to rock formations and each other. Negative space as well as positive space is considered. In some cases the petroglyph is an addition, as the image pecked on one of the stones in the east wall of the heiau at Kamoʻoaliʻi, where the heiau is clearly the dominant element (Figure 2.1).

Certain locations were considered sacred throughout Polynesia. These included hills, rocks, caves, odd rock formations, natural markings, and the like. The Hawaiian Islands as well as other islands in the Pacific abound with such sites, and many unusual but naturally-formed rocks are believed to have a life force residing within them, such as *kūʻula*, fish gods. At times petroglyph sites are located in places of great beauty, sweeping vistas, mysterious caves, or where some legend or myth indicated they should be (Figure 2.2).

Petroglyphs were neither insignificant markings nor were they placed randomly in the landscape. It appears they were deliberately created in those places where some ritual was involved, or where the petroglyphs, as prayers or offerings, would be the most efficacious (Figure 2.3). Lava domes, like that at Puʻuloa, became a center for petroglyph making as did lava tubes, such as at Kalaoa. Low

8

mounds of pāhoehoe at Puakō and Ka'ūpūlehu became centers or focal points for petroglyph carvings. Thus natural lava domes and caves were attractive locations, probably due to mythical associations or ritual use. Small humps or bubbles in the lava were particularly attractive to petroglyph makers. Was the choice of location due to a real or perceived break in a feature-less plain of lava, or might there have been earlier legends that brought the site to attention? We don't know the answers but many sites have special natural attributes that surely led the petroglyph maker to them (Figure 2.4).

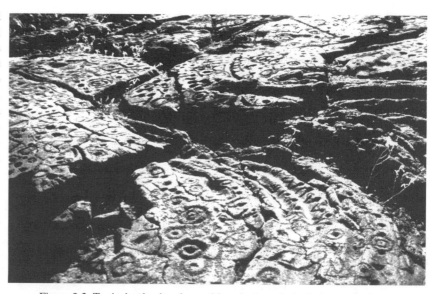

Figure 2.3. Typical pāhoehoe lava with *poho* (cupules), circles, and other geometric designs. Anaeho'omalu, Hawai'i Island.

Different types of rock affect the end result. Pāhoehoe is relatively soft as compared to boulders of basalt and thus the former tends to be more deeply pecked. The crusty surface found in some lava tubes breaks out easily, so that petroglyphs in these locations may be rough in form.

The bulk of petroglyphs in Hawai'i are made by pecking that varies from very fine and precise to bold, rough strokes. Techniques included pecking, and pecking with abrading in order to create deep smooth grooves. Some petroglyphs, especially on dense basalt boulders, are merely abraded or bruised and are very shallow. Occasionally one encounters incising, but these examples appear to be later and possibly made with metal tools. Bas relief, so common on Easter Island, is seldom found in Hawai'i; this technique is, according to Cox and Stasack (1970:61), the 'next logical step' in petroglyph production, so the few examples we encountered were studied with considerable interest. In bas relief, the pecking around a form allows the motif to protrude above the rock. With one notable exception, bas relief petroglyphs in Hawai'i are quite shallow. The exception is a remarkable boulder from the island of O'ahu, now in the Bishop Museum (See Chapter 10).

It has been assumed that superimposition of Hawaiian petroglyphs over older, often badly eroded images was an indication that once carved, the transaction was complete and of no further consequence and that the act of creating the petroglyph was not just the important thing, it was the <u>only</u> thing. This probably is a correct assumption in some cases. Some of the superimposed Hawaiian petroglyphs could be a way of indicating that times and conditions had changed. Overlays, then, may signal evolution.

Figure 2.4. Large sails carved on pāhoehoe with natural "waves" on the surface give a feeling of wind in the sails. Ka'ūpūlehu, Hawai'i Island.

Petroglyphs may have been made exclusively by men since women were severely restricted in certain activities and privileges, particularly in access to sacred sites. Females held an ambiguous position in ritual and hierarchical systems in Hawai'i (Valeri 1985:19). Although constricted in many areas of life, women of royal birth might assume roles of power in the society. Hanson (1982:371) notes that women had the capacity to remove kapu and that females attracted the gods by erotic dancing (as in the maka-hiki festival) in order to arouse Lono so that he might transform his generative powers into children.

While women may have been excluded from sacred sites, such as heiau, the women may have been in charge of placing the *piko* (umbilical stump of a newborn) in *poho* (cupules) that dominate the petroglyph fields, such as Pu'uloa. The piko[1] ceremony itself involved placing an umbilical stump into a man-made depression or natural crack with the purpose of insuring long life.

A scramble to place piko on Cook's ships was described in Dr. Samwell's journal: ". . . the Women seemed to have the chief hand in this mystic Affair" as they directed men to where on the ship they should place the piko (Beaglehole 1967:1225). This recorded historical event was sparked by the arrival of Cook's ships and, as he was believed to be the god Lono, what better place to deposit a child's piko!

Nevertheless, it is likely that men, perhaps kahuna, were in charge of petroglyph-making, and may have stood apart by virtue of their artistic skill and ability to invent images. Boulders and lava were the 'bones' of the land, not to be casually pulverized. Petroglyph-making likely was a sacred enterprise and a "properly" made one—that is, created with the correct ritual prayers and offerings—would have been embodied with considerable mana.

Engaging or commissioning a master carver increased the odds that the ritual would be performed correctly and perfect execution was an absolute requirement for a successful cere-mony. For example, a chanter who made a mistake would be severely chastised because an incorrect action generates an unwanted result. It would not occur to a master carver to make any designs or even sharpen a tool (itself imbued with spiritual power and life) without the proper invocation and prayers that would provide guidance and inspiration leading to the de-sired result. Accuracy dominated religious ethics. The word for fault or sin (*hala*) means error, as in a false stroke of an adze. Should a priest err in recital of a prayer or spell, the effective-ness would be negated and a carving thrown away or abandoned (Handy 1940:319).

A few informants, when asked about the origin of petroglyphs, said that they were made by someone else or they had "always been there." This consistent denial may be due to peri-odic lapses in petroglyph making. Although not provable at this distant point in time, it may be that the carving of petroglyphs occurred in 'waves' with intervals of inactivity. Major trends may be introduced by particularly gifted individuals; temporary retreats into past styles may signify the clinging to old traditions.

PRIOR ROCK ART RESEARCH

Hawaiian petroglyphs were mentioned in various archaeological surveys, but these sel-dom were comprehensive studies. One by Bonk was an early effort to photograph the entire site at Pu'uloa, in Hawai'i Volcanoes National Park. Another project at Puakō by the Bishop Museum, also on the Big Island of Hawai'i, sketched the petroglyphs from photographs (see Chapters 3 and 7). These undertakings were ambitious but not fully successful: the Pu'uloa project was not completed, and drawings from photographs contain serious errors. Earlier documentation efforts at Puakō missed some motifs as well as several peripheral sites, and drawings made from photographs resulted in problems similar to those at Pu'uloa. As impor-tant as photography is, for purposes of documentation it works best when combined with scale drawings.

These comments are not intended to denigrate earlier studies, but standards of recording have changed. The practice of making rubbings and the chalking of petroglyphs were once common methods of recording. Since they can physically change the rock art in addition to adversely affecting any potential dating efforts, and are often inaccurate, they are no longer condoned.

CURRENT RESEARCH

The Hawaiian petroglyph documentation project was begun in 1988, under the auspices of the University Research Expeditions Program, University of California, Berkeley and, in association with Edward Stasack (Ka'ūpūlehu and Kaho'olawe Island), continued through 1997. The sites studied range from small caves with around 100 petroglyphs to enormous fields of petroglyphs such as at Pu'uloa. Each had special attributes and problems.

When the project began, it was clear that few petroglyph sites in Hawai'i had been studied scientifically. Aside from one site in Kaua'i (Kikuchi 1994) and an uncompleted archaeological project at Kahalu'u on the Big Island (Tuggle 1990), none had been given full coverage which could be interpreted as one-hundred percent of all motifs, drawn to scale, measured and photographed and recorded in their context.

Figure 2.5. A stick figure from Lāna'i. Although simple in form, many figures display movement and personality.

The Hawaiian project followed on the heels of a previous study on Easter Island (Lee 1992). An assistant on the Easter Island project, Sidsel Millerstrom, subsequently became involved in intensive research on Marquesan petroglyphs. Millerstrom not only worked on the Hawaiian project, but kindly shared her Marquesan data. Thus considerable comparative Polynesian material has been compiled. From first study, it was obvious that we were dealing with a different aggregation of design types than is found on Easter Island, but one that more closely resembles the rock art of the Marquesas (see Chapter 11).

As a result of this comparative research, it can be suggested with confidence that petroglyph making began shortly after the Polynesians arrived in Hawai'i; that the early forms (i.e., stick figures) and the images of dogs that we see in Hawai'i bear an astonishing correspondence to similar motifs in the Marquesan Islands. If hundreds of years had elapsed before petroglyph making began in Hawai'i, surely there would be more variation between the rock art of these two widely-separated island groups.

It appears certain that the first figure type for anthropomorphs was a linear archaic style called stick figure (Figure 2.5). Over time, the style for depicting a human form evolved in Hawai'i, and a triangular-torso body type developed (Figure 2.6) (a stylistic evolution that did not happen in the Marquesas). The triangle figure may have appeared around AD 1400-1600, possibly due to a new concept in the society. Dates calculated for the lava flow at Pu'uloa (Holcomb 1987; Ladefoged, et al., 1987) give us a general period for initial use of that site. Those dates coincide with our intuitively determined time-frame for the site, based on figure types and weathering. The Hilina Pali site (Cleghorn 1980) and Kalaoa Cave (Hammatt and Folk 1980) both have revealed dated stratigraphy in association with figure types that supports this sequence of development.

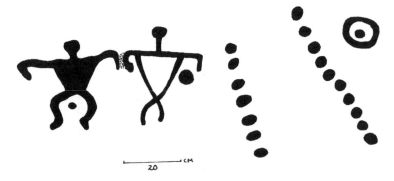

Figure 2.6. Two triangle torso figures from Pu'uloa, Hawai'i Island. One is solidly pecked, the other in outline. Individual cupules (poho) are associated, as well as those that form two lines. A cup-and-ring motif is on the right.

The next progression in figurative representation was the addition of muscles. Muscled figures clearly are later and lend bulk and character to the anthropomorphic images. Some have all the extremities muscled; a few also have muscles shown across the chest (Figure 2.7). These could be efforts to depict warriors or status indi-

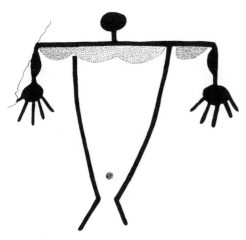

Figure 2.7. A muscled figure (130 x 135 cm) from Puakō has pectorals as well as muscled arms. Note the out-sized hands and fingers. This figure form is known as "open base".

viduals and are a variation on the theme of triangle forms. Many exhibit very fine pecking and nuanced edges suggesting that skillful craftsmen were at work. Some bear a close resemblance to the well-known sculptures in human form, carved in wood.

Excluding modern graffiti, the apparent final phase in petroglyph making was 'copperplate' lettering (Figure 2.8). The source of this kind of lettering is obvious; it resembles the early printed material brought to the islands by missionaries. Several examples of copperplate lettering in Hawai'i show the letters in reverse order, like mirror writing. This can be explained by practicalities among 19th century Hawaiians: Often a group circled the only copy of a book and students had to learn to read from any angle, even upside down (Rubellite Kawena Johnson, personal communication 1993). At Pu'uloa on the Big Island, a few examples of attempts at script writing are found.

Initial research was begun on the island of Lāna'i. With the earlier study by Emory (1924) as a basis, sites were mapped, scale drawings made, and photographs taken. A tentative typology was begun to help systemize the data and provide for organization of distribution patterns. Following Lāna'i, two seasons were spent at the site of Puakō on the Island of Hawai'i, and several other sites on the Kona side of the island were examined. A working typology was achieved and the entering of the petroglyphs into a computerized data base began. The petroglyphs on the island of Kaho'olawe were studied next and finally a study at Pu'uloa, in Hawai'i Volcanoes National Park was initiated; it took two field seasons to complete most of this huge site.[2] The Hawaiian database now includes 31,640 petroglyphs (see Statistics in Chapter 12). This is an adequate size from which to make concrete statements in regard to the rock art of Hawai'i.

Although petroglyph sites on Kaua'i, O'ahu, Moloka'i and Maui have not been formally documented, most sites have at least been viewed by one or both authors. Thus the reader should note that this report does not encompass all the known rock art sites in the Hawaiian Islands.

This study is the first of its kind in Hawai'i, as it was on Easter Island, in that we documented each petroglyph at the sites that were studied, in their contexts. As the data base increased yearly, unusual patterns of distribution for some of the motifs and sites became obvious. These variations were intuitively felt, but the data base provided real numbers. It became clear that distinct motifs occurred at certain sites. These data highlighted the variations in the universe of design motifs suggesting that we were not only dealing with change over time, we were experiencing differences related to site function.

The collection of motifs that comprise the totality of Hawaiian rock art has much to reveal. (See Chapter 12 for methods of recording, typology, and statistics).

Figure 2.8. An example from Pohue Bay of copperplate lettering, introduced by the missionaries.

FOOTNOTES

[1] The *piko*, according to Mary Pukui (John Charlot, personal communication 1991), has three aspects: the umbilical cord, the genitals, and the fontanel. The fontanel is the connection to the ancestors; the navel to the immediate previous generation (the mother); and the genital *piko* to future generations. The three *piko* locations, in the Hawaiian tradition of hidden meanings, have counterparts. Each person has three levels of spiritual existence or consciousness: the self; the higher self; and the lower self. The self inhabits the body and is recognized as a particular individual; the higher self is that which is associated with the gods, the creator, and the source (*kumu*). Certain analogous relationships are suggested. The self was embodied (given its existence) through the connection of the navel with the immediate ancestor, the mother. The connection to Papa, the earth mother, would be through the lower consciousness; to Wakea, the sky father, through the higher consciousness.

[2] As this book goes to press, the western portion of Pu'uloa field is being recorded by Diane and Edward Stasack with the help of Professor Peter Mills and his students from the University of Hawaii at Hilo, and Rowland Reeve, and with the cooperation of Hawaii Volcanoes National Park rangers and staff from the Cultural Resources Management division. Another 1000 units are expected to be added to the total of petroglyphs from Pu'uloa.

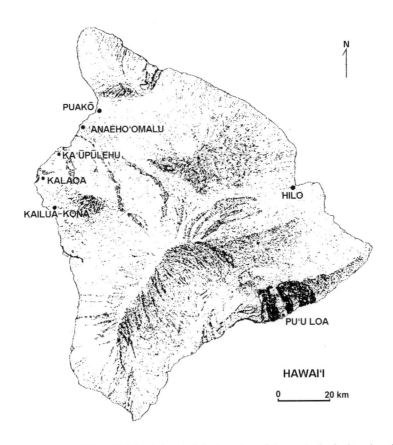

Figure 3.1 Map of Hawai'i Island showing the location of the petroglyph sites described for this island, and their position in relationship to the cities of Hilo and Kailua-Kona.

3

PUAKŌ: HAWAI'I ISLAND

Puakō is located in South Kohala (Figure 3.1), on the leeward coast of the island of Hawai'i—a hot, dry area that contained little vegetation in aboriginal times. Today the area is thickly forested with imported kiawe (*Prosopis pallida*) that forms tangled masses of scrub forest. A reef that runs along this portion of the coast provides excellent in-shore fishing.

Archaeological dates from the southern part of Kohala suggest temporary occupation from around AD 1000 or earlier. No traces of a village have been found near Puakō but Stokes (1991:178-9) mentions three heiau for human sacrifice in this area: Mahiki-hia, Kauhuhu and Kapo Heiau. The last two are names of minor deities. He also mentioned another heiau, Pahauna, for this area. We found no evidence for these; probably all traces have disappeared due to modern-day developments. Without doubt, the presence of four heiau indicates that one or more villages were located in the vicinity.

Some agricultural complexes have been identified inland from Puakō Bay and Kirch (1979) excavated a lava tube shelter at Paniau that yielded a collection of fishing gear, indicating occupation from around the 1400s. A stratified midden has been reported (but not dated) from the western point of Puakō Bay (Smart 1964).

No early references to Puakō's petroglyphs have been found; one mention in Beckwith (1970:350) has the name Puakō in relation to the dog-thief Puapualenalena but this may refer to other places on the island with the same name. The word *puakō* means sugarcane blossom which appears to have little relevance in this non-agricultural area.

The main petroglyph sites, which are some 800 meters inland from the coast, were formerly accessed from Puakō Beach Road. This entry has been closed. Visitors now reach the site through the grounds of the Mauna Lani Resort where a *mālama* (preservation) walking trail has been established. Thus today one reaches Kāeo 1, the main part of Puakō, after a ten-minute hike through the forest from an established parking area.

Puakō's sites are on reddish tinged pāhoehoe that appears to be ancient, and has been dated to around 3,360 years ago.[1] Most of the pāhoehoe takes the form of smooth, low waves of lava but some parts of sites are upraised so that tilted sections of rock have provided slanted panels for petroglyphs.

Previous reports on the Puakō sites were made by the Bishop Museum (1964), Tuggle (1962), Cox and Stasack (1970), Kirch (1973, 1979), Tomonari-Tuggle (1982), and Welch (1984). The Bishop report was the first to suggest that the Puakō sites indicated a trail. However the report also mentions two land divisions and that the petroglyphs might have marked a boundary. Since the publication of that report, the area north of the main section of the site has been called the "Kāeo Trail". However, we searched for any evidence of a trail and concluded that the suggestion of a boundary is more likely correct; there certainly is no trace of a trail northeast of the main site and all but two of the sites are on the boundary between Lalamilo and Waikoloa ahupua'a. The boundary is suggested by a dashed line (bearing 60°) in the 1982 USGS topographical map.

The Puakō sites were given letter designations by the earlier Bishop Museum survey. In order to accommodate additional loci that we found and recorded, these sites were renumbered.[2] All the sites were originally located with compass and tape. Later, four sites, including the datum, were rechecked with GPS measurements.

The location of the Puakō sites are shown in Figure 3.2. The four sites located by GPS are Kāeo 1, Kāeo 9, Kāeo 18 and Kāeo 35. The distribution of these as well as the other Kāeo sites located by compass and tape lies along the Lalamilo-Waikoloa boundary indicated on the topological map by the dashed line. The datum for all of Puakō , 19° 57.46' N, 155° 51.34' W, was located in Kāeo 1 (as shown in Figure 3.27) because Kāeo 1 appeared to be the focus containing the largest cluster of petroglyphs. This datum lies approximately 25 meters NW of the boundary line drawn in the topographic map, a distance within the error of the GPS measurement. An additional 49 small groups and individual units extend a distance of two kilometers along the boundary NE of Kāeo 1 on smaller areas of pāhoehoe or slightly raised lava domes. Beyond Kāeo 39, the lava gave way to soil and no more petroglyphs were found.

A second large cluster of units is at a locus called Paniau 1 (formerly Paniau C), northwest of Kāeo 1. Paniau sites 3 and 4 (formerly A and B), located west and southwest and Paniau 2, 5, and 6, are to the west and closer to the coastline; some are situated at or in collapsed lava tubes. Many of these have been destroyed by construction or vandalism and some were pulverized by bulldozers during attempts to create a firebreak. One additional small site, referred to as the Mālama Trail site, was discovered in 1990 during the creation of a new entrance pathway to Kāeo 1.

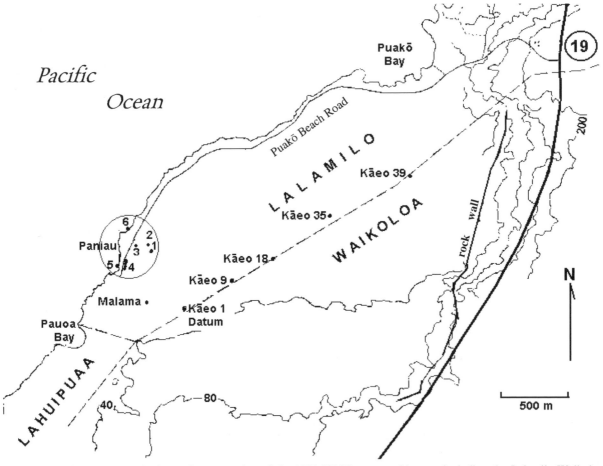

Figure 3.2. This map is drawn from a portion of the 1982 USGS topographic map including the Lalamilo-Waikoloa boundary (dashed lines). Those Kāeo sites which were located with GPS are plotted on the map. It can be seen that these sites lie along the boundary, suggesting that, in addition to other possible uses, the Kāeo sites served as boundary markers.

Figure 3.3. Aerial view of Kāeo 1 showing the west side viewing platform (right center), east side platform (far left) and a scale marked in meters (center). The circle indicates the area of highest petroglyph density. The perimeter of the site is outlined with a low stone wall (Photo: Don and Elaine Dvorak).

KĀEO 1

The part of Puakō known as Kāeo 1 is approximately 2,200 square meters of weathered pāhoehoe (Figure 3.3). It is nearly covered with petroglyphs and appears to have been the 'center' of petroglyph making in this area. The area is bordered by a stone wall erected in the 1960s to hold back wind-blown overburden. Some of the stones in the wall contain petroglyphs. The wall at the south end of the site held back several feet of loose dirt. This wall was removed in 1995 exposing more petroglyphs that had long been buried. In recent years two viewing platforms (Figures 3.3 and 3.4) were constructed on the west and east sides of the site in an effort to reduce foot traffic on the pāhoehoe, and former openings in the surrounding stone wall have been eliminated.

Naturally tilted areas of pāhoehoe form a boundary on the south and southeast borders of the area. These tilted sections are in poor condition and appear to be eroding more rapidly than the level areas (Figure 3.5).

Figure 3.4. Kāeo 1 as seen from the west side viewing platform, looking northeast. The second viewing platform can be seen to the right of the sign. The surrounding low stone wall, added in modern times, is clearly visible.

Figure 3.5. Tilted sections of pāhoehoe were choice locations for petroglyphs at Kāeo 1.

Kāeo 1 is remarkable for many reasons. Not the least is the intensive activity that resulted in the application of at least 2717 petroglyphs in this one discrete area. The most heavily carved is the south-central section that encompasses a slight mound of pāhoehoe located by the circle in Figure 3.3. At first inspection, many motifs appear to be indecipherable (Figure 3.6). It took weeks of patient scrutiny to sort out the individual designs. The intensity of activity suggests to us that Kāeo 1 was special, and most likely sacred. When we observe that nearby surfaces of smooth pāhoehoe are devoid of petroglyphs, it leaves little doubt that some singular activity was focused at Kāeo 1.

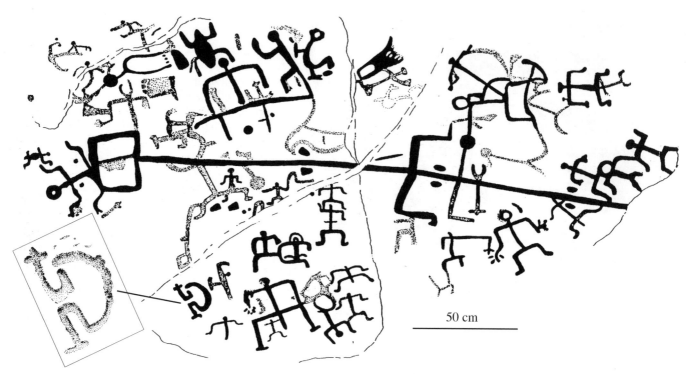

Figure 3.6. The main panel at Kāeo 1 is shown extending over pages 16 and 17. This portion measures 7 meters in length. It is heavily carved with numerous overlapping forms and figures including a long lizard-like form that continues across both sections. Underlying (older) forms are more lightly drawn. This is the area of dense petroglyphs indicated in Figure 3.3 and in Sections 17 and 19 in Figure 3.27. The unusual crouching figure is 35 x 22.5 cm.

The design motifs at Kāeo 1 have certain special features. For example, superposition is fairly common—but is rare at Paniau and the boundary sites. At Kāeo 1, many anthropomorphic figures are "compound", that is, they share arms, legs, or torso lines with nearby anthropomorphs. In contrast, there are many disjointed arms and legs that do not connect with bodies, as well as incomplete human forms. Whether a figure is incomplete or is deliberately made in that manner is subjective; however, enough examples were recorded to give the impression that something specific was intended.

Petroglyphs of human footprints (149 at Kāeo 1; 201 for all Puakō) are prominent; these range from very large to tiny, baby-sized feet. Most are fully pecked out (intaglio). The tiny feet often appear in pairs and when they do, they are usually the same size. Other motifs of feet are pecked in outline with toes carefully delineated (Figure 3.7).

Figure 3.7. Instead of intaglio, this foot motif is pecked in outline. Note the six toes. Petroglyphs of feet with six toes were also recorded on Easter Island (31 x 20 cm).

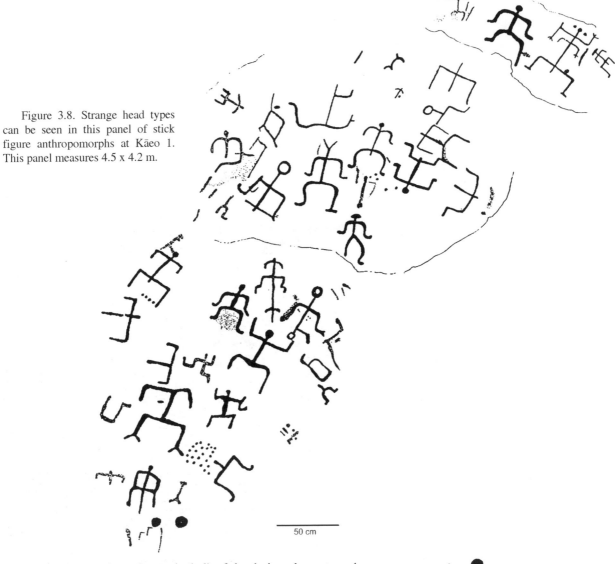

Figure 3.8. Strange head types can be seen in this panel of stick figure anthropomorphs at Kāeo 1. This panel measures 4.5 x 4.2 m.

50 cm

Anthropomorphs make up the bulk of the design elements and many display unusual features such as a dot on each side of the head or neck, or a head that is formed by a curved or forked line (Figure 3.8). Geometric motifs are rare at Puakō. There are some cupules, but in far smaller numbers than at ʻAnaehoʻomalu and Puʻuloa.

The few cupules recorded at Puakō (209 at Kāeo 1) appear to have served some function other than as receptacles for the piko of an infant. For the most part they are quite small and shallow, and may be on sloping or vertical surfaces. Some are parts of figures or are associated with them in some way (Figure 3.9).

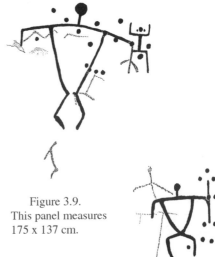

Figure 3.9.
This panel measures
175 x 137 cm.

Figure. 3.10. A female figure (40 x 65 cm) with feathered headdress and prominent vulva. The emphasis is on the face (with eyes) and genitals.

There appears to be a focus on family concerns at Puakō, with figures shown as a unit; smaller figures may be enclosed by the arms of a larger figure. Some human motifs have outsized heads with eyes and several have vulvae. Depictions of vulvae are rare in Hawaiian rock art, thus the examples from Kāeo are noteworthy. These leave little room for doubt as they are placed on figures in anatomically correct positions (Figure 3.10). When Yoshiko Sinoto first saw this site, he dubbed it "maternity hill" (Krauss 1988:357).

We were impressed by the numbers of figures at Kāeo 1 that are connected to one another: of the 1,860 human figures, 463 (25%) are connected (Figure 3.11). Although stick figures are made with few basic lines and may be static, others can be lively and some appear to be dance postures (Figure 3.12). There are only two open-base triangle figures at Kāeo 1 (13 for the entire Puakō area). As for the triangle torso figures, considered a later development, there are only 39 at Kāeo 1 (157 for all Puakō). This distribution of human figure designs is in considerable contrast to the petroglyph motifs at the site of Pu'uloa in Hawai'i Volcanoes National Park.

Figure 3.11. Connected figures are common at Kāeo 1, where figures share arms, legs, or torso line. The foreground figure (50 cm wide) has exaggerated toes.

Figure 3.12. Some anthropomorphs appear to be in a dance or active posture. Note polissoir grooves formed by tool sharpening and smoothed areas where implements were honed (left center). The feet on the image (left) have been partially erased by this activity. The figure in central foreground is 56 x 33 cm.

Of particular interest is the occurrence of profile anthropomorphs (15 at Kāeo 1), with knees bent and in squatting position (Figure 3.13 and Figure 3.6). This is another unusual form in Hawaiian rock art although Kikuchi (1994:27-32) has recorded some on Kauaʻi and others are found at the Puʻuloa site and in a cave in Kaʻū. Note the bird-like characteristics and long arm with three digits. A nearby anthropomorph has a forked head. Other faint traces are associated.

A few motifs are in shallow bas relief. Although not fully in relief, these have sufficient pecking around them to suggest that some modeling of form was being attempted (Figure 3.14).

Figure 3.13. A profile figure from Kāeo 1 (32 x 80 cm).

Figure 3.14. Examples from three different locations of shallow bas relief at Kāeo 1.

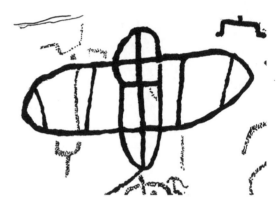

Figure 3.15. A rare image of a Polynesian kite (86 x 60 cm) at Kāeo 1. This is the only kite petroglyph at Puakō.

Only three dog images were recorded at Kāeo 1 (10 for all of Puakō and 11 for all the sites recorded on Hawaiʻi island); this contrasts with other Hawaiian islands, particularly the island of Lānaʻi, which has 105 images of dogs. Another rare image is that of a Polynesian kite (Figure 3.15). Only four others are known for the Hawaiian islands, at Kaʻūpūlehu and at Kaʻū. The kite motifs bear similarities to an extant kite from New Zealand (Poignant 1967); but these examples are unique in Hawaiʻi. Hawaiian legends of the demi-god Māui include one about kite flying as a way to demonstrate control of the wind, or as a means of reaching the heavens to ensnare the souls of those who have done evil (Beckwith 1970:109). The Hawaiian god Lo-lupe was a kite, stretched on a frame in the shape of a fish with wings, tail, etc. (See Chapter 6 for more on kites).

Despite such oddities, Kāeo 1 in general has a strong thread of continuity, lineage, family identification, succession, and perhaps longevity, as human figures emerge from or branch off from a central image. Tiny figures beneath the shoulders of larger anthropomorphs suggest family concerns (Figure 3.16). The numerous footprint motifs, particularly those depicting baby footprints, indicate family or clan concerns. The intensive superposition of designs suggests that the place itself was more important than clarity of the motif.

Figure 3.16. Perhaps these figures refer to parental concerns; note tiny forms below each arm of the larger one (44 x 48 cm).

Figure 3.16. An owl (?) may represent an 'aumakua.

Some images, such as owl (Figure 3.16) and turtle (Figure 3.17) may be 'aumakua (Ho 1988:64). *Akua 'aumakua* were a class of deities related to kinship groups. They could be acquired individually, but usually they were transmitted to one's descendants and thus associated with either 'personal gods', or ancestral deities of a family. Owl is one of the most important manifestations of 'aumakua (shark is another). Turtle is less clear but, as a creature that intersects ocean and shore, it may be a metaphor between the living and the dead (Valeri 1985:23).

Figure 3.17. Turtle motifs are not common in Hawaiian rock art.

KĀEO BOUNDARY

Earlier surveys assigned letter designations to some of the 39 sites that extend from Kāeo 1 (Kirch 1979, Figure 2). However, four of these loci are shown on the early map to be on a line perpendicular to and south of the tribal boundary and extending into an area of *'a 'ā* (rough, broken lava) that obviously could not support petroglyphs. Our survey corrected this error. Only loci 12 and 13 lie slightly to the east. We ran into considerable difficulty trying to correlate the early survey numbers given by the Bishop Museum with the sites we located and, because we found many more sites, we have renumbered them. The only motifs shown on the Bishop drawings that we could not account for are those labeled 'Kāeo F, Part 2, Figure 4G'. These should be southeast of our site Kāeo 14 but we found nothing in that (or any other) area which matches the illustrated figures in the report. Included are '7 units,' three of which appear to be triangle torso figures, one T-figure, two stick figures, and fragments of figures. There is no suitable rock surface where these are presumed to be located.

In March of 1990 a blaze in the kiawe forest brought in fire-fighting bulldozers to cut a firebreak through the area. In one day more petroglyphs were destroyed than had been damaged by years of individual acts (Figure 3.18). The firebreak that was created zigzags erratically through a number of sites leaving a few individual elements surrounded by tread marks. Site Kāeo 28 was nearly obliterated. As these sites had not yet been documented (recording of this area was done in October and November 1990), there is no way of knowing precisely what has been lost.

Figure 3.18. Anthropomorph damaged by bulldozer tracks, Kāeo boundary, Site 28.

The sites that stretch northeastward from Kāeo 1 seemingly had other functions than that of Kāeo 1, and we might search for those by examining the idea of boundary in ancient Hawai'i. In the Hawaiian way of thinking, the word for boundary, *palena,* would have three levels of meaning in addition to a literal one. Breaking the word down, *pā* is defined as a fence or enclosure; *lena* means to stretch out, to sight or aim. Lena also means to bend, which is an interesting modification of its primary definition. A palena thus could be thought of as a stretched-out fence: a boundary.

The concept of boundary has symbolic and abstract potential plus severe practical and psychological connotations. It implies an end and a beginning, separation from something, limits and warnings, and more. In the visual realm it implies edges and contours. The boundaries at Puakō separate the ahupua'a of Lalamilo from that of Waikoloa, and they were kapu. Travel across them was forbidden except during the makahiki (November through January). The boundary between these ahupua'a was not marked in any other way and thus we cannot be sure if the petroglyphs are to one side or the other. Either way, there can be no doubt that the residents of both areas knew the boundary, in particular the residents of the *'ili* or subdivision adjacent to the line.

Perhaps the petroglyphs marked a neutral zone between the two ahupua'a, free of kapu. We can eliminate geological constraints, such as lack of adequate surfaces, as a rationale for this 'line' of petroglyph sites: for tens of meters on either side of the boundary and for nearly its entire length, large areas of smooth pāhoehoe exist—devoid of petroglyphs.

Figure 3.19. Muscled anthropomorphs are more common along the boundary sites. This figure, at Kāeo 18, is 78 x 76 cm.

At the Kāeo boundary (exclusive of Kāeo 1) we recorded 44 loci and 872 petroglyphs. Individual sites have wide numerical distribution, from 1 element to 144. Forty one percent are anthropomorphs. This may be compared to Kāeo 1 where 53% are anthropomorphs and, of these, 2.7% are triangle torso. The Kāeo boundary inventory also contains far fewer 'unidentified' petroglyphs but this may be related to the rarity of superposition: there is less ambiguity when motifs are spaced and separated from each other.

The farther one travels along the trail from Kāeo 1, the higher the proportion of triangular figures vs. stick figures and the more triangular anthropomorphs with exaggerated muscles (Figure 3.19). This fact, and the prolific over-carving, suggests to us that the "center" (Kāeo 1) predates the boundary petroglyphs. More on the statistics of Puakō is presented in Chapter 12.

For the Puakō sites in general, there are enough differences between the design inventories of Kāeo 1, Paniau, and the Kāeo boundary sites to suggest that they might have been function specific, possibly dedicated to special purposes. Kāeo 1 is, of course, the most heavily worked of the three and has a preponderance of the so called "stick" figures. The next largest group, "unidentified" could not be placed into any particular category. The remainder consists of other types of images such as feet, sails, fishhooks, geometric designs, or cupules.

While it is possible that the proliferation of stick figures may have been due to personal preference among the image makers, the evidence doesn't support that hypothesis. It seems that the high point of petroglyph making at Kāeo 1 was, in fact, earlier than most major sites on the Island of Hawai'i and, served a different function than sites that occur on trails and boundaries. However, the presence of Hawaiian names carved in the pāhoehoe at Paniau and at a few sites on the Kāeo boundary, plus the ship motif at Kāeo 9 (Figure 3.20) indicates that at least parts of the site were still used into the 19th century.

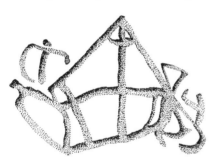

Figure 3.20. An historic ship motif at Kāeo 9 (70 x 67 cm).

Paniau

Paniau is northwest of Kāeo 1. The Paniau sites were divided into three loci and designated as A, B and C by the early Bishop Museum survey.[3] Due to problems correlating our sites with previous surveys plus the addition of other loci, new designations were assigned to these sites.

Paniau 1 is on a large level area of pāhoehoe. Paniau 5 and 6 are at the ocean's edge; the remainder of Paniau's sites are on broken ground, inland from the ocean and in or near lava tubes or jumbled areas of lava, made nearly impenetrable by the heavy growth of kiawe. Portions of this area are now built up with homes and other developments. Puakō Beach Drive is the main access to this area and formerly ended at a turnout just past the old walking trail into the site; today it continues south to a new development, cutting through the sites.

The Paniau sites (including the Mālama trail) have 269 units; 84% are anthropomorphic figures. Virtually all of the others are either in the unidentified category or are cupules. It is fruitless to compare and contrast the ratio of Paniau's figure types to those at Kāeo because so many petroglyphs have disappeared from Paniau in recent years. But by including the information contained in the earlier Bishop report, it is clear that anthropomorphs were the dominating motifs. Superposition is rare. Lines of

Figure 3.21. One of several long lines of anthropomorphs at Paniau. This group measures 7.4 x 1.8 m.

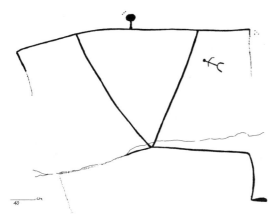

Figure 3.22. A large 'spindly' type anthropomorph from Paniau (2.8 x 2.2 m).

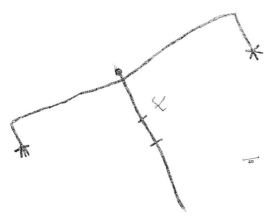

Figure 3.23. This may represent a Lono figure. Paniau, Site 1 (3.5 x 2.0 m).

Figure 3.24. Mālama trail site. Vandals have scratched fake figures and other markings on the petroglyph boulders.

figures were deemed important (Figure 3.21); this suggests some sort of organized activity or, as Ho (1988:78) proposed, a genealogical record.

A very large 'spindly' type of figure (Figure 3.22) appears to be centered at Paniau 1 and these provide considerable contrast to the usual "chunky" and well-proportioned stick figures that are more in the stylistic norm. It is possible these out-sized figures referred to chiefs and smaller ones indicated commoners. Lono images also can be postulated from this site (Figure 3.23). Triangle bodied anthropomorphs holding paddles aloft are a common motif at Paniau. These might indicate status, ceremony, or warfare. Or perhaps all three.

Paniau's petroglyphs have suffered from bulldozer damage, vandalism and theft. Three panels have been stolen from these sites in the past few years (*Rapa Nui Journal* 10 (3):62). The missing petroglyphs have not been recovered.

MĀLAMA TRAIL

The final locus at Puakō is known as the Mālama Trail; this site was discovered during construction of the new walking trail into the site from the grounds of the Mauna Lani Resort. The Mālama petroglyph site may or may not be sites ES-33 or ES-34 (Kirch 1979); Kirch reported archaeological sites in this vicinity but he did not note petroglyphs in the report. This is the first site that visitors reach as they go along the new trail from Mauna Lani Resort and, when they were discovered in 1990, they were in pristine condition. Unfortunately, the site has since been vandalized; scratched names and other graffiti are now to be seen on the petroglyph boulders (Figure 3.24).

DISCUSSION

Nearly 100% of Puakō's sites have been recorded, although more figures may lie beneath the overburden around the perimeter of the sites or may be hidden by brush and detritus. The Kāeo boundary sites have lost many petroglyphs due to bulldozer activity that churned the pāhoehoe into gravel. Paniau's sites have been badly disturbed and problems continue in those areas as developments crowd the sites. Despite these uncertainties, 3,829 petroglyphs have been documented for Puakō.

Throughout the area, variation in pecking is evident. Some elements appear to have been crudely hacked into the rock with large tools while others were made with much delicacy and control. At times it is possible to deter-

mine which design was carved
first and which one cut through
an earlier motif. The variation in
pecking suggests that the act of
making an image was equal to or
more important than the final
result.

Human motifs face in all
directions if they are located on
flat and level surfaces (Figure
3.25); angled surfaces tend to
have the figures placed in an
"up" position. There is no evidence to support a statement on
the viewing platform sign at
Kāeo 1, erected by the Mauni
Lani Resort, that describes the
figures as being oriented to a
mountain.

Former studies of Puakō
(Bishop Museum 1964:6-7) suggest that this is an early site,
based upon the lack of historical
elements in the rock art, the intense superposition of the designs, linear stick figures (as opposed to triangle torso figures)
and the presence of profile/
crouching figures. This judgment on Puakō appears to be correct, particularly as applied to Kāeo 1. Comparisons suggest that activity at the Puakō sites is earlier than that
at Puʻuloa.

Figure 3.25. Anthropomorphs on a horizontal surface face in all directions at Kāeo 1.

Tuggle (1982:2) suggested that Puakō dates from AD 1200-1600. Dates for two
petroglyphs at Puakō are AD 1400 with a range of 1307-1421; and AD 1660 with a
range of 1641-1950 (R. Dorn, personal communication 1994). However, the petroglyphs that were tested may lack a claim to antiquity and the amount of vandalism,
including chalking, could skew dates. At this writing, the dating efforts at Puakō remain unpublished.

It is clear from several documentation projects spanning many years that the universe of designs at the Puakō sites is different from nearby ʻAnaehoʻomalu and different still from Kaʻūpūlehu, a bit further to the south. It is even more at variance with the
great site at Puʻuloa in Hawaiʻi Volcanoes National Park on the south end of the island, a site dominated by cupules (See Chapter 7).

Perhaps rituals commemorating or ceremonially initiating the transformation of a
special individual to the status of family ʻaumakua were performed at Kāeo 1. Tiny
footprints (wāwae) may be records of new additions to the ʻohana. Judging from the
number of adult size footprints accompanied by smaller ones, it may signify a family
record; there are 201 images of feet at Puakō, which is 60% of the feet recorded on the
entire island. Only ʻAnaehoʻomalu was close in number with 109 examples.

Although Kāeo 1 may have functioned as an early record of vital statistics, history and legend, images of feet in other parts of Polynesia had a different meaning.
One of the frontal stones of the *langi*, Malaʻe Lahi (ʻUiha Island), Tonga, has a petroglyph of a human foot. Langi were sacred resting places of divinely descended kings:
it is suggested by Burley (1994:511-12) that a foot is a potentially powerful symbol
and may represent an act of respect reserved for the highest chiefs. Gifford (1929:118)

reports that the act of respect involved touching the soles of the feet of Tongan chiefs, thus the symbolic connotations of a foot on a tomb was the ultimate respectful action. Although Puakō may be a sacred place, it is interesting that in other parts of Polynesia an image of a foot can be a powerful symbol; perhaps the petroglyphs of footprints at Puakō had a deeper meaning than is apparent.

The profile or "crouching" form that we recorded at Puakō has corollaries throughout Polynesia (see Chapter 11); whether this posture referred to burial and death, prayer or dance, or rebirth is unknown.

To compare Puakō's sites with others along the Kohala Coast, as well as the site of Puʻuloa, it is clear that something special was occurring here, particularly at Kāeo 1. The incidence of female images, the baby feet, connecting figures, suggest family links, maternity, ʻohana. This apparent focus on family is absent from most of Paniau's sites where the outstanding motifs are long lines of figures, or triangle torso figures with paddles raised as if in ritual pose or warfare (Figure 3.26). Sites on the boundary have still wider variations, as well as historic elements.

During our final documentation project in 1997, we were interested to note a young Hawaiian family arrive to Kāeo 1, bringing an offering bundle. After walking around the site and considering various options, the bundle was set down in the center of the slight mound where the carving is the most dense. Even today this location appears to radiate a force.

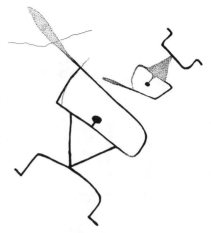

Figure 3.26. Two triangle-torso anthropomorphs with paddles at Paniau 1 appear to be involved in some ritual dance posture or are involved in warfare (panel is 1.5 x 1.3 m).

SITE DESCRIPTIONS

KĀEO 1

Kāeo 1 was gridded in ten meter squares (referred to below as 'sections'), oriented N-S, E-W (Figure 3.27). Within each 10 meter division, individual panels were given additional designations. The most heavily carved portion of the site is in Sections 16, 17, 19; 27-28; these areas encompass a slight mound and appear to have been the major focus of activity and perhaps was the first part of the site to be used. A secondary mound of pāhoehoe is located at Sections 1 and 2 as well as the east side of the site in Sections 5 and 6 where there is a definite slope. Tilted rock surfaces seem to have been a popular locations for petroglyphs.

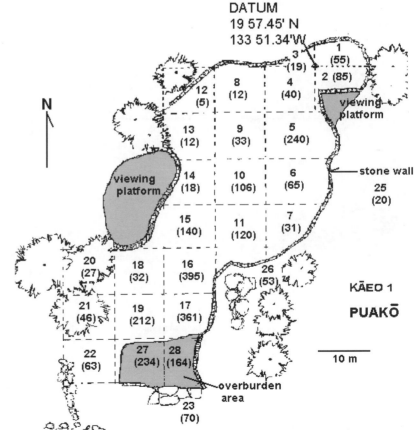

Figure 3.27. Map of Kāeo 1 showing the area as surveyed into 10 m sections. The datum selected for the entire Puakō site is indicated and the number of petroglyphs in each section is shown in parentheses. The area which was covered by overburden has been cleared and the exposed petroglyphs recorded.

Figure 3.28. Stick figures from Section 1, Kāeo 1.

Figure 3.29. Photograph of Section 2 (see also drawing, 3.32).

Kāeo 1, Section 1 (panels A-I, 55 units): the north end of the site, defined by the modern stone wall. Sloping sections of pāhoehoe contain a variety of stick figure anthropomorphs (Figure 3.28) and a turtle motif (Figure 3.17). Most of the figures here are very roughly pecked. Sharpening grooves (polissoir) were noted, interspersed with petroglyphs. Polissoir are not particularly common at Hawaiian rock art sites; these are of a width and length to definitely suggest that tools were being sharpened.

Kāeo 1, Section 2 (panels A-J, 85 units): surfaces slope slightly to the southeast. Most petroglyphs are roughly pecked. One sail with ribbing is an exception, being deeply pecked and abraded. The majority of the motifs are faint, and numerous examples of superposition make it difficult to separate out the individual elements. One panel has a stick figure that has been abraded over its surface, and two curved lines seem not to relate to the figures themselves (Figure 3.30). Two deep foot prints with prominent toes as well as an unusual anthropomorph with unconnected body parts can be seen at the base of the panel (Figures 3.29 and 3.30).

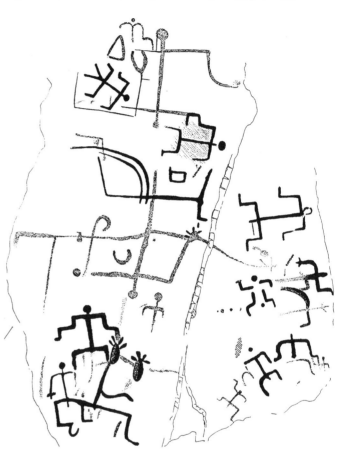

Figure 3.30. This panel measures 2.8 x 2.2 m. Deeply carved feet are superimposed on stick figures. Shading indicates intentionally abraded areas.

Kāeo 1, Section 3 (panels A-E, 19 units): faint, roughly pecked figures. One of these, directly in a former pathway, has been eroded by foot traffic. This section also contains a polissoir.

Kāeo 1, Section 4 (panels A-I, 40 units): located mainly on the east portion of the quadrant where the pāhoehoe uplifts slightly. An abraded circular area, apparently used for polishing a stone implement, has partly worn away a figure. The pecking is mostly rough with the exception of one carefully made figure that resembles an owl. This unique motif (see Figure 3.16) has been a popular target for visitors who have tried to make rubbings, leaving the petroglyph covered with traces of paint and crayon.

<u>Kāeo 1</u>, <u>Section 5</u> (panels A-M, 240 units): located mainly on the eastern portion of the section where the pāhoehoe slopes upward. A stone wall defines the eastern edge; on the western side is a lower flat section of rough ropy lava that makes a poor surface for petroglyphs. Only three motifs are located in the latter; one of these is notable. It has two cupules on each side of the head and what appears to be a vulva partially formed by a natural hump in the lava (Figure 3.31).

Several fine panels are located on the east side of the section on sloping pāhoehoe; unfortunately these have been a target for rubbings and attempts to make resin or latex molds. Some of the most attractive petroglyphs have been severely damaged. Cupules (on sloping surfaces) are associated with several figures (see Figure 3.12). Many small cupules are scattered in this area but, as these are on sloping surfaces, we assume they had some symbolic value and were not meant to hold the piko. Six panels in this section have abraded basin-like areas that partially obliterate stick figures. Two deep polissoir are also located here (Figure 3.32). One panel (Figure 3.33) has an oversized foot and a variety of figures including one with extraordinary legs. Note the small figures under the arms of the large anthropomorphs. The border of sections 5-6 contains two joined figures, one with an arc over the head (Figure 3.34).

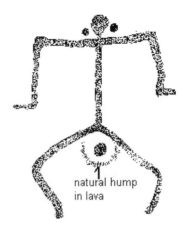

Figure 3.31. (69 x 56 cm). Note cupules on each side of the head.

Figure 3.32. The central large figure is 100 x 34 cm. Polissoir (sharpening grooves) can be seen right center where they cut through some petroglyphs.

Figure 3.33. This panel (2.1 x 2.1 m) has some of the few triangle torso figures at Kāeo 1.

Figure 3.34. A panel of two joined stick figures measures 50 x 40 cm. Note line over head of left figure.

Kāeo 1, Section 6 (panels A-L, 65 units): the stone wall and some rough tilted surfaces form the east border. Stick figures in all sizes and variations decorate the panels; some showing extra limbs. One deeply pecked figure has distinct fingers on one hand and a tiny figure under one arm (Figure 3.35). Nearby is an odd form, shaped like an adze (27 x 14 cm). This form, always shown in bas relief, was recorded several times at Kāeo 1; two other examples are in Section 27. A stick figure on the left side of the panel strikes an active pose. Section 6 has little superposition. Much of the surface is not suited for making petroglyphs.

Kāeo 1, Section 7 (panels A-G, 31 units): a wedge-shaped area at the southeastern portion of the section, bordered by the modern stone wall that curves around at that point. Relatively few figures are located here, and there are little superposition. One notable figure is a huge human foot, pecked out in intaglio. It measures 43 x 23 cm and has its toes clearly indicated. Just off the heel of the footprint are two tiny baby-sized prints. The anthropomorphs are stick figures but with a variety of form. Some have an extra set of legs and many suggest action, with wavy arms and legs. One is a running figure.

Kāeo 1, Section 8 (12 units): at the north central portion of the section. This sparsely carved section contains only two panels. A stick figure has what looks like a beak. It is deeply pecked and has smears of paint from attempts to make rubbings.

Kāeo 1, Section 9 (panels A-G, 33 units): petroglyphs are spread out and isolated with no superposition. The northeast corner is very rough which is the reason for the scarcity of elements. One petroglyph combines a form in partial bas relief with a stick figure. Two of the associated anthropomorphs are open torso triangle figures (Figure 3.36).

Kāeo 1, Section 10 (panels A-J, 106 units): most of the petroglyphs cluster on the east side, with none in the northwest section. Although some are scattered and solitary, as one approaches the eastern edge the more dense the petroglyphs and the superposition become. Several of the motifs are unusual: one is a female figure with a face, wavy arms and legs, fingers and toes which reminds one of a hula dancer (Figure 3.37). Other special features in this section are oversize human feet associated with baby-sized feet.

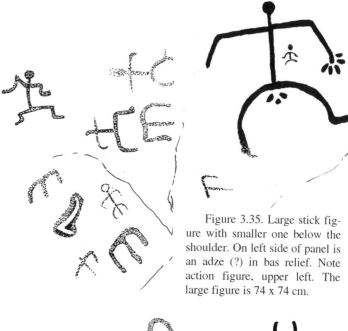

Figure 3.35. Large stick figure with smaller one below the shoulder. On left side of panel is an adze (?) in bas relief. Note action figure, upper left. The large figure is 74 x 74 cm.

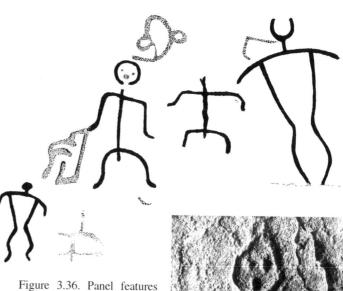

Figure 3.36. Panel features "open base" triangular torso figure, a stick figure with a face, and a small bas relief motif (panel is 136 x 96 cm.).

Figure 3.37. This has been called a hula dancer (64 x 34 cm).

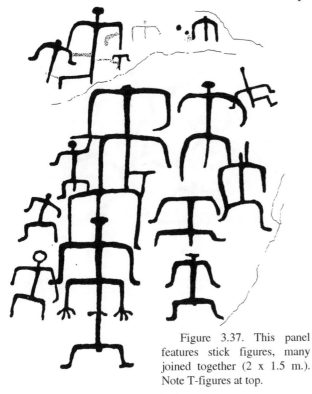

Figure 3.37. This panel features stick figures, many joined together (2 x 1.5 m.). Note T-figures at top.

Figure 3.39. A female figure with headdress, face, and vulva (72 x 48 cm).

Figure 3.40 (80 x 80 cm). This unusual figure has what is called "shelf-like" feet. Note dots on each side of neck.

Kāeo 1, Section 11 (panels A-K, 120 units): a heavy concentration of motifs on the eastern side and a lesser number in the rest of the section, a distribution probably due to a rough surface in the west-central portion. The eastern portion slopes upward and presents a fine and very visible surface for designs.

Panel H is particularly interesting for its connected anthropomorphs which may display the concept of family or generation themes (Figure 3.37; see also Figure 3.11). Anthropomorphs grow out of other figures; torsos become legs, and so on.

Figure 3.38. Anthropomorph with oversized legs, Section 11.

There is considerable variety in the size of some of the units in this section: the largest anthropomorph is 115 cm high (Figure 3.38). Panel K includes a stick figure with vulva, headdress and facial features (Figure 3.39; see also Figure 3.10). A small extension of Section 11 encompasses an area that is mostly covered over by dirt and a curving stone wall. Only the north end is visible. There are two interesting panels plus a few scattered units. Some continue beneath the wall. Two figures are shown in profile: a rarity in Hawaiian rock art .

Kāeo 1, Section 12 (5 units): bounded by the stone wall which leaves a wedge-shaped section with few petroglyphs. Two units are outside the wall.

Kāeo 1, Section 13 (12 units): over half of its area covered by overburden; the surface here is rough and seemingly not an attractive one for petroglyphs. One stick figure is notable for the long wavy attachments to the arms (Figure 3.40). Note small cupules on each side of the neck.

Kāeo 1, Section 14 (18 units): lacks good surfaces for petroglyphs; all petroglyphs are located on the eastern side.

Kāeo 1, Section 15 (panels A-P; 140 units): the eastern portion has
many designs; the western part is basically devoid of petroglyphs. Some figures are quite large, up to 279 x 665 cm. Although many are scattered around and not superimposed, the
closer one approaches to the eastern side, the more superposition
and the more densely packed are the images. Aside from the
many stick figure anthropomorphs, this section has a sail with
ribbing and a very large profile figure with a bird head[4] (see Figure 3.16). This latter figure is extremely interesting as its basic
form echoes the bas relief petroglyphs on a boulder found in the
Moanalua Valley, Oʻahu (now in the Bishop Museum), petroglyphs at Kauaʻi (Kikuchi 1994), at Puʻuloa, and in a cave at
Kaʻū (see Chapter 10).

One small grouping, part of a larger panel, has connected
figures, one with an oddly shaped head and a piko cupule in the
crotch, perhaps indicating a female. Another figure has legs that
end in a circle, and one has a detached head and long penis line.
Note how forms are connected (Figure 3.44).

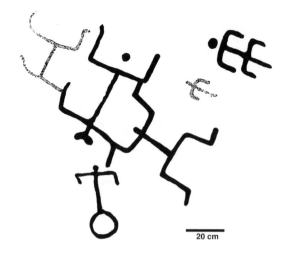

Figure 3.44. This grouping (128 x 112 cm.)
features three connected stick figures, plus other
variations, including a figure with circle legs.

Kāeo 1, Section 16 (panels A-Y; 395
units): part of the 'center' of the
site and, along with sections
18/19, has the major concentration of motifs. Virtually every
square meter in this quadrant
contains petroglyphs. The stone
wall marks the southeast corner
of the site. The density of petroglyphs made documentation
very difficult and time consuming (Figure 3.45). In addition,
erosion is severe from foot traffic over the years. The petroglyphs range from finely pecked
to very rough, and from faint to
deep. Some figures are grossly
oversized while others are small.
One long spindly figure with a
flat head is 192 cm long (see
Figure 3.25).

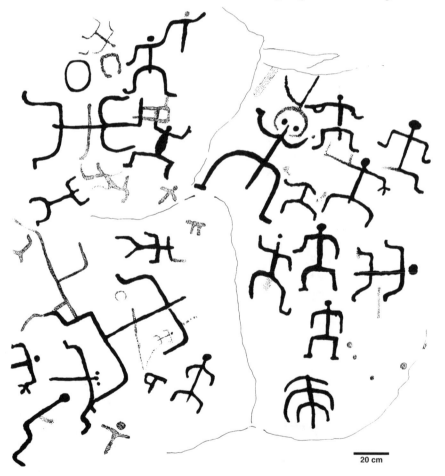

Figure 3.45. This portion of a larger group measures 2.6 x 2.5 m. Note the profile
figure at lower left, stick figures with detached heads, and one with a "face" and eyes.
Many are connected. Variations in pecking are indicated by lightly dotted motifs.

Figure 3.46. This panel, another portion of Section 16, measures 2.2 x 1.9 m. One motif resembles a comet.

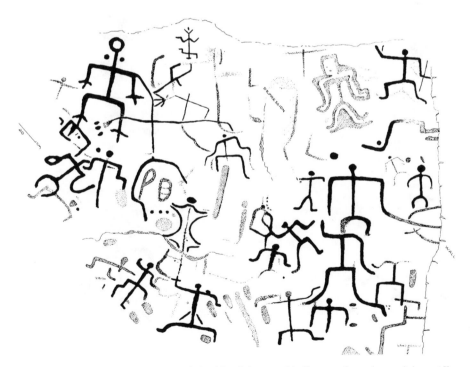

Figure 3.47. The line up the right side of the panel indicates where the retaining wall at the south send of the site used to be. Many foot motifs are found in this area, usually these are shown in pairs. This panel measures 3.2 x 2.3 m.

Triangle torso figures are not observed in Section 16—all are stick figures of one sort or another and many connect with each other (Figure 3:46). Note the comet-like motif at upper left.

Kāeo 1, Sections 17-19 (panel 17, A-I, 361 units and panel 19, A-R, 212 units): located near the south end of the site. These sections have numerous motifs and are, basically, a continuation from Section 16; superposition, varying quality of carving, and 'panels' all flow together. The motifs run from one panel to another and across breaks in the pāhoehoe to form an amazing display of stick figure petroglyphs, many connected to each other. Interspersed are feet (mostly intaglio) and cupules. Triangle-bodied anthropomorphs are conspicuous by their absence (see Figures 3.7 and 3.8).

These two sections need to be discussed as one, for the major motif—a giant mo'o (lizard)—runs across them both. The mo'o figure measures 64 x 440 cm. Starting with a round head, arms branch off and, as the long torso stretches out across the slight rise of the lava dome, other lines branch out. A pair of legs (opposing the direction of the arms) gives it the appearance of a giant reptile. The form ends in an open rectangle, out of which projects an anthropomorph. Along the torso line are pairs of baby-sized feet. There is nothing comparable elsewhere in Hawaiian rock art. Mo'o were 'aumakua or guardian spirits and considered as huge black lizard-like creatures. Associated with feminine equivalents, they supposedly lived in ponds or rivers. Small reptiles furnished the natural model and had the same taboos. Lizards relate in general to ancestry, backbone, and are metaphors for genealogy (Valeri 1985:22; Ho 1988:67). The early Bishop Museum Report (1964:17) mentions the possibility of mo'o representations at this site.

Sections 17-19 are covered with petroglyphs for the eastern two-thirds of the quadrant and again at the western edge where the lava rises upward. In between is a low-lying area with poor surfaces. At the time of our initial site documentation in 1989, petroglyphs ran up to and under the wall that defined the southwest section (Figure 3.47). The 1997 field season documented those formerly covered over and added another 457 petroglyphs to the data base.

It is clear, particularly in the main center of this section, that we are dealing with layers of petroglyphs (Figure 3.48). By using a raking side light, faint images can be seen beneath more deeply carved figures, with still more recent ones overlaid (Figure 3.49). Evidently this has been a special part of the site for a long period of time, with the same, seemingly sacred, area being used. Few phallic anthropomorphs are present, but many figures have vulvae (Figure 3.50). Several odd images appear to be abbreviated crouching figures. Others here include two large anthropomorphs, one with dots on each side of the neck and an unexplained appendage (Figure 3.51), and a figure with an angled line serving as a head (Figure 3.52). Both have 'shelf-like' hands and feet.

Figure 3.50. A female figure with fingers (82 x 57 cm).

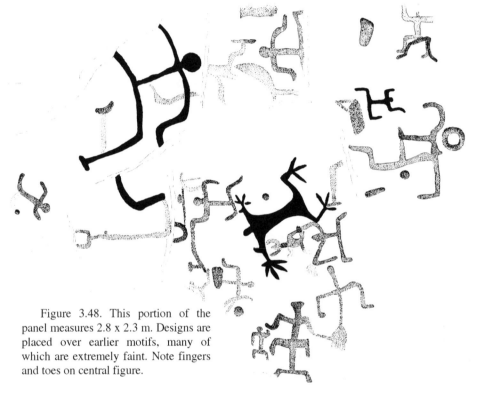

Figure 3.48. This portion of the panel measures 2.8 x 2.3 m. Designs are placed over earlier motifs, many of which are extremely faint. Note fingers and toes on central figure.

Figure 3.51. Note dots on each side of neck area. The appendages in the genital area are unexplained (62 x 62 cm).

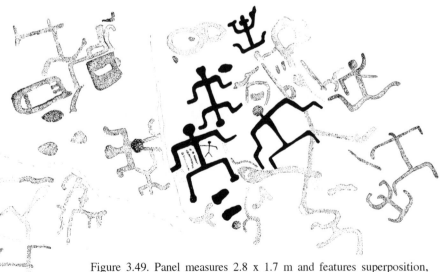

Figure 3.49. Panel measures 2.8 x 1.7 m and features superposition, stick figures and footprints. Note the lightly pecked running figure on the upper right.

Figure 3.52. A "hook" headed stick figure with shelf hands and feet (58 x 42 cm).

Kāeo 1, Section 18 (panels A-J, 32 units): nine panels are located on the eastern portion and one is on the far western side where the rock tilts upward. The rock surfaces between are unsuitable for carving. Some bulldozer tracks are visible in this section. All the motifs are stick figures.

Kāeo 1, Section 20 (27 units): on a slightly raised portion of pāhoehoe; only the southeast corner of the section is visible. Three small panels contain stick figures and one triangle body figure. These are not deeply pecked. One figure is in a running posture (Figure 3.53)

Kāeo 1, Section 21 (panels A-P, 46 units): some panels have only one motif. The eastern side of the section contains petroglyphs; the remainder is hidden beneath overburden and underbrush. The surface of the pāhoehoe here is very broken and segmented. All but two of the anthropomorphs are stick figures and most are extremely faint.

Figure 3.53. Running stick figure (58 x 48 cm).

Figure 3.54. A natural feature in the lava suggests a vulva (70 x 36 cm).

Kāeo 1, Section 22 (panels A-G, 63 units): the pāhoehoe is very rough and ropy with petroglyphs scattered on the few smooth areas. Panel C, at the northwestern part of the section, was nearly destroyed when a dead kiawe fell and its roots tore the rock apart. One faint stick figure utilized a naturally raised oval located in the genital area (Figure 3.54).

Kāeo 1, Section 23 (70 units): bounded by tilted pāhoehoe at the end of the site, the panels face north. These motifs are weathered and difficult to see. The most interesting feature here is a bas relief figure (Figure 3.55) at the base of the tilted panel. Aside from this figure, all but two are stick figures. The clearing of overburden revealed more motifs including many connected figures. However, the clearing process also damaged some of the pāhoehoe and thus impacted a few petroglyphs. Section 23 also includes the vulva form seen in (Figure 3.56).

Figure 3.55 This grouping is on a tilted section of pāhoehoe at the south end of the site; it measures 2.1 x 1.3 m. Some figures are connected. A small bas relief anthropomorph which appears to have sheep ears is at the bottom.

Figure 3.56. A boulder in Section 23 at south end of site has a small vulva form at upper right.

Kāeo 1, Section 27 (237 units): east of section 22. This area was hidden by overburden until 1995. Some remarkable petroglyphs are located in this section, including some unique stick figures, mostly interconnected, as well as some circles and enclosures (Figure 3.57).

Other motifs include a female figure with breasts and two curious forms in bas relief that are not securely identified, but appear to resemble adzes or shark tooth implements; one is inside a circle motif. Numerous feet can be seen, some with toes. A few figures are very deeply pecked (see also Figure 3:37).

Figure 3.57. This portion of Section 27 measures 4.2 x 2.7 m and is located on a slight slope. Densely carved, it has layers of motifs. Note presence of feet, and emphasis on female attributes. Two bas relief adze-like motifs are found on the panel, one can be seen inside the circle at lower left.

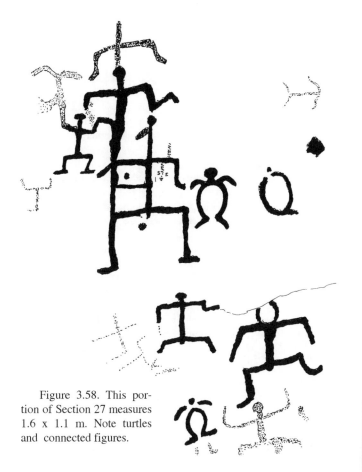

Figure 3.59. Deeply carved anthropomorphs in Section 27. See also Figure 3.57.

Figure 3.58. This portion of Section 27 measures 1.6 x 1.1 m. Note turtles and connected figures.

Section 27 also contains three turtles (Figure 3.58) and a kite (see Figure 3.15). Many petroglyphs are deeply carved (Figure 3.59 and 3.60).

Kāeo 1, Section 28 (164 units); east of section 27, formerly hidden by overburden. This section continues up to the tilted rocks in section 23. Petroglyphs are more spread out along the eastern portion, near a wall. As one moves west toward the "center", the density increases and superposition is the rule. Machinery used for clearance damaged parts of the pāhoehoe that are just below the present stone wall (Figures 3.61 and 3.63). Some of the forms here are most unusual (Figure 3.62).

Figure 3.60. A deeply carved anthropomorph from Section 27 dominates one panel.

Figure 3.61 (64 x 52 cm). A curious figure with eyes, head, and shelf hands and feet. The diagonal line below the right shoulder results from machinery damage during the recent clearing of overburden.

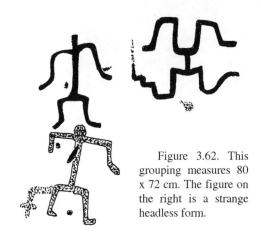

Figure 3.62. This grouping measures 80 x 72 cm. The figure on the right is a strange headless form.

Figure 3.63. This portion of Section 28 measures 2.8 x 2.7 m. Note gouge marks from machinery.

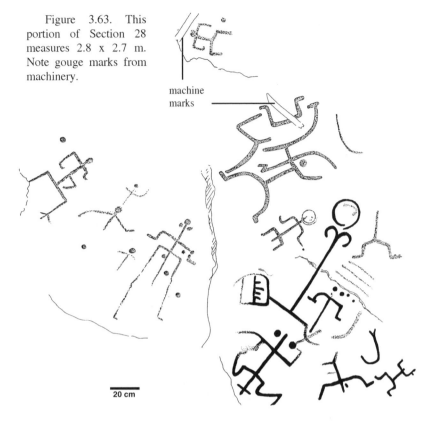

machine marks

20 cm

Section 28 also contains an unusual panel (Figure 3.63) with a long form that has one large foot, partially carved in bas relief, and a circle above a forked 'head'. Note the long legged anthropomorph with two cupules on each side of neck. This panel was damaged when overburden was cleared, as shown on the drawing. A fish-hook is in the lower right corner.

Kāeo 1, Section 24 (60 units): west of Section 22, upslope and under kiawe trees. The scattered motifs are on a series of small areas of pāhoehoe. Some are found on up-tilted areas, others are level. The forest cover here is heavy and the sites are difficult to locate. Notable are figures with extra limbs or joined to other figures, small baby feet and cupules. An unusual feature is a small smooth oval inclusion in rougher lava which contains a T-figure petroglyph in the middle of the smooth area (Figure 3.64).

Kāeo 1, Section 25 (20 units): east of Section 7 and outside the stone wall. Here there are scattered small areas of fairly rough pāhoehoe, containing a few motifs. The site was discovered following a fire which burned off the heavy brush. The petroglyphs are mainly crude stick figure anthropomorphs. However, there is one large (30 cm) intaglio footprint with toes.

Figure 3.64

Kāeo 1, Section 26 (53 units): east of Section 17. These upright sections of pāhoehoe are decorated by some very faint and eroded motifs. Many are quite large. Because these rocks are in heavy shade, it is very difficult to see the designs clearly (Figure 3.65). Simple stick figure anthropomorphs are predominant. One small motif may be a vulva form.

Kāeo 1.1 (2 units): an outlying site found after the fire burned off the underbrush in that area. It is east of the main site of Kāeo 1 on small sections of pāhoehoe. Two anthropomorphic stick figures.

Figure 3.65. View of Section 26 showing tilted surface with petroglyphs on east side of the site.

Figure 3.65. Kāeo 4 petroglyph measures 29 x 22 cm. The "outline" around it is an attempt to remove the figure from the rock.

Figure 3.66. This figure (88 x 96 cm) from Kāeo 4 is not shown in the Bishop Museum Survey, suggesting that some portions may result from recent vandalism.

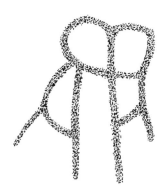

Figure 3.67. A unique abstract figure measuring 60 x 52 cm.

KĀEO BOUNDARY SITES

Kāeo 2 (7 units): a large area of smooth pāhoehoe with many inviting surfaces for petroglyph making; however, there are few units here. Given its proximity to Kāeo 1, which is heavily carved, this contrast provided evidence that something existed there that made it the favored location. Perhaps the slight mound near the center was attractive, or some long-lost motivation that we are unlikely to comprehend. In any event, Kāeo 2 has only six petroglyphs, one polissoir, and one clear fake: a clumsy anthropomorph made with a chisel. One figure has been ruined by attempts to make a resin mold. We noted a great deal of spilled paint and residue from rubbings made in the past.

Kāeo 3 (15 units): a small site not included in the Bishop Museum Survey. The surface of the pāhoehoe is very weathered and cracked. All motifs are stick figures, some partial or perhaps unfinished. Additional nearby petroglyphs designated as Kāeo 3.1, 3.2 and 3.3 were found after the fire which burned off the brush in the area; two footprints and one stick figure were damaged by bulldozer treads.

Kāeo 4 (Bishop Museum Survey designation B, 118 units): a border site northeast of Kāeo 1 and 3. Kāeo 4 has the distinction of having a great deal of vandalism which, unfortunately, is continuing. The north end of the site contains two raised lava domes with sloping surfaces; these appear to have been attractive locations for petroglyphs. Vandalism is apparent: the rock surface around one handsome petroglyph has been cut where removal was attempted (Figure 3:65), and paint traces remain on the rock from rubbings. This site has several strange forms—some of which appear to have been tampered with in historic times. For example, a stick figure has additions made with a different tool and a lesser degree of patination is clear. Another strange figure does not appear in the Bishop Museum Survey drawings although it would have been hard to miss had it been there originally (Figure 3.66).

Kāeo 4.1 In the middle of the firebreak, 56 m northwest of Kāeo 4, surrounded by bulldozer tracks, two small stick figures were found. Whether others were there in the past is impossible to determine.

Kāeo 5 (3 units): a small site, on tilted sections of pāhoehoe. Figures include crudely made anthropomorphs; one is a unique design that does not fit into any defined category (Figure 3.67).

Kāeo 6 (24 units): on pāhoehoe that is very cracked and irregular, with many folds and ripples and a poor surface for carving. Some of the units appear to have been made along natural cracks. One is a fat-bodied anthropomorph holding a paddle aloft.

Kāeo 7 (68 units): partially damaged by the bulldozer incident: the petroglyphs along the west edge have suffered the most damage. One stick figure has tread marks through it (see Figure 3.20). The pāhoehoe here is broken, rough and ropy—not an ideal surface for petroglyphs. Of particular interest are some large figures, one holding a paddle (Figure 3.68). This element appears to have been reworked.

   Some of the petroglyphs have beveled areas as if used for polishing some object; this action has nearly eradicated the designs, and one small figure has some pecking around it to suggest bas relief was attempted.

Kāeo 8 (Bishop Museum Survey K, 7 units): a small site 100 meters to the south of the boundary line sites, containing a few stick figures and two human feet.

Kāeo 9 (Bishop Museum Survey C, 36 units): the east side of the site is damaged by bulldozers. Notable motifs here are a ship (see Figure 3.22), a figure in partial bas relief, and a very deeply pecked anthropomorph. The figures are a mix of stick and triangle bodied, some with muscles.

Kāeo 10 (Bishop Museum Survey D, 57 units): a large site with petroglyphs spread out in discrete clusters. Many of the motifs are very faint; some can be seen only in the late afternoon light. The pāhoehoe varies from smooth to ropy, with several areas being unsuitable for carving. In contrast, many fine surfaces are untouched.

   Discrepancies were noted in the Bishop Survey report: a large triangle torso figure shown at their grid No. 10 F-E must have been accidentally transposed from somewhere else in the drawing. Physically, there is no place at the site for this size figure due to the nature of the pāhoehoe. The Bishop Museum Survey drawings were made from photographs, thus we assume likely that this figure was incorrectly placed in the drawing.

   In contrast, some motifs missed in the Bishop Museum Survey were recorded by us. The units here show varying degrees of skill; some are very faint and ill-formed while others are deep and well made. Several figures have rayed heads (Figure 3:69a, b and c).

Kāeo 11 (15 units): circles and some odd and ungainly anthropomorphs. These units were located after several inches of debris were removed from the surface.

Kāeo 12 (Bishop Museum Survey E; 16 units): This site, mostly stick figures which are incomplete or eroded, is 100 meters south of the boundary line sites. One figure appears to be an attempt to show a profile or crouching figure.

Kāeo 13 (3 polissoir): These polissoir, a few meters northeast of Kāeo 12, were not recorded on paper.

Figure 3.68. This panel of two figures from site Kāeo 7 measures 132 x 108 cm. Note the exaggerated fingers and toes. The club/paddle form has been altered.

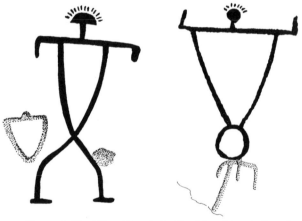

Figure 3.69a (76 x 43 cm); 3.69b (96 x 54 cm). Rayed heads are not common thus it was interesting to find this feature on many of the anthropomorphs at Kāeo 10..

Figure 3.69c, site Kāeo 10 (48 x 44 cm). A stick figure with rayed head.

Kāeo 14 (Bishop Museum Survey F; 50 units): a large site spread out on various levels. Part of the site is on a rise; other sections are lower. All figures shown on the Bishop Museum Survey drawing were relocated except for one figure; others were found that were missed in the early survey. Some are very well-made muscled anthropomorphs (see Figure 1.1). One enormous stick figure has a single massive foot (Figure 3.70). It was found buried beneath several inches of detritus. This figure appears to be a combination of several features: the right foot ends in a torso line that forms a head and arms; the head area is a conglomeration of lines that may have been part of an earlier figure. There is no 'head' per se. The figure has enormous hands with fingers and the left foot is completely oversized. Tucked under the right arm is a small stick figure superimposed by a human footprint.

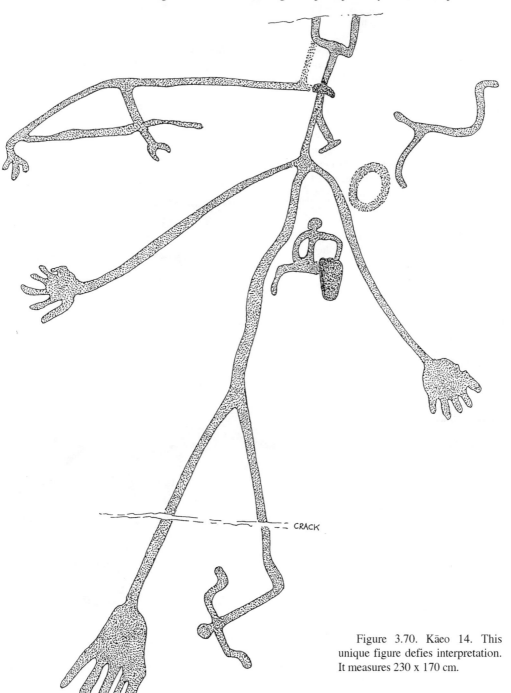

CRACK

Figure 3.70. Kāeo 14. This unique figure defies interpretation. It measures 230 x 170 cm.

Kāeo 15 (11 units): a raised mound of pāhoehoe with smooth sections on the downslope. Part of the rock has exfoliated leaving portions of a large figure; more figures were subsequently pecked on the newly exposed surface. Aside from this oddity, a beveled and polished area contains a cup and ring motif, rare at these sites.

Kāeo 16 (16 units): a small isolated site with 2 anthropomorphs and a unique circle composed of dots with a center cupule (Figure 3.71). One figure appears to be unfinished as it is missing part of its torso line.

Kāeo 17 (21 units): spread out on a long flat section of pāhoehoe. Most figures are triangle torso, some open-base, and a few superimposed. One figure is placed inside a beveled area, and another is a wonderfully whimsical little figure with outstretched arms (Figure 3.72).

Kāeo 18 and 19 (Kāeo G and H, 12 sections, 212 units): on two very large contiguous areas of pāhoehoe that can be taken as one large site. Today these are separated only by a few kiawe trees which were not present when the petroglyphs were made. The area was divided for convenience in recording.

Some images are very faint. In an effort to extract more information, several of these were studied by lantern at night but we were unable to see more details than in daylight.

One of the better known images from this site is the "birth scene of an aliʻi child" as described in Cox and Stasack (1970:48). This grouping of four figures is very suggestive of a family unit: the triangle torso male is fully pecked out in intaglio and was made first; the female figure's left arm is pecked over the hand and body of the male. Not noted by Cox and Stasack in either the text or figure is a small human foot pecked in the center of the female torso (Figure 3.73). They interpret the scene as follows:

> The father and mother are side by side. The figures are larger than the average petroglyphs, about 3 feet high and somewhat more elaborate, which probably indicates their importance. The male's body is a wide triangle, the surface of which is entirely pecked out. The female's body is equally wide but rounded rather than angular, the vulva is shown as a large circular cavity, much deeper than any other marks in the area. On her shoulder is a girl child, judging by the open torso. The father is holding another child by the feet with the head down. The head of this child is of particular importance. It is stylized as a horizontal bar with vertical comb-like bars rising from it, perhaps the crest symbol of a high chief.

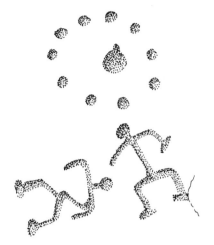

Figure 3.71. This small group of petroglyphs measures 72 x 62 cm.

Figure 3.72. (44 x 40 cm) An amusing little figure at Kāeo 17.

Figure 3.73. A family group from Kāeo 18. The panel measures 1.7 x 1.0 m. It seems to represent a male, a female and children. Note small footprint pecked in the body of the female.

Figure 3.74 (32 x 28 cm). Geometric forms such as this grid-like motif are rare at Puakō.

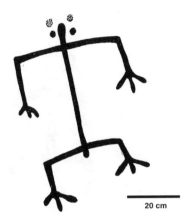

20 cm

Figure 3.75. A stick figure from Site 19 has cupules associated with the head and exaggerated fingers and toes.

Some of the motifs featured at sites 18-19 are sails, dogs, rows of cupules, concentric rings (rare at Puakō), nine muscled figures, and a rooster-like form. A deep 'grid' like form is an oddity (Figure 3.74).

One large triangle torso figure has the area between the legs pecked out, apparently a later addition, to give the feeling of muscles. Some of the anthropomorphs have cupules placed on the sides of the heads (Figure 3.75) and triangle figures tend to have muscles indicated (Figures 3.76).

Sails are present in a variety of sizes and some have small anthropomorphic figures in association (as we noted also at Ka'ūpūlehu). Site 19 also has the famous Kūkini or "running man" (see Figure 1.4) (Cox and Stasack 1970: Fig. 89).

One panel contains feet that have tiny cupules for toes. These are associated with a roughly pecked circular depression and a flat-headed open-body anthropomorph. An odd form attached to the left arm of the figure appears to be a flying bird. This grouping is very suggestive of a family unit, perhaps with the bird as 'aumakua. A fishhook petroglyph is located nearby (Figure 3.77).

Missionary-style lettering is found at both of these sites: "LUKA LUAHINE" at Site 18 and "NAZAWAHA" carved into a panel of motifs at Site 19.

Figure 3.76. These two figures at Site 18 measure 1.4 x 1.0 m. The muscles are in outline form. Note the three-toed feet.

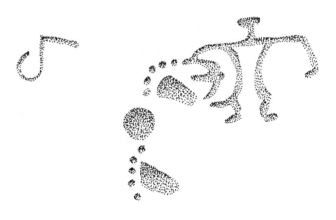

Figure 3.77. A Site 19 panel measures 110 x 66 cm. It includes feet with toes, a fishhook and an open base anthropomorph which may hold a bird in its hand. Note the unusual head shape.

Kāeo 20 (16 units): spread out on an expanse of pāhoehoe. Most are simple stick figures, although one has 2 sets of arms, a round head and upturned legs (Figure 3.79).

Kāeo 21 (1 unit): on a sloping surface of pāhoehoe; the name "IoKoPa" was found, made with irregular rough pecking.

Kāeo 22 (2 units): on contiguous sections of pāhoehoe. The anthropomorph has a circle head, open torso and shelf feet. The wavy contours suggest a feminine figure.

Kāeo 23 (1 unit): a most interesting little anthropomorph. It consists of an open torso with what appear to be breasts and a circle that goes around the head (Figure 3.80).

Kāeo 24 (Bishop Museum Survey, Site I, 35 units): scattered small petroglyphs on the north end of the site. Bulldozer tracks can be seen only a few feet from the panels. The main focus (the south end of the site) has some large and complex figures; the most elaborate are sails, a large stick figure holding an adze, and some interconnecting motifs (Figure 3.81). A close study of the figure holding the adze reveals that the two motifs were carved with different tools and not at the same depths. The adze apparently was added later. The sail also has a different style of pecking, which suggests that the creation of this "unit" was on-going over a span of time.

Kāeo 25 (28 units): three triangle torso anthropomorphs interspersed with many stick figures and partial figures, circles, a large roughly pecked squared shape, and a line of cupules. Some of the petroglyphs were placed on abraded areas; one of these resembles a profile anthropomorph.

Kāeo 26 (12 units): on irregular, tilted sections of pāhoehoe containing a variety of figures, including one large triangle torso anthropomorph with upturned feet—a rare feature (Figure 3.82).

Kāeo 27 (24 units): on undulating pāhoehoe in poor condition. Petroglyphs are eroded and indistinct. A few geometric motifs were recorded, two triangle figures (one with an open base) and 17 stick figures—two of which have forked heads. One motif is very unusual: it appears to represent some sort of structure (Figure 3.83).

Kāeo 28 (5 units): Bulldozers have pulverized most of the pāhoehoe destroying much of the site. Only two small panels were located, one on a tilted surface. Two anthropomorphic figures remain along with one foot pecked in intaglio and a faint circle. A photograph taken in 1989 shows another anthropomorphic figure nearby which could not be relocated.

Figure 3.79.
(48 x 27 cm)

Figure 3.80
(30 x 26 cm)

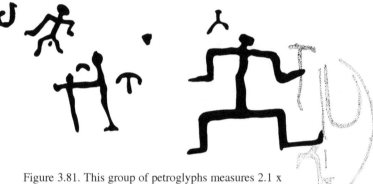

Figure 3.81. This group of petroglyphs measures 2.1 x 0.9 m. Note the fishook on the left.

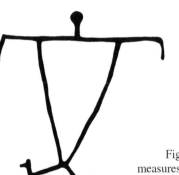

Figure 3.82. This group at Kāeo 26 measures 2 x 1 m. The up-turned feet on the anthropomorph on the left are uncommon features.

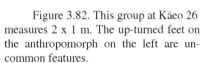

20 cm

Figure 3.83. A strange motif at Kāeo 27 that appears to resemble a structure.

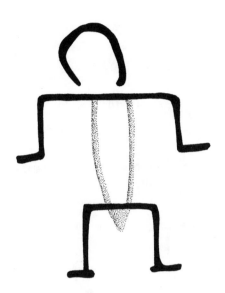

Figure 3.84 (96 x 76 cm). This figure at Kāeo 33 has shelf hands and feet and a detached head. On an upright piece of lava facing southwest along the boundary, it stands out dramatically.

20 cm

Figure 3.85. Kāeo 36 anthropomorphs, on a sloping surface, with wavy arms, fingers and toes.

Kāeo 29 (1 unit): a sloping surface. The petroglyph is a large triangle-bodied figure with four fingers on each end of the shoulder line. The legs are atypical in that they angle out and appear to end in ball-like shapes. Two cupules appear above the head.

Kāeo 30 (6 units): one unit is a single cup and ring motif; the other consists of two stick figures and a long curved line (somewhat canoe shaped) which connects to the head of one of the figures. Along the boundary line to the north is a roughly pecked partial figure.

Kāeo 31 (12 units): a fairly large section of pāhoehoe around a natural basin-like cavity. Motifs are anthropomorphs, fishhooks, and feet. A small lava tube is associated.

Kāeo 32 (5 units): a large expanse of fine level surface with few figures. Two of these are scattered on a large flat section of pāhoehoe; nearby are 2 human feet, pecked in outline style.

Kāeo 33 (3 units): one huge anthropomorph is dramatically positioned on an upright section of rock. The head is unconnected to the body/shoulder line, or perhaps eroded. The figure has shelf-like hands and feet (Figure 3.84). Under a nearby tree is a large (2 m long) sail with a tiny human figure inside.

Kāeo 34 (1 unit): a very faint single long-arm figure on a sloping surface; the legs are atypical in that they angle outward.

Kāeo 35 (22 units): around a tilted section of pāhoehoe. The major figure here is a gigantic triangle-bodied anthropomorph with arm and pectoral muscles clearly delineated, large hands and long fingers (see Figure 2.7). There is one sail and a few geometric motifs; all others are anthropomorphs.

Kāeo 36 (8 units): on separate tilted surfaces. It is possible that there are more petroglyphs at this locus as the rock surfaces are surrounded by heavy kiawe growth, covered with detritus, and very little light penetrates the forest at this point. The petroglyphs at this locus are all stick figures, some very animated with wavy arms (Figure 3.85).

Kāeo 37 (2 units) and Kāeo 38 (1 unit): both sites have been torn up by bulldozer activity. One of the surviving figures has bulldozer tracks running through it.

Kāeo 39 (4 panels; 7 units): isolated. One panel has three typical Polynesian-style fishhooks. It is at this point that the pāhoehoe disappears.

PANIAU SITES

Paniau 1 (Bishop Museum Survey designation, Paniau C; 122 units) is the largest of the sites in the Paniau area. Paniau 1 is inland, approximately 200 meters east of Puako Beach Road and 500 meters northwest of Kāeo 1. The petroglyph area is located on a large section of level pāhoehoe, approximately 40 x 40 meters, and surrounded by a mass of kiawe trees that encroach upon it. A well-worn path used to lead into the area from the road; this has been closed in recent years.

The area was divided by N-S and E-W string lines forming 10 meter squares (Figure 3.86). Each petroglyph was documented and located with respect to the squares. It is possible that more petroglyphs may be found in the vicinity, buried beneath overburden and debris. Many of the motifs here are extremely faint and some that lie near the middle of the site (Sections 3, 7 and 11) have been worn down by modern-day foot traffic. There has been distressing vandalism at Paniau; attempts to make molds have left latex material over one of the most attractive units, and many others have grooves filled with crayon, paint and chalk.

Paniau 1 designs generally were made with light pecking. Some barely can be seen with the aid of a raking side light and others are visible only because lichens grow in the peck marks. Motifs are spread out in the site, with little or no overlapping of figures.

Paniau 1, Section 1, north end of site: 1 stick figure petroglyph.

Paniau 1, Section 2, northwest portion of site: 1 panel with two triangle torso figures and the name: KEKOOLANI. It was the only historic element noted at this site (Figure 3.87).

Paniau 1, Section 3, northeast section of site: two panels, one with one triangle figure and a large figure. The latter, an elongated stick figure without legs (T-figure), this motif has been called a representation of the god Lono. Lono figures were carried in procession around the island and were part of the makahiki celebration. Although there are many T-figure motifs in the rock art at these sites, this figure is unusually large (175 x 364 cm), but not unusually large when compared to several other huge anthropomorphs here. Each hand has 5 distinct fingers. A tiny faint figure is below the right shoulder (see Figure 3.23). A nearby panel in Section 7 is also suggestive of a Lono image (Figure 3.88)

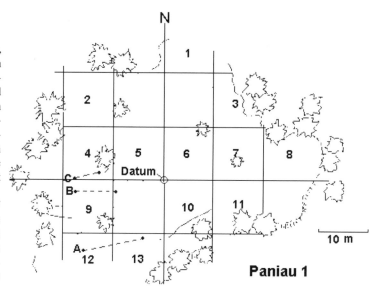

Figure 3.86. Map of the site.

Figure 3.87. This panel features lettering and measures 161 x 83 cm.

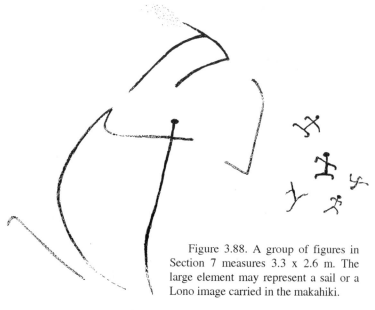

Figure 3.88. A group of figures in Section 7 measures 3.3 x 2.6 m. The large element may represent a sail or a Lono image carried in the makahiki.

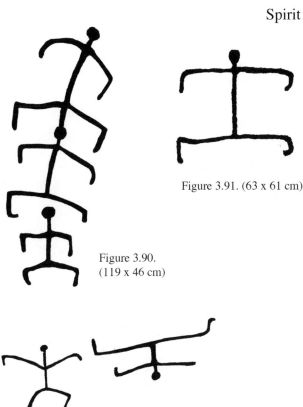

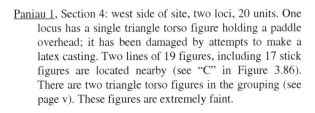

Figure 3.91. (63 x 61 cm)

Figure 3.90.
(119 x 46 cm)

Paniau 1, Section 4: west side of site, two loci, 20 units. One locus has a single triangle torso figure holding a paddle overhead; it has been damaged by attempts to make a latex casting. Two lines of 19 figures, including 17 stick figures are located nearby (see "C" in Figure 3.86). There are two triangle torso figures in the grouping (see page v). These figures are extremely faint.

Paniau 1, Section 5: near the center of the site, one panel with three stick anthropomorphs in a line, plus one partial figure (Figure 3.90). Two of the figures are connected.

Paniau 1, Section 6: near the center of the site, three panels with four units. Two anthropomorphs are large ungainly figures; one has widespread arms (see Figure 3.24). Another stick figure is more compact but still displays exaggerated arms and legs (Figure 3.91).

Paniau 1, Section 7: five panels, nine figures. A partial figure plus indeterminate pecking and a modern-appearing triangle torso figure are in this section, as well as a cluster of three active figures (Figure 3.92) and a huge active anthropomorph (Figure 3.93), associated with the images in Figure 3.88.

Paniau 1, Section 8: east end of site, two panels with three anthropomorphs. One is very large and is associated with a tiny figure; the other is a jaunty open base triangle torso figure (Figure 3.94). The latter was discovered under several centimeters of detritus.

Figure 3.92. This panel of what appears to be three dancing stick figures measures 108 x 108 cm.

Figure 3.94 A jaunty figure from Section 8 (63 x 49 cm).

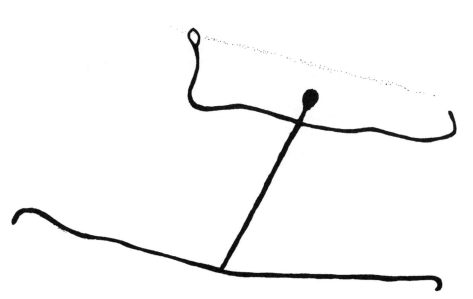

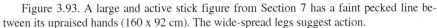

Figure 3.93. A large and active stick figure from Section 7 has a faint pecked line between its upraised hands (160 x 92 cm). The wide-spread legs suggest action.

Figure 3.95 from Section 9 may represent a dancer (118 x 110 cm).

Figure 3.97. One of the remaining panels at Paniau 3 measures 165 x 71 cm. Severe damage is shown by hatching.

Paniau 1, Section 9: west end of site, four panels with 28 figures, including a long line of 23 stick anthropomorphs labeled B in Figure 3.86, and five other figures, some very large. One of the latter (a very faint motif) appears to be a dancer (Figure 3.95).

Paniau 1, Section 10: four panels, eight anthropomorphs. Three of these are in lively poses. One triangle figure holds a paddle aloft.

Paniau 1, Section 11: two panels, four units. Two triangle figures with paddles aloft (see Figure 3.28). Another huge spindly triangle figure has a tiny stick figure below its right arm.

Paniau 1, Section 12: southwest end of site, one large stick figure and part of the long line of anthropomorphs which extends into Section 13 (Figure 3.96) and labeled A in Figure 3.86.

Paniau 1, Section 13: the other end of the line of figures that continues from Section 12. The panel contains 30 stick figures in a row with three more offset to one side; this grouping has been referred to as "marching men" by Cox and Stasack (1970:45) who state this ". . . can only be a line of men in single file on a trail."

The lines of small stick figures at Paniau 1 are unusual. These consist of symmetrical anthropomorphs that line up, one after the other and form straight or curving lines as they meander across the pāhoehoe.

Aside from the long lines of stick figures, there is remarkable variation in figure sizes at this site, ranging from small (12 x 20 cm) to very large (276 x 236 cm). The many large figures, most rather ungainly, contrast with smaller compact ones. The large anthropomorphs have very narrow lines for torsos, wide-apart legs that often indicate action such as running or perhaps dancing. Arms are as wide, or wider, than leg spread. Sex is not indicated and the heads are round and often on a long neck; a few have fingers and it is fairly common to find a tiny stick figure associated. Some large spindly figures are also in triangular-bodied form and may hold a paddle aloft. No cupules were found at this site.

Paniau 2 (1 unit): lies north of Site 1 and east of a destroyed site, Paniau 3. It consists of a single petroglyph at the edge of the kiawe forest. It is nearly surrounded by tread marks from bulldozers so it may be that other motifs were here at one time.

Paniau 3 (Bishop Museum Survey, Paniau B; 13 units): the site is relatively close to Puakō Beach Drive. In fact, the residential developments are all that lie between the site and the road. This site is virtually destroyed. When the original mapping was undertaken by the Bishop Museum Survey (1964), the drawings showed a considerable collection of figures. Only 13 were relocated, and some of these are remnants. Most that remain have been damaged. As near as could be determined, some 40 units have disappeared. Bulldozer tracks can be seen on what is left of the pāhoehoe.

Cement covers part of one panel at this site; apparently this was the corner post for a pigpen. From what remains, and from a study of the Bishop Museum report, the main elements were anthropomorphs. One line of four stick figures drawn in their report is now gone, as are two possible profile figures. A particularly fine set of triangle torso anthropomorphs that originally comprised seven in a row plus two more on the right, is now reduced to five, and nearly all are damaged or partially broken. Only traces remain of the two off to one side, (Figure 3.97).[5]

Figure 3.96. The so-called "marching men" panel from Sections 12-13 is 11.60 m long.

Paniau 4 (five separate loci; 78 units): The early Bishop Survey found 136 petro-glyphs in this area. Despite considerable effort, only 78 could be relocated. These sites are scattered around among collapsed lava tubes, dense kiawe growth and heavily disturbed areas—a nightmare for the researcher. Those found do not necessarily correlate with drawings made by the Bishop Museum in 1964, and thus we have no way of knowing whether we were at their sites labeled A-1 or A-4, etc.

In one instance an entire section of petroglyph-bearing rock at Paniau had been broken off and carried away; by studying the Bishop Museum sketches it was determine that the missing section of rock contained 12 pet-roglyphs.

It is possible that some of the "missing" petroglyphs were overlooked due to the difficulty of crawling through the kiawe forest and collapsed lava tubes. There has been considerable disturbance here: pipelines, electrical poles, and a new road leading to a development now run through this area.

One of the panels at Paniau 4 (called 5A on the Bishop Museum draw-ing) was still extant when we recorded the site, but it was a mere three me-ters from the new road and clearly visible from it. It was notable for its clus-tering of stick figures and placement of cupules in relation to the figures (Figure 3:98). This panel was stolen by vandals in 1996 (*Rapa Nui Journal* 10(3):62).

Figure 3.98. The stolen panel measured 110 x 75 cm. Note cupules in association with the figures.

Paniau 5 (1 unit): a single petroglyph on a beach rock, facing inland; it was not possible to correlate this figure with the Bishop Museum drawings. In 1995, we were unable to relocate the boulder and it is assumed that it had been removed by vandals.

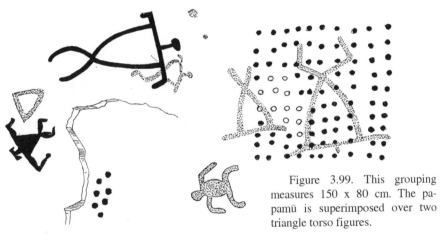

Figure 3.99. This grouping measures 150 x 80 cm. The pa-pamū is superimposed over two triangle torso figures.

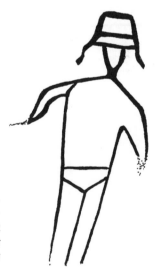

Figure 3.100. Paniau 6 (80 x 50 cm). This human figure wearing a hat has been dubbed Captain Cook by locals.

Paniau 6 (30 units): on pāhoehoe, only 15 meters from the ocean's edge at the end of a beach ac-cess path; it is not shown on the Bishop Museum Survey map. This site is particularly vulner-able due to its highly visible location at that point where the public gains access the beach. It has been vandalized and it appears that many of the petroglyphs have been embellished over the years. Some clearly are modern. The rock is very dark and the petroglyphs are not clearly visible.

The only known papamū[6] (pecked game board) at Puakō is located here, and superim-poses two figures (Figure 3.99). There is one deep cupule plus a cluster of small pits that may have been the start of another pāpamu, and some faintly pecked names and initials. One of the more problematic units is a human figure wearing a western-style hat. Although it is patinated and is made with strong outline and deep pecking, the form surely is historic (a local resident stated that it represented Captain Cook). It is curious, and one of a kind (Figure 3.100). Oth-ers here, such as the faint triangular anthropomorphs beneath the papamū and some other small human forms appear well within the normal range for prehistoric carvings. Due to its exposed location and lack of protection, this site no doubt will continue to be vandalized.

Figure 3.101 (80 x 60 cm). These two anthropomorphs from Mālama appear to represent a couple.

Mālama Trail Site

<u>Mālama site</u>. (14 loci; 24 units): Nineteen of the figures are anthropomorphs. Three stick figures feature prominent toes and/or fingers and a pair of triangle torso figures appear to be a 'couple' (Figure 3.101). Aside from the petroglyphs there are four deep and narrow polissoir and other polishing areas in the form of rounded and smoothed depressions.

Footnotes

[1] Charcoal from beneath lava flow near the upper highway has been dated by ^{14}C to 3360± 200 years (Geological Map of the Island of Hawaii 1996).

[2] Puakō site correlation between the letter designations of the Bishop Museum Survey (1964) and the current study are listed below. The Bishop Museum Survey also refers to sites represented by the letters J, K, L and M which were added to their map but not illustrated in their report. Lacking illustrative material, we have not been able to correlate them with our sites. Kāeo A = 1; B = 4; (L?) = 6, 6.1; (M?) = 7, 7.1; (K?) = 8; C = 9; D = 10; E = 12; F = 14; G = 18; H = 19; I = 24.

[3] Bishop Museum's Paniau A = 5; B = 2 and 3; C = 1. The Museum did not give a designation for 5 and 6.

[4] This petroglyph has been damaged by many rubbings; layers of paint can be seen on it.

[5] See Figure 2, Cox and Stasack (1970) for a view of this panel prior to the damage.

[6] Papamū were used for playing *kōnane*, a game similar to checkers. Papamū are composed of small pecked cupules that run in lines, and are laid out in a square pattern. They are found at many sites in the islands, although there are variations in the numbers of cupules in the rows and numbers of lines in the square.

4

KALAOA AND OTHER CAVES: HAWAI'I ISLAND

KALAOA

Kalaoa cave is on the Kona side of the Big Island and south of Puakō in the Keahole area (see Figure 3.1). The site is entered from a large collapsed section of lava tube; the tube itself was excavated by Hammatt and Folk (1980).

The cave at Kalaoa consists of three major lava tubes that radiate from a sink or collapsed area approximately 30-40 meters in diameter. The caves were used over a long time-span for a burial place, habitation, and refuge. The north tube, which contains petroglyphs, extends N-NE for approximately 124 meters. Its west wall contains 12 meters of petroglyphs and a few are located on the east wall.

Hammatt and Folk's (1980) report[1] describes their research and illustrates one section of a petroglyph panel that is located within the cave. In 1990, as part of a larger recording effort at Puakō (Lee 1990), all the petroglyphs inside the cave were documented.

Petroglyphs are located only within the area exposed to natural light coming from the collapsed sink area and not beyond. Hammatt and Folk (1980:34) excavated a platform built against the cave wall, revealing portions of a petroglyph panel. They determined that at least some units were made prior to the placement of the platform against it. Their report (ibid.:32) states: ". . . this segment of the platform showed that only one section, approximately one meter long, actually had platform slab paving rocks contacting the petroglyphs. This trench . . . was excavated first. The loose framework slab platform was removed to a depth of approximately 55 to 60 centimeters exposing 30 centimeters of the lower part of three petroglyph figures . . . . By this relationship it was determined that the making of the petroglyphs preceded the construction of the platform."

Hammatt and Folk (1980:36-7) also cite the "petroglyph phase" as the earliest use, but ". . . the making of the petroglyphs may overlap with the domestic occupation phase . . . ." which appears to be the second use of the site. Evidence of occupation involving domestic craft activities suggests use by more than one family unit. The use of the cave as a place of refuge postdates the domestic occupation. A date from basaltic glass was obtained from the

Figure 4.1 Triangle torso figures at Kalaoa. Note unusually long and widespread arms. The crusty surface of the cave walls results in rough outlines.

domestic phase, ca. 1700 AD. No attempts were made to date the burials which remained undisturbed.

The cave presented significant difficulties for petroglyph documentation. Obtaining adequate light was a problem as the cave opening is partially blocked off by a stone wall, leaving only a narrow entry passage to illuminate the decorated areas. These loosely piled stones served to secure the cave when it was used for a refuge.

Many of the petroglyphs are barely visible against the cave walls which are fractured and coated with calcium deposits, with some stalactites on overhead horizontal strata. Most of the petroglyphs are pecked into a crusty surface which tends to break easily, leaving an uneven line or ragged shape (Figure 4.1). Thus they are less clearly defined than many that are found on pāhoehoe. In contrast, Cleghorn (1980:7), describing the cave at Hilina Pali, notes that the vitreous surface of the natural ledges inside that cave allowed for a delicate, fine-lined technique that made small and detailed petroglyphs possible, including such features as fingers, hair or headdresses.

Figure 4.2 Recording the petroglyphs at Kalaoa was difficult because of the lack of light and the mineral deposit on the cave walls.

Due to moisture and deposits on the walls as well as the undulating surfaces, gridding the panels for documentation was not practical. Thus on-site drawings (Figure 4.2) or direct tracings on Pliofilm were made with marking pens. The tracings were photographed with slide film and the slides projected onto paper for final drawings, which were made by comparing with sketches and slides of the actual petroglyphs. Those petroglyphs that had been chalked at some time in the past were particularly difficult to see clearly as this practice obscures and confuses the images. Panel designations were made based upon natural divisions on the rock walls.

Beginning at the south end of the west wall, petroglyphs are scattered along at approximate eye level and are very difficult to see. Parts of the wall have exfoliated and some figures are incomplete.

DISCUSSION

Although there is some variety within the universe of figure motifs at Kalaoa, few exhibit fine details. We recorded 107 elements on the west wall and two on the east wall. Why the west wall was the preferred locale for petroglyphs is unknown. It may have been cultural, location of petroglyphs may have been related to some activity inside the cave or, perhaps because more light strikes the west wall during certain times of the year.

Although some of the petroglyphs consist of partial figures (legless, armless, or headless) and many are crudely pecked, all those that are identifiable represent anthropomorphs. Fifteen others are unidentified. Some in this latter category were probably anthropomorphs also but, due to the condition of the surface of the cave wall, are now unclear. Of the figure types, 44 are stick figures and 37 are triangle torso anthropomorphs; 4 others are in the 'other body' category. There are ten cupules (all on vertical surfaces); two of these are placed within the leg area of figures, one near the crotch. It is possible these refer to the genital piko, rather than sex markers.

Because of the crusty surface of the rock and rough pecking, little could be determined with regard to the great deal of superimposition present. Some figures connect and overlap which suggests that the panel was made over a period of time. Other panels here tend to have figures 'free-floating' without reference to each other. At least eleven figures in the long final section have paddles raised above their heads. These 'paddle figures' bear a strong resemblance to petroglyphs reported by Carter and Somers (1990: Figure 10) from the Puna-Kaū area which has a group scene of men holding a steering paddle above their heads. Holding a paddle aloft in a static position can be distinguished from holding a paddle at an angle, as if in a threatening gesture or dance posture. Many examples of the latter can be seen at Ka'ūpūlehu and at the Paniau section of Puakō. A comparison between the motifs found at Kalaoa with those from the Hilina Pali petroglyph cave (Cleghorn 1980) and a cave near Pahala, Ka'ū (Cox and Stasack 1970:12) shows considerable variations from those at Kalaoa; the 'paddle dancers' at Apua, Puna (ibid.), are stylistically closer to those at Kalaoa.

Kirch (1985:169) suggested that the Kalaoa panel with its upraised canoe paddles or war clubs was executed as a single work and that this panel may depict either a dance or battle scene. However it is unlikely that a panel that was carved at one time would have so many figures superimposed upon others in this manner.

Paddles had enormous significance for the sea-faring peoples of Polynesia and were replete with overtones of status and founding ancestors. Symbolically, the paddle becomes an extension of the man; the more expert he becomes the greater importance it assumes. Buck (1938:34-5) notes that paddles were given names and even the canoes of the gods had their steering paddles named. Paddles were the weapon of choice for those in fighting canoes. Further, dance paddles are known from Easter Island, Ra'ivavae, Tonga and the Cook islands. Religious dancing was a prominent feature in ancient Polynesia and closely related to the offerings and feasts in honor of the gods (Handy 1927:210). Given the importance of paddles and their ceremonial use, it is likely that some sort of ritual was being commemorated, perhaps connected to a status burial placed in the cave, or veneration of a famous canoe paddler or renowned warrior.

Our study of the petroglyphs at Kalaoa confirms Hammatt and Folk's determination that the petroglyphs were made before the cave had a refuge wall, based upon the light factor which appears to verify that the carvings were made prior to that time. They may be concurrent with the use of the cave as a burial site. Few attempts have been made to establish dates; it is hoped future dating efforts will provide a more secure time-frame for this small but interesting site.

SITE DESCRIPTIONS, KALAOA

WEST WALL

Panel 1 (7 units): vertical wall. Lower figures are easier to discern. One legless figure has a line arching overhead, like a rainbow. It is possible that it had legs originally but the area between the legs was removed in the pecking process. Five of the seven are clearly triangle torso anthropomorphs. The other two are unclear traces of figures.

Panel 2 (4 units): vertical wall. Two are fairly complete anthropomorphs, and one of these appears to be phallic. There is one triangle shape which may be the beginning a figure and another shape consisting of two opposing triangles which probably were intended as the torso and legs of another figure.

Panel 3 (19 units): vertical wall. On the upper part are four units, including a triangle with head, but neither arms or legs. Adjacent is a group of at least three forms that appear to be figure fragments. Below and right is an anthropomorph with arms up, joining at the head. The lower portion has six visible figures; a partial one; and some indecipherable marks. A large exfoliated area is located on the lower right side and, with the proper side lighting, three or four very faint figures can be made out. Two of the anthropomorphs have triangle torsos; one is a stick figure with detached head, and the others appear to have square torsos.

Panel 4 (13 units): vertical wall. This panel has four full figures, several incomplete anthropomorphs and fragments. One stick figure has a line overhead.

Panel 5a and b (15+ units): vertical wall. Petroglyphs are heavily chalked and disfigured. The main large figure in 5a appears to have one arm up and one down, with an object held aloft. Lines continue across the base of the figure crossing a natural ledge in the wall, and encompassing another partial figure. The other four figures are incomplete in one way or another, and a pecked area above is not complete enough to describe. Panel 5b was the panel uncovered by Hammatt and Folk (1980). The panel has been damaged by erosion, exfoliation and chalking. Most of the motifs are variations on human figures and superposition has resulted in some strange figures, particularly the group in the lower left section (see Figure 9 in Hammatt and Folk). A row of small cupules runs above the panel and a few isolated figures are located above. These were not noted in the drawing by Hammatt and Folk.

Panel 6 (45+ units): vertical wall. This is the most complete group of figures (Figure 4.3). The long intricate panel has anthropomorphs holding paddles aloft plus other figures that appear to be integrated into the 'action'. A small grouping on the lower right includes a figure with its arms out, seemingly sheltering two smaller figures (see also Figure 4.1). This panel is neatly divided by natural ledges in the wall, giving the impression of a frieze.

EAST WALL
Panel 1 (two units): vertical wall. Approximately 90 cm apart, both figures are incomplete.

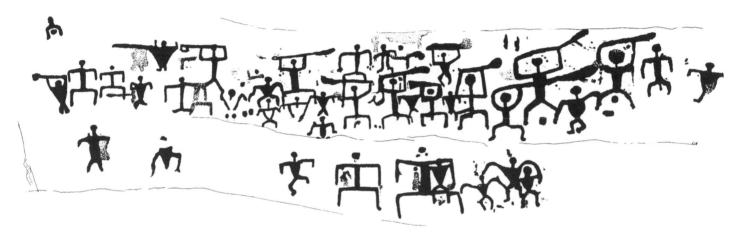

Figure 4.3 The main panel on the west wall of Kalaoa; it measures 4.2 x 1.2 m.

OTHER CAVES SITES, HAWAI'I ISLAND

Eight years after our documentation of the cave at Kalaoa, we were provided with information and photographs of other caves on the Big Island. Although one of these has not yet been recorded, it is interesting to note similarities as well as differences in the design inventories. One of the sites is located near Kalaoa (here designated Kalaoa II). Two others are located in the Ka'ū desert (Cleghorn 1980; Stasack and Stasack 1997).

KALAOA II
In an initial report by Walker and Rosendahl (1989), few photographs of the petroglyphs are provided. Slides of this remarkable site were kindly supplied by Rowland Reeve. Despite the fact that it is difficult to study a site from photographic images only, it is apparent that this site contains a remarkable collection of petroglyphs, in two separate sections of a lava tube (Figures 4.4 and 4.5).

Figure 4.4 A portion of the panel at Kalaoa II. Most figures have triangle torsos. Sizes vary and many figures are connected. Note that some have wide curved arms similar to Kalaoa I. (Photo: R. Reeve)

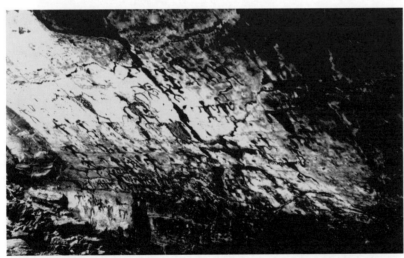

Figure 4.5 Another view of Kalaoa II. Some of these figures have prominent phalli. (Photo: R. Reeve)

The Walker and Rosendahl report (1989:A-16) mentions human figures but adds that some represent pregnant women, birthing women, men displaying sexual prowess, and figures copulating. From studying the photographs, this interpretation may be in doubt. Clearly there are figures with prominent phalli, but a fat anthropomorph may or may not be a pregnant woman, and nothing appears to represent either birth or copulation. Although three figures are in a prone position, they are not interacting (Figure 4.6) and may just as well be interpreted as fallen enemies.

Triangle torso figures clearly are in the majority and many of these have muscles indicated. This obviously is an important site, and in need of documentation and preservation. This area is marked for development and once this begins, these remarkable petroglyph panels will be impacted by visitors and construction.

Figure 4.6 This panel displays a variety of anthropomorph types including three stick figures in a prone position. (Photo: R. Reeve)

Figure 4.7. Hilina Pali petroglyphs are located on horizontal and vertical surfaces. (Photo: Gordon Morse)

HILINA PALI

The Hilina Pali site is located in the dry Kaʻū desert, in a most inhospitable spot. The survey and fieldwork by Cleghorn undertaken in 1975 included mapping and excavations (Figure 4.7). The latter revealed objects of material culture and dates.

The petroglyphs are located along the cave walls for some 17 meters from the opening (Figure 4.8). Although all the units were not documented, approximately 550 were recorded (Cleghorn 1980:7). Elements include human and zoomorphic figures, cupules and straight lines, seven turtles and possibly some images of dogs. There are two

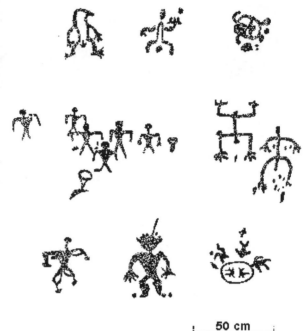

Figure 4.9. A few of the motifs from Hilina Pali showing the variety of figure types (from Cleghorn 1980). Note bird-headed figure and a turtle. Both stick and triangle torso anthropomorphs are represented. An odd group at lower right is described by Cleghorn as a cock fight.

fishhooks, and nine motifs of human feet. Figure 4.9 illustrates some of the forms at Hilina Pali (from Cleghorn 1980).

Radiocarbon dates from the excavations indicate the site was occupied around AD 1540-1720 (ibid. 20). Building activities inside the cave led to the construction of an artificial floor that buried some of the petroglyphs. The lower levels feature stick figures, higher levels feature triangle torso figures. The conclusion by Cleghorn (1980:30) is that the depiction of the human form changed from stick figure to triangle torso figure around AD 1600.

Figure 4.8. Drawing of the petroglyph panels at Hilina Pali (Cleghorn 1980).

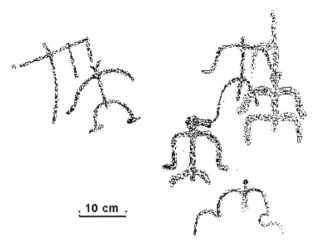

Figure 4.10. Stick figures from Kaʻū. Some are attached. Note wavy arms on lower right anthropomorph (Stasack and Stasack 1997).

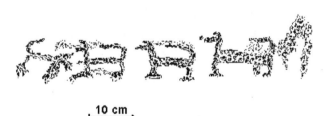

Figure 4.11. A panel of dogs and what appears to be a horizontal headless anthropomorph at Kaʻū (Stasack and Stasack 1997).

KAʻŪ CAVE

Kaʻū Cave is located in the southern part of the Kaʻū desert near the ocean's edge, and apparently it has been affected in the past by earthquakes and tsunami, according to Stasack and Stasack (1997).

Two hundred-twenty petroglyphs were recorded at this cave site (ibid.: 33). Nearly 60% are anthropomorphs, but none of these are triangle torso figures (Figures 4.10, 4.11 and 4.12). This is an important variation and suggestive of an early date for the site.

Eight dog figures were documented (Figure 4.11) (rare in this part of the island), and one turtle. Of significance are anthropomorphic figures with bird heads and one squatting profile figure. The latter is identical in form to those from Kāeo 1, Puakō. Indeed, the stick figures most resemble those from Kāeo 1, which is also considered to be an early site.

Although this is a tentative conclusion, it appears from a study of secondary sources—and the incidence of stick figures *v.* triangle torso figures—that the cave sites in the Kaʻū are earlier than those in the area of Kalaoa on the Kona coast. Other cave sites remain to be documented on the island of Hawaiʻi. Given the disturbances of geology and development that have occurred in the past, it is imperative that they be recorded soon.

FOOTNOTE

[1] Hammatt and Folk erroneously refer to the long panel as being on the east wall and the opposite as the south wall. Their map (1980: Fig 8) shows the correct orientation, however.

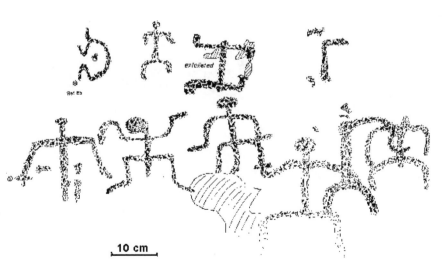

Figure 4.12. A group of stick figures at Kaʻū. Note profile squatting figure (upper left); it is nearly identical to the one found at Puakō (see Figure 3.6). (Stasack and Stasack 1997).

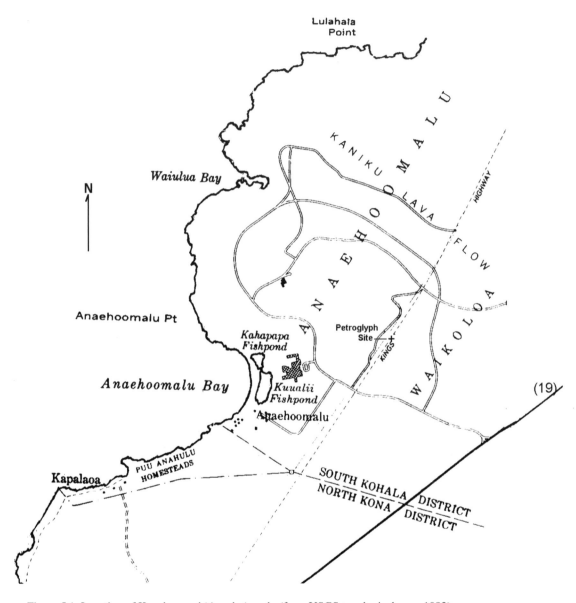

Figure 5.1. Location of Kapalaoa and 'Anaeho'omalu (from USGS topological map, 1982)

5

'Anaeho'omalu and Kapalaoa: Hawai'i Island

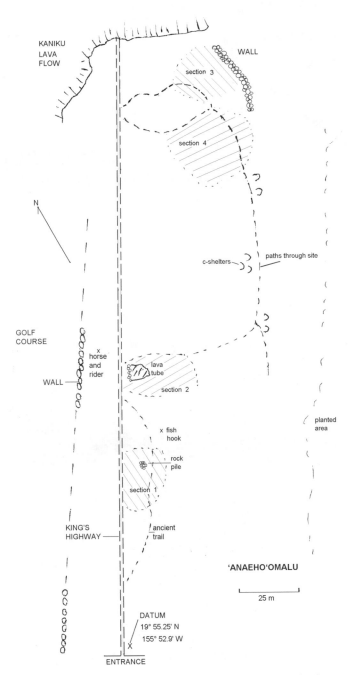

Figure 5.2. Map of the petroglyph site at 'Anaeho'omalu showing the Kings Trail, an earlier footpath, and our designated sections.

Before large resorts were constructed in the area of South Kohala, the land was barren pāhohehoe interspersed with flows of 'a'ā. An ancient trail—and the historic King's trail—ran through the area. Other than that, for miles nothing but blackish fields of lava were to be seen. Once tourism became a focus, things changed. Land that formerly appeared barren and of little commercial value, blossomed—with a little help from bulldozers and top soil, and a great deal of money.

Today one approaches 'Anaeho'omalu through lush golf greens, spreading across acres of land, blooming bougainvillea, and palm tree-lined boulevards that stand out against barren miles of surrounding lava flow. Large tourist hotels, resorts, and condominiums are seen along the newly created lake and at the ocean's edge. An upscale shopping center is located slightly inland from the hotels. A paved path leads into the remains of the petroglyph site.

'Anaeho'omalu's petroglyphs formerly covered a much larger area, but portions of the site were destroyed to create the golf course. Today the black lava contrasts with vivid green golf links water hazards, and palm trees.

The oasis of 'Anaeho'omalu (a nearby sandy bay with sheltered ancient fishpond) is located to the south of the hotels, and it also contrasts sharply with adjoining fields of 'a'ā and pāhoehoe lava. Figure 5.1 is a map of the area and Figure 5.2 shows a map of the petroglyph site including a modern path as well as the remains of C-shelters and a collapsed lava tube. The latter appears to have been the focus of the site. Modern stone walls separate the site from the surrounding golf course.

Coming into the site of 'Anaeho'omalu's petroglyphs today is a far different experience than it was originally (Figure 5.3). Because the site was undocumented prior to development, it is hard to estimate what has been lost. It is said that approximately three acres of carvings existed (Krauss 1988:356), and Kirch (1985:169) refers to more than 9,000 figures; J. H. Cox (1961) suggested there were 9,400 petroglyphs. Today, only the center portion of the site remains, surrounded by golf links (Figure 5.4).

The southern border of the Kanikū Lava Flow marks the northern end of the site. Bisected by the Alaloa trail, 'Anaeho'omalu's petroglyph site is also the ahupua'a boundary between Waikoloa and 'Anaeho'omalu.

Excavations have revealed dates that indicate 'Anaeho'omalu was settled as early as the 10th century, probably as a small fishing camp. Later, a large permanent settlement existed here, with the inhabitants focusing on marine exploitation of the fishpond.

The presence of mullet at 'Anaeho'omalu may have aroused the envy of potential conquerors and visitors who sought its sacred gifts and mana. Barrera (1971:106) places the initial use of the majority of sites at 'Anaeho'omalu as not before the late 14th century and he suggests the major activity in the petroglyph fields to be at the same time. He postulates new occupations at four sites in the 1700s, but these were subsequently abandoned, as were seven others. Only two sites were still occupied as late as the 1800s but they, too, were forsaken by the middle of the 19th century.

'Anaeho'omalu lies five kilometers south of Puakō but, despite the proximity, there is a world of difference between them. Although 'Anaeho-'omalu has its share of anthropomorphs, it is chiefly known for the multitude of geometric motifs.

Figure 5.3. 'Anaeho'omalu's petroglyphs formerly were found in a desolate stretch of pāhoehoe. This picture was taken by Edward Stasack around 1960, prior to development in the area.

Figure 5.4. The petroglyph site of 'Anaeho'omalu today with its encircling golf course. The collapsed lava tube is a central feature of the site and is surrounded by petroglyphs.

Figure 5.5. Grinding area partially obliterates one petroglyph; subsequently, another petroglyph was made within that depression. Note linked circles and open-base triangle figures. A small quadruped is seen at lower right corner.

Some grinding basins at 'Anaeho'omalu (one of which has a petroglyph inside it) have been dated between AD 1400 and 1600 (Ross Cordy, personal communication 1992) (Figure 5.5). Increasing evidence suggests that there was a peak population during this period of time.

'Anaeho'omalu undoubtedly was a sacred area which seems to account for the variety and great numbers of petroglyphs carved there. Because of its nearby fishponds, it was more of a destination than either nearby Kapalaoa or other sites along the Kona coast, such as Puakō and Ka'ūpūlehu. Barrère (1971:109-110) states that "Most, if not all, of the trails into and within 'Anaeho'omalu were surely marked out by the prehistoric inhabitants of the land. They led to clusters of houses and to water pools within the area, and to the inland coastal trail that led to the uplands of Waimea, from whence came *poi* and whatever other necessities or 'luxuries' gift-exchanges of fish might bring. Foot travelers making the trek between Kohala and Kona on this inland trail no doubt frequently used the branch trails into 'Anaeho'omalu."

In ancient times, a southward journey along the Kona coast by canoe was propelled by favorable winds. But the return trip often was made by foot along the Alaloa trail. Such travel no doubt had an impact on the petroglyphs carved at 'Anaeho'omalu. Except for the time of the makahiki when tribute collectors (*ho'okupu*) went around the island, crossing the borders of the ahupua'a from Kona into Kohala was kapu. Makahiki also was the time of year for Kona storms, when the winds switch direction. The experienced observer could spot the *makani pua'i hale*, the wind that "goes around the house"; swirling clouds over Waimea would predict that the next day would have winds coming from the other direction and, for the next week, a return trip could by made by canoe. Kona winds were the exception, however, and thus there was a fair amount of overland travel during winter months. For travelers, then, the period of access to 'Anaeho'omalu was during the time of tribute collecting and a welcome relief from the severity of kapu. Keeping in mind that 'Anaeho'omalu was a sacred place, there was probably some genuine anticipation.

When the primary purpose of the area became that of keeping and maintaining the king's mullet ponds, petroglyph activity may have ceased. Perhaps the pond-keepers preferred to live at nearby Kapalaoa, an attractive shaded setting that supported a resident population later than did 'Anaeho'omalu.

All of this changed when kapu was lifted. Horses were brought to the island in 1803—a gift for King Kamehameha—and cattle, sandalwood, and crops began to be moved along coastal trails: the 'King's Trail' was constructed around 1800, bisecting the site.

Opportunities for exchange of ideas increased, and now there theoretically was unrestrained access to all the petroglyph sites, al-

Figures 5.6 a) 'Anaeho'omalu. The ancient Alaloa trail cuts across and over some of the petroglyphs. The traffic in the 19th century was heavy, and included shod horses. Much of the abrasion probably happened after 1819, when the kapu was lifted and, for some Hawaiians, access to sacred areas was no longer forbidden; b) A drawing of the area shown in the photo. See also Figure 1.3.

though many still clung to the old religion and respected boundaries and kapu, as before. After 1819, travel was open to all who chose to accept the new freedom (Figure 5.6 a, b).

It is possible that 'Anaeho'omalu was a rest stop for those traveling the trail; coming from the north, the site is in a large depression at the end of a rough stretch of 'a'ā. There are sheltering caves as well as 'C-shaped' shelters made of piled up stones in the shape of a half-circle.

As we noted, in former times the petroglyphs were part of a desolate sea of pāhoehoe that stretched for miles. Today the site presents an entirely different vista: tightly hemmed in by the golf course, visitors are in danger of being bombarded by stray golf balls. Indeed, the north part of the site has danger signs suggesting that one should not venture further into the petroglyph areas.

The original size of the petroglyph site is unknown. The apparent 'center' was preserved while the perimeter was bulldozed to allow maximum space for the golf links. Thus what can be seen now is assumed to have been the site's focus.

DISCUSSION

According to Cox and Stasack (1970:85) 'Anaeho'omalu contains several thousand units, a low number compared to Kirch's (1985:169) estimate of 9,000. As our brief study managed to document 2126 petroglyphs with several sections still unrecorded, the actual total today probably falls somewhere between the two.

The reader is urged to keep in mind that any tally for 'Anaeho'omalu is made from a sample only. Most common elements (81%) are cupules, circles and variations

Figure 5.7. A horse and rider from ʻAnaehoʻomalu. Cowboys were brought from Mexico in 1832 by King Kamehameha III to teach Hawaiians how to ride horses and herd cattle. According to locals this example probably is a more modern effort.

Figure 5.8. ʻAnaehoʻomalu. A one-armed figure that appears to be a woman wearing a muʻumuʻu. Note the bird-like feet.

of circular elements; only 5.8% are human figures. The numbers of triangle-bodied anthropomorphs and stick figures are roughly equal. The remainder are feet, lettering, fishhooks, and historic elements such as sailing ships. A modern horse and rider (Figure 5.7) was added in recent years. There is an image that appears to be a woman wearing a *muʻumuʻu.* (Figure 5.8).

ʻAnaehoʻomalu has many instances of superimposition, such as the image of an aliʻi with feathered headdress engraved over the older, very faint triangle torso figure (Figure 5.9).

In several places the worn footpath overlaps and occasionally obliterates the petroglyphs, clearly indicating the petroglyphs had preceded the trail and that, over time, any proscription protecting them had expired. The proliferation of motifs around the collapsed lava tube suggests that this was the center of spiritual power. It includes a raised area and a cave: both situations appear to have had some kind of numinous essence.

The elaborate circular motifs with interior designs were noted with interest. The circle was a constant theme which we believe was carved throughout all periods. There are thousands of variations of this

Figure 5.9. ʻAnaehoʻomalu has a few well-carved anthropomorphs, such as this example with a plumed headdress and muscled arms. It is pecked over an earlier, fainter image and has some deep scattered peck marks in association.

universal symbol on Hawai'i Island. They may refer to a concept of completion, a journey, life's journey, or encompassing by forming a ring around otherwise separate units. Whatever their significance, they appear to have been of considerable importance. In a quick survey, 48 of these motifs were recorded. Figure 5.10 shows some examples of these circles. In addition to circles, large 'enclosures' have been pecked around various motifs. What this signifies is unknown although an enclosure may have been intended as a means of giving the designs special presentation by isolating them. Enclosures are not common in the islands, but they are also found at Pu'uloa, where they are also associated with a trail.

It is noteworthy that all of the names carved here are Hawaiian, despite the fact that much of the traffic during the mid-nineteenth century included foreigners. Some of the carved words and names are puzzling, particularly those made in mirror writing: OKAUP and INIHUAK. The former is Puakō, in reverse (Figures 5.11a,b). The latter may be, in part, Kaū, a place name. Ka'u has multiple meanings and is a place-name for the southern *moku* (land division) of Hawai'i.

This site is in need of comprehensive documentation. Despite its protection now that it is part of a luxury resort and surrounded by a golf course, erosion continues. Recently, signs were erected forbidding rubbings of the motifs, and requesting the visitors not to chalk the images. Visitation is not heavy, despite the new walking trail into the site. The focus is now on resort activities such as golfing, and little notice is paid to petroglyphs by those whizzing past in golf carts.

20 cm

Figure 5.10. A sampling of circles and variations on the theme of circles from 'Anaeho'omalu. Some have intricate interior patterns.

a   b

Figure 5.11 a) Hawaiian words carved at the south end of the petroglyph field by the Alaloa trail, 'Anaeho'omalu. The words Puakō and Kauhini are written in reverse: b) A close-up of the carving.

Site Descriptions: 'Anaeho'omalu

Time constraints prevented a complete recording of all the petroglyphs at 'Anaeho'omalu. The few days that were available allowed only enough time to document a sample (2126 units). The site was divided arbitrarily into four sections (see Figure 5.2).

Section 1 (14 panels, 985 units): directly on the ancient foot trail at the south end of the site, near the present-day entry to the petroglyphs. This section has most complete coverage. This portion of the site has an ancient footpath that has worn down the petroglyphs, leaving fragments of motifs on either side. A stone cairn is located close to the path and approximately in the middle of this section. The footpath meanders and is a separate feature from the King's Trail, which runs on a straight line through the site (see Figures 1.3, 5.2 and 5.6).

Much superposition is evident in Section 1 and most panels are a mass of pecking, including some recent vandalism. The pāhoehoe is in poor condition in general, and erosion has made some elements very unclear. Modern graffiti and attempts to make rubbings and castings have left paint and latex on the panels.

An outstanding panel in Section 1 was "dissected" by Kenneth Emory (Cox and Stasack 1970: Figure 71 a-d); he theorized how this collection of motifs and lines might have been built up over time. This panel seems to have begun as a large stick figure but subsequent additions over time transformed it. Of particular interest is the square head on the figure which echoes the square form on the mo'o figure from Puakō (Figure 5.12).

To the east of the old foot trail and slightly to the north, we recorded petroglyphs near a 'C' shelter, and the historic letters 'KA'. This area has a few open-base triangular figures, a few stick figures, and an outstanding fishhook, similar in form to petroglyphs recorded on Easter Island (Figure 5.13). However, the bulk of the petroglyphs are cupules, circles and variations thereof.

20 cm

Figure 5.12. Panel in Section 1 showing a variety of motifs and much superimposition. Compare to Figure 71 a-d in Cox and Stasack (1970). Note the large and small foot motifs, circles, and anthropomorph with two dots on each side of neck.

Figure 5.13. Petroglyphs of Hawaiian fishhooks are very similar to those found on Easter Island.

Section 2 (15 panels, 783 units): north along the trail and on a rise where a lava tube has collapsed, forming a cave shelter. Petroglyphs surround the lava tube and some are inside the depressed area. The petroglyphs in this area appear to be some of the oldest at this site because of the design elements, weathering, and their density. Two panels were divided with a grid prior to drawing and others were sketched and measured. We estimate that 3/4 of this area is documented. The designs here are mostly circles and cupules (Figure 5.14). This part of the site has many natural bubbles in the lava that were utilized as part of the design (Figure 5.15). The surfaces around the collapsed lava tube are crowded with designs; the rule seems to be that the 'best' or most ceremonially appropriate places are chosen first. Several 'enclosures' were noted. Dominant motifs include circles, concentric circles, and cup and ring motifs.

Section 3 (12 panels, 206 units): the north end where a path turns east from the King's trail and runs toward the adjacent maintenance yard; a stone wall defines the boundary of the site. Petroglyphs continue beneath the wall. The east-running path divides Section 3 into a north and south component. The western part of the area is more 'open' with fewer motifs which are spread out and isolated; on the east side, petroglyphs are more densely placed and superposition is the rule. It is estimated that only a small portion of the total has been documented.

Some very unusual motifs are seen here: a cape of the type worn only by ali'i (Figure 5.16) and some zigzags. Several large anthropomorphs were recorded but this area is notable for the numbers of circular elements that contain interior designs or divisions.

Section 4 (4 panels, 111 units): an extensive area of pāhoehoe which is literally covered with anthropomorphs and geometric motifs, historic lettering, and other petroglyphs. One hundred-eleven motifs in four panels were recorded in this sector, but in proportion to its area, we found the least number of units in this section.

Other: A random collection of 41 circular motifs was added to the data base from the vast central area that lies between the collapsed lava tube and northern end of the site.

Figure 5.14. Cupules (poho) and circles at 'Anaeho'omalu. Some are concentric rings and a few have enclosures around them. Every possible space has been heavily carved.

Figure 5.15. Detail of poho cluster and concentric rings carved around a natural lump in the lava. Use of natural features is common in the rock art. As can be seen, the cupules are on sloping surfaces and thus would not be suitable for containing the piko of an infant.

Figure 5.16. This petroglyph appears to depict a cape. Capes, made from thousands of brilliant feathers, were worn only by high ali'i.

KAPALAOA

Kapalaoa is located approximately 1.6 kilometers south of 'Anaeho'omalu, near a small cove paved with water-worn coral that would have provided an excellent canoe landing. Today it is accessed by a short walk south along the beach from 'Anaeho'omalu. At present the area is overgrown with kiawe, various native trees and ground cover. Many rock walls, house sites, and corrals are present, along with a few hundred petroglyphs that are strung along the pāhoehoe patches just north of the village site. The petroglyph site at Kapalaoa has not been documented, other than a few photographs, but is mentioned here to illustrate the impact that western contact—and culture—had on the traditional society of Hawai'i.

The main petroglyph area is on a natural rise of fairly smooth pāhoehoe surrounding a collapsed lava tube. From this vantage point the nearby bay can be viewed with ease (Figure 5.17).

The petroglyphs, which range from stick figures to historic elements, appear to cover an extended time period, possibly the same time span as those at 'Anaeho'omalu. There are certain 'themes' evident: sailing ships, a few names and dates, and a preponderance of triangle-bodied figures that seem to describe family connections or hereditary lines. There are also cupules, pāpamu (Figure 5.18) for playing kōnane, circles and variations thereof, groupings with and without figures, and meandering lines. One motif resembles a horse.

The most prominent designs, however, are those of sailing ships (Figure 5.19). About 15 are visible with the possibility of more beneath the kiawe and ground cover (Figure 5.20).

There were many ships in this area in the early part of the 19th century. Almost all of those photographed depict one and two-masted ships. There is one attempt at a three-masted ship but the design appears to have been too demanding for the pāhoehoe and the carver. The contours of the two-masted

Figure 5.17. From the petroglyph site at Kapalaoa one has a commanding view of the ocean and the bay at 'Anaeho'omalu. Kapalaoa was inhabited during the time of the sailing ships of Cook, Vancouver, and others, and has over 15 images of sailing vessels. One such ship can be seen near the center of the photograph. Long wavy lines traverse the pāhoehoe.

ships suggest they may have been representations of whalers. Most of the commerce along this coast in the early days dealt with either whaling or sandalwood (Figure 5.21).

One of the ship petroglyphs has some similarity to *Cleopatra's Barge*, a ship sold to Kamehameha II in 1820. Numerous ships were known to be in these waters in the 1800s: for example, in the year 1838, 110 vessels arrived at O'ahu (Ward 1967:141).

DISCUSSION

Petroglyphs of Polynesian canoes and of sails (with or without a canoe attached) are reasonably familiar design elements for the Hawaiian petroglyph maker. The ship, a vehicle for transportation, the conveyance of power and the bringing to the island of new technology undoubtedly possessed mana in the eyes of the islanders; it was a 'floating island.' A petroglyph of a sailing vessel or gun ship may have been an effort to simply make a record or to perhaps tap into its power. But probably there was much more significance than that. The impact of Cook's arrival by ship with sails reminiscent of the tapa hung from a wooden cross, symbol for the god Lono, could and probably did carry on and become perpetuated in ways that would be consistent with the veneration Hawaiians held for the ali'i. Recalling the many women who directed their men folk to place piko stumps into cracks and crevices on Cook's ships, it is clear that Hawaiians believed the mana of a man-god could be extended to his possessions. A ship, under certain conditions, could be seen as a holy tabernacle. Thus a sailing vessel was a suitable subject for the petroglyph, fulfilling one of its most sacred functions: to succor and gain the favor of the gods.

Figure 5.18. Small pecked depressions forming a pāpamu; this example is near the beach at Kapalaoa.

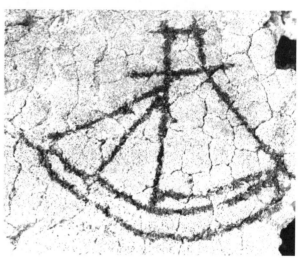

Figure 5.19. Petroglyph of a schooner from Kapalaoa area, now relocated to a nearby shopping center.

Figure 5.20. Petroglyphs of sailing vessels from the Big Island; these date from the late 18th to early 19th century. The images are found along the coast from Puna to Kohala. There are none at Kealakakua Buy where Cook anchored, perhaps because there is little suitable rock surface in that area.

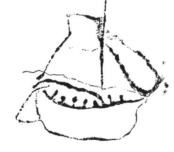

A structure as important as a ship would also qualify among the Hawaiians to have all four levels of meaning which pertained to most Hawaiian words: as well as a literal depiction, the ship could be seen as a moving, floating heiau; a conveyor for the gods; the way to the "source" over a distant horizon, to *kumu* itself; a symbol for female and male duality, the hull and masts; and kaona, 'hidden meanings.' The value of the image was not visual but metaphorical.

Like 'Anaeho'omalu, Kapalaoa is in need of full documentation. Some motifs already have been damaged by attempts to make copies and display latex spills, paint traces, and so on. Aside from the value of a record, it would be an interesting study to compare this site with nearby 'Anaeho'omalu and other sites on the Kona coast.

Figure 5.21. A sailing ship of the period under discussion, late 18th to early 19th century . At first, the ships appeared to be 'floating islands' to the Polynesians.

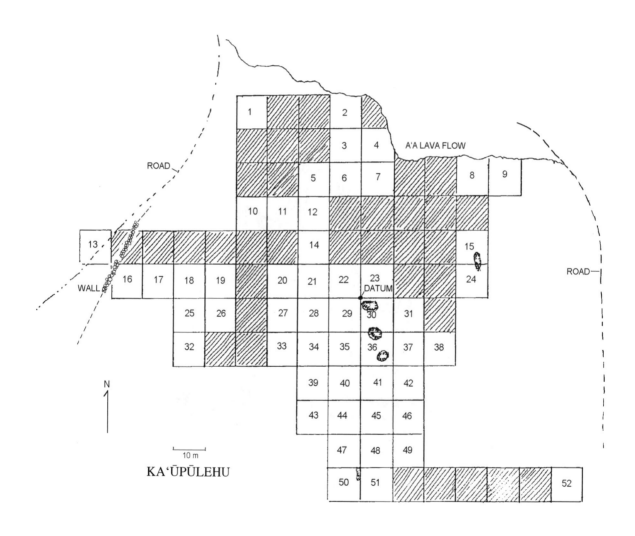

Figure 6.2. Grid map of the Ka'ūpūlehu Site.

6

KAʻŪPŪLEHU: HAWAIʻI ISLAND

North of Kailua-Kona and the Kona airport is Kaʻūpūlehu (Figure 3.1), an outstanding site that, like ʻAnaehoʻomalu, is associated with a delightful lagoon (Figure 1.1) and attractive beach. The site is accessed through a desolate stretch of barren pāhoehoe and ʻaʻā.

The lagoon and beach are now occupied by the exclusive Kona Village Resort. The site is within the Resort grounds on a fairly level stretch of pāhoehoe, inland from the lagoon (Figure 6.1). Because the Resort is not open to the public, the petroglyphs have received relatively little impact from tourists.

According to legends, a spring of fresh water bubbles out of the sand along the edge of the sea and divine intervention by Kāne named the site: Kaʻūpūlehu literally means "oven in which the God was roasted" (Maguire 1966:29-33). Historical references (Kuykendall 1938:24) refer to a chief called Kameeiamoku who lived here; surely he was but one of many who found this refreshing oasis to be a prime place to live.

The Kaʻūpūlehu site has distinctive features that set it apart from most other petroglyph sites on Hawaiʻi Island: extraordinary design motifs and excellent quality of craftsmanship. We are unaware of any heiau here, but any such structures may have been lost when lava overtook part of the site, for Kaʻūpūlehu was very nearly destroyed in 1800-1801. Surely a part of the petroglyph site was covered at that time because a high wall of ʻaʻā encroaches on the northeast side of the site and petroglyphs are located at its base. At the north edge of the petroglyph area is a collapsed pile of lava rocks. This structure is unidentified.

The dominant tree today is kiawe which forms a forest around the site and intrudes upon it. Some tree roots have broken up the lava and disturbed the petroglyph carvings.

Figure 6.1. A portion of the Kaʻūpūlehu petroglyph site. Surfaces are fairly level with some slight mounding of the pāhoehoe. The foreground panel has several sail petroglyphs.

A datum was established at a high point on the north end of a collapsed lava dome near the "center" of the site (Figure 6.2). A string grid running NS/EW was constructed of 10 meter squares totaling 8300 square meters of which 5200 square meters contained petroglyphs. Petroglyph panels were located with respect to the grid within each 10 m section, detailed drawings were made by constructing a 20 cm string grid over the panels.

At the time of documentation, a low stone wall defined the entry.[1] Two isolated petroglyphs are located outside the wall in Section 13; one is an Hawaiian name, *mailou*, which figures in a legend. All other petroglyphs are located east of the wall. During the project's second phase, additional clearing of the kiawe forest by the resort crews revealed more petroglyphs and it is possible that others, still beneath foliage and debris, await discovery.

Because of the compact nature of the petroglyph site, the motifs are discussed by subject matter.

SAILS

It is clear that sails are the dominant motif and sailing is the commanding theme at Kaʻūpūlehu. Only the sails are shown, not the canoes. It may be that if one had a full sail, it was understood that there had to be a canoe beneath it. These large, elegant, and well designed motifs are displayed with sweeping curves (Figure 6.3) and often are associated with small anthropomorphic figures (a tendency also noted at Puakō). Some anthropomorphs are within sails, or on the edges, or next to them. Perhaps this is an identification marker of the owner of the sailing canoe. A few sails have pennants flying from them and at times sails are superimposed, with smaller ones inside larger

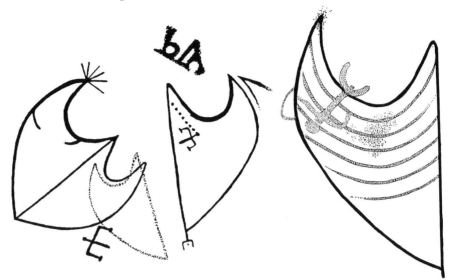

Figure 6.3. Sails have sweeping curves and elegant designs. This group (240 x 210 cm) shows a double sail with tassel, single sails, small partial anthropomorphs, a row of cupules, and modern graffiti at upper right. Note the inverted 'U' on the base of the sail at right.

Figure 6.4. Some sails show ribbing. This example also has a very faint figure beneath the sail. Rough pecking can be seen near the middle of the sail. The sail measures 168 x 100 cm.

examples or placed on the lines of one another. Some have ribbing indicated (Figure 6.4) although there seems not to be any set number for ribs; up to 26 were recorded on a single sail. A few have an inverted 'U' at the base as seen in Figure 6.3.

A panel of seven large and elegant sails in a row is without parallel in the islands. Two of these display ribbing and some have pennants flying (Figure 6.5). Other lines may have been beginnings for more sail images. On the far left side of the row of sails are lines projecting outward; one is a paddle and one appears to represent a trident or perhaps a type of fishing spear.

Crab-claw sails went out of fashion by 1800, two decades after contact. From that time on, sprit sails were used. Based on form, it can be stated with confidence that the sail petroglyphs are earlier than 1800, and surely date from prehistoric times.

Figure 6.5. This panel is without parallel in all of Hawaiʻi. Crab-claw sails are interspersed with anthropomorphs, an oar and a trident far left. Two sails show ribbing, one with a tassel. Two figures at far right appear to be holding objects and the figures themselves display variations: one has a detached head, four others have fingers, and one on the right has an open body form. Note the circle and cupules near the sail on the right. This panel measures 9.0 x 2.5 m.

PAPAMŪ

At least 18 papamū for playing kōnane were recorded; the tiny depressions that form the papamū range from clear to barely visible. Some are beneath other petroglyphs and a few have been vandalized by gross pecking. Papamū have varying numbers of rows and pits; many of the rows are not in straight lines.

KITES

Two motifs represent kites (Figure 6.6) and bear similarities to an extant kite from New Zealand (Poignant 1967) (Figure 6.7). These motifs are rare; however, one other kite image has been recorded at Puakō (see Figure 3.17) and two others are in Ka'ū (Stasack and Stasack 1997).

Hawaiian legends of the demi-god Māui include one about kite flying as a way to demonstrate his control of the wind or a means of reaching the heavens to ensnare the souls of those who have done evil (Beckwith 1970:109).

Similar stories are found elsewhere in Polynesia. Kites made of tapa cloth with painted bird heads (*manu hakarere*) are cited from Easter Island (Métraux 1971:353). In New Zealand kites were not only for play but were used in ritualistic magic, being flown for divination purposes by priests, and it is said that Tawhaki ascended into the sky world by means of a kite (Barrow 1984:103). In Mangaia (Cook Islands), the god Rongo was the patron of kite flying (Poignant 1967:66).

In Tahiti, kites were used to propel rafts. Haddon and Hornell (1975:143) mention a story about the district of Vairao on Tahiti which had a debt of revenge to pay to the people of Varai (now Papeari), a village across a broad bay. They loaded rafts with food and sent them across the bay by means of kites. This was ostensibly a gift, but in reality it was intended to lead the people from Papeari to return the compliment by coming unarmed to Vairao with a return gift. The ruse succeeded and the people of Vairao had their revenge.

The use of kites as a means of propelling rafts was noted also by Corney (1915:324): "Kites have been used for towing rafts of timber and bamboo at this part of the coast—Mataeai and Papeari." In regard to kites, many men were involved in maintaining them in flight (Henry 1962:279) and it is mentioned that their sizes were ". . . of truly large dimension . . . their manipulation undoubtedly posed no difficulty in the sea for the masters of the knowledge and use of winds" (Guiot 1995:21). The use of kites in traditional navigation is equally demonstrated by a legend concerning the double canoe of Māui which was pulled by a kite (Poignant 1969:66).

Early missionaries mention kite flying by Tahitians as one of the "useless" diversions practiced by the natives, and one they stamped out.

Although little research has been done regarding Polynesian kites,[2] their use may have been over a wide area: Bidault (1945:73) mentions kites made from braided palm leaves that were used to propel bamboo rafts in the Banda Sea (southeast of

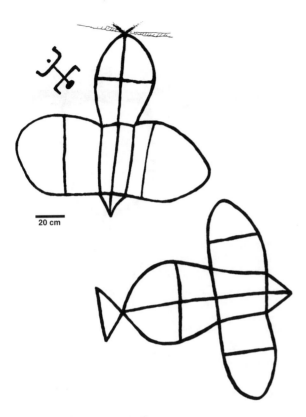

20 cm

Figure 6.6. Kite motifs are rare in Hawai'i. Another kite, at Puakō, is shown in Figure 3.15.

Figure 6.7. A kite in the shape of a bird, from New Zealand. Kites have ritual overtones throughout Polynesia (drawn from Poignant 1967).

Indonesia).

It was extraordinary to find images of kites in the petroglyphs of Hawai'i Island. The Hawaiian god Lo-lupe was shaped like a stingray—*hīhīmanu* in Hawaiian (Beckwith 1970:109, 121) and thus kites were stretched on a frame in the shape of a fish with wings, tail, etc. Lo-lupe took charge of those who spoke ill of the king and consigned them to death while the souls of those who were not guilty were taken to safety. Maui's grandfather showed him how to make a kite from feathers, *ti* leaves and *'ie'ie* vines.

In another legend, Kawelo angered his fellow Hawaiians by outdoing Kauahoa in managing toy boats and kite flying. The place where he defeated Kauahoa is called Ka-ho'oleina-a-pe'a (the kite caused to fall) (Beckwith 1970:109, 121, 233, 407).

Westervelt relates the following legends:

> Maui called for the priest who had charge of the winds to open his calabash and let them come up to Hilo and blow along the Wailuku river. The natives say that the place where Maui stood was marked by the pressure of his feet in the lava rocks of the river bank as he braced himself to hold the kite against the increasing force of the winds which pushed it towards the sky. Then the enthusiasm of kite flying filled his youthful soul and he cried aloud, screaming his challenge along the coast of the sea toward Waipio—

> *O winds, winds of Waipio*
> *In the calabash of Kaleiioku,*
> *Come from the ipu-makani,*
> *O wind, the wind of Hilo,*
> *Come quickly, come with power.*

(Westervelt 1910:116)

And,

> Maui soon learned the power of his kite when blown upon by a fierce wind. With his accustomed skill he planned to make use of his strong servant, and therefore took the kite with him on his journeys to the other islands, using it to aid in making swift voyages. With the wind in the right direction, the kite could pull his double canoe very easily and quickly to its destination. (ibid.:118).

In Hawai'i, the kite had two meanings. Some folk customs pointed to the dread of death. Children should fly kites only in open spaces and never at night in the fear that Death might seize the kite and thereby claim the youngster (Pukui 1972:147). A kite that flew high, unimpeded and untangled, meant wealth, fame, or attainment (Pukui 1979: 180). Pukui's Proverb No. 1226 says, "It is the tail that makes the kite fly"—meaning that it is the number of followers that raises the prestige of the chief (Pukui 1983: 133).

TRANSFORMATIONAL FIGURES

Interesting transitional or transformation-like figures that appear to depict a combination of human and animal form were recorded. Some are anthropomorphs with turtle-like bodies (Figure 6.8) and one is a fish-human combination (Figure 6.9). Transformation creatures are those that have a magical ability to cross boundaries such as from earth to sky to water or travel from one dimension to another. These may have been intended to represent 'aumakua or to have some supernatural connotations. When a human takes on the attributes of a creature, he acquires power from it. In the same way, kahuna were held in awe for their ability to communicate between the gods and the mortal world (Rolett 1986:87).

Figure 6.8. This motif (46 x 44 cm) appears to be part turtle, part human. Note flipper-like feet and fingers on one hand.

Figure 6.9. A few motifs at this site appear to be transformational: note the triangular bodied anthropomorph with fish tail. This panel measures 252 x 165 cm.

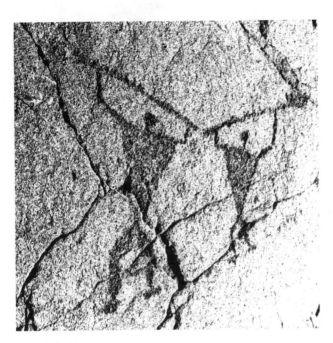

Figure 6.10. Two 'paddle dancers' or warriors from Ka'ūpūlehu; compare active stances to the more static figures at Kalaoa Cave. These two figures are carefully pecked out, with muscled legs indicated on one figure.

Figure 6.11. Funeral or sacrifice? A fairly descriptive grouping of figures shows two anthropomorphs seemingly carrying a body slung beneath a long pole. Unfortunately the petroglyph has been defaced by someone trying to make a latex copy. This panel measures 55 x 24 cm.

ANTHROPOMORPHS

Kaū'pūlehu has 17 T-figures and 101 triangle torso anthropom (including muscled figures). Those with triangle bodies outnumber stick figures almost two to one. Only eight are clearly phallic but six have a cupule in the crotch area which may represent a female sign or could refer to the genital piko. Compared to Puakō, for example, the percentage of figures with sexual images is low.

Two sets of triangle torso anthropomorphs with raised paddles at Ka'ūpūlehu (Figure 6.10; see also Figure 1.9) no doubt have connotations relating to sailing, but also may refer to either battles or ceremonies. These are active figures, not static like those at Kalaoa's cave.

Figure groups showing an activity are rare, but not unknown, in Hawai'i. Ka'ūpūlehu has a startling tableau of two figures conveying a body suspended from a carrying pole (Figure 6.11). Because sacrificial victims were carried in this manner to the *luakini heiau* (sacrificial heiau), this panel may represent a human sacrifice. Another possibility is reference to a burial in a lava tube, known to contain the remains of several persons. Perhaps it commemorates the death and burial of the captain of the 19th century schooner, *Fair American,* reputedly buried in a nearby cave.

The story of the *Fair American* has been told by Kuykendall (1938:24):

> The *Fair American* . . . while making its way down the west coast of Hawai'i was becalmed near a place in North Kona where the chief Kameeiamoku was residing. This chief had once committed some petty offense on board the *Eleanora* for which he had been struck with a rope's end by Captain Simon Metcalfe. Smarting under this affront to his dignity, Kame-eiamoku, who was living at Kaupulehu at the time is said to have sworn that he would have revenge on the next foreign ship that came his way. As fate would have it, the next ship was the tiny schooner, *Fair American*, commanded by Metcalfe's son and having a crew of only five men. Kameeiamoku and his followers, after gaining admittance to the vessel by pretense of friendly trade, had little difficulty in throwing the captain and crew overboard, killing all of them except one, and seizing the vessel. The sole survivor, Isaac Davis, was taken under the protection of Kamehameha, who by this time had become king of the northwestern half of the island of Hawai'i and who is said to have rebuked Kameeiamoku for his barbarous deed. Kamehemeha likewise

took possession of the schooner and it became the first foreign style vessel in his war fleet.

There has long been unsubstantiated talk about the burial cave located near Ka'ūpūlehu. There may be a connection between our strange petroglyph group and the story of the *Fair American* for, in 1968, human bones mingled with fragments of clothing, a pocket watch, and spectacles could still be seen in the cave, which also held a canoe cut in half with one part used as the cover as in a coffin. Inside was a skeleton of a very tall person, and alongside were the bones of two equally tall men flanking the coffin. This is the traditional method for burial of a chief. If the body of the captain were recovered from the ocean, it might have been carried to the cave near Ka'ūpūlehu . With Kameeiamoku in residence there, and considering his vow for revenge, it is not unlikely that a petroglyph was made in commemoration of his moment of triumph.

The akua-type (god-like) human images at Ka'ūpūlehu are close to the wooden sculptural forms of Hawai'i in their mass, fine finish, and solid muscular conformation. There is little doubt that we are dealing with motifs that relate to status and, likely, kingship. There are petroglyphs at Ka'ūpūlehu of elegant anthropomorphic figures wearing feathered headdresses which seem to refer to crowns reserved for ali'i and/or gods. One is a very evenly pecked large muscled figure with an elaborately plumed headdress (Figure 6.12); the others include a figure with fish line, fishhook and *ulua* on the line (Figure 6.13) and a muscled spear thrower wearing a headdress (Figure 6.14).

One "status" figure with muscled legs and headdress has a 270 cm long fishing line with hook and fish—possibly an *ulua*. Ulua is a species of jack crevalle that was an important food fish. The term can also refer to supernatural fish-beings. This grouping suggests the legend of Māui fishing up the islands, for Māui is said to have invented the barbed fishhook as well as the kite and these symbols seem to suggest a connection with that demi-god. Two unusual designs flank the major figure on this panel: pole-like forms with knobs on the ends and what appears to be feathered tops. We suggest they represent kāhili (Figure 6.15).

Ellis (1782:II:156) was the first to write of the ceremonial objects known as kāhili:

> They have also a kind of fly-flap, made of a bunch of feathers fixed to the end of a thin piece of smooth and polished wood: they are generally made of the tail feathers of a cock, but the better sort of people have them of the tropick birds feathers . . . . The handle is very frequently made of one of the bones of the arm or leg of those whom they have killed in battle, curiously inlaid with tortoise-shell: these they deem very valuable, and will not part with them under a great price.

Figure 6.12. A finely pecked chiefly figure with muscles, elaborate headdress, and an unusual mushroom-shaped head. This petroglyph measures 130 x 83 cm.

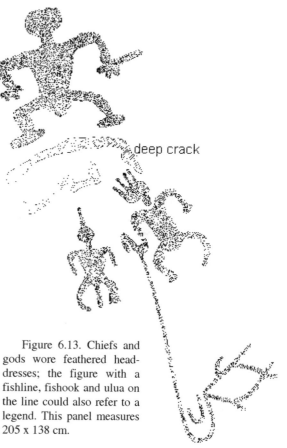

deep crack

Figure 6.13. Chiefs and gods wore feathered headdresses; the figure with a fishline, fishhook and ulua on the line could also refer to a legend. This panel measures 205 x 138 cm.

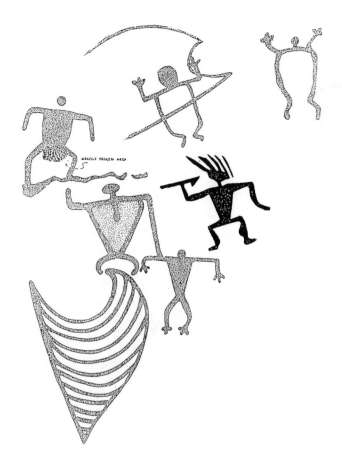

Kāhili were collected by Cook and other early visitors. Chiefly individuals were accompanied by honored retainers who carried kāhili. Some kāhili were used like fly whisks, but others were standards indicating status and authority. The most complete description of these objects can be found in Rose et al., (1993).

FISHING

Figures with fishing lines and fishhooks are unusual in Hawaiian rock art. But, as we have shown, several were found at Ka'ūpūlehu. One petroglyph shows a fisherman holding a line attached to four fish hooks and standing on a platform-like shape; perhaps this portrays a legendary fisherman, one whose successes were unequaled, rather than a god or king (Figure 6.16). The mana of a great fisherman was sought after and hooks were carved from his bones if they could be obtained, a custom practiced throughout Polynesia. Earlier photographs of this design show that the line and hooks were hidden beneath debris, thus the anthropomorph and platform were mistaken for a surfer on a surfboard.

Figure 6.14. A muscled spear thrower with feathered headdress is a dominating figure in this panel, although it is now covered with latex, the result of an attempt to make a mold. Note the ribbed crab-claw sail in association, and other figures, two with open bodies. This panel measures 233 x 172.

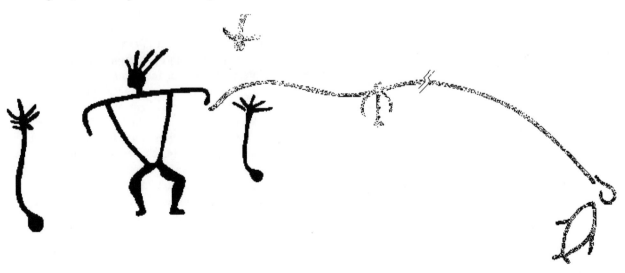

Figure 6.15. A chiefly figure with headdress, long fish line, hook and ulua. The line is curtailed in the drawing for ease in presentation. The two unusual forms on either side of the figure appear to be feather standards (kāhili). This panel measures 279 x 121 cm.

Figure 6.16. Muscled fisherman with line and four hooks. A segment of the line has been damaged by gross pecking. The figure appears to be standing on an object or platform. This panel measures 134 x 114 cm.

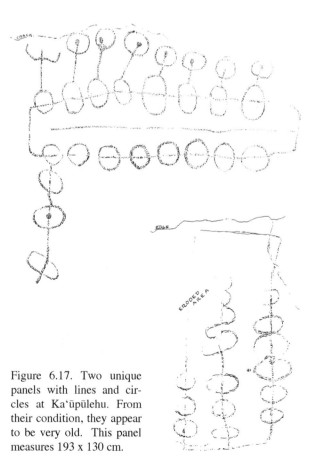

Figure 6.17. Two unique panels with lines and circles at Ka'ūpūlehu. From their condition, they appear to be very old. This panel measures 193 x 130 cm.

OTHER

Two units at Ka'ūpūlehu are puzzling and without known parallel in Hawaiian rock art (Figure 6.17). These two groupings of motifs resemble circular elements arranged in rows on a rectangle shape, with connecting lines running through the circles. One unit has three lines with circular elements (the northeast corner of the petroglyph has been worn away by foot traffic). However, the other is elaborated and somewhat more clear. Two rows of circles run along the sides of a divided rectangle. On the north side, the circles are actually legs of stick figures with their arms raised and, in all but one example, the arms join over the heads forming another row of circles. The line of circles on the south end of the motif lack the anthropomorphic extensions although at the southwest end, three additional circles extend on a line. The upper row of figures resemble seated forms in a rectangular structure. The composition, interestingly, echoes the arrangement of Hawaiian chiefs and kahuna in an engraving by Webber that shows Captain Cook being feted by Kalaniopu'u at Kealakakua Bay in 1778 (Feher 1969:127). That the circles grade into anthropomorphs was only discovered after intensive study of the forms under varying light conditions. It is tempting to suggest that the unadorned row of circles may be a form of "shorthand" or abstraction, and represented to the artist a second row of seated figures. However, caution must be exercised in making such postulations: we have no way of penetrating the mind of the person who made these motifs. We can say about them that, as far as we know, they are unique to this site; they appear to be very ancient because of their condition. Without a raking side light, they are nearly invisible.

LETTERING

Ka'ūpūlehu probably had continuous use from ancient times to the historical period. The latter time frame is established by dates and names pecked into the pāhoehoe. Many of these are made in the style of copperplate letters, and several overlay more ancient motifs. One group is associated with a nicely carved turtle (Figure 6.18). The letters appear to include a backward 'N' (or the letter 'I' in Russian). The amount of superposition has made this set of letters unintelligible.

Another group of letters spells LELE IOH KI and is over earlier motifs including a sail, and LIWAI is over a sail as is the date "1820" (Figure 6.19). There was no alphabet nor even standardized symbols for the local language until 1826, although some printing was done in English in 1822. The New Testament was translated into Hawaiian ten years later and the entire Bible by 1839.

The date of 1820 is the arrival time of the first company of American Protestant missionaries in Hawai'i although we have nothing to tie the petroglyph to that event except to note that the Kona coast was the area where the missionaries first landed.

Heavily pecked/damaged area

Figure 6.18. A turtle from Ka'ūpūlehu superimposed over an older image. In the photograph, note the faint rectangular forms at the upper right of the turtle. In the drawing the extent of the undeciphered lettering can be seen. Additional heavy pecking has damaged part of the lettering.

Figure 6.19. A Polynesian crab-claw sail overlaid with a copperplate date. This date is significant in Hawaiian history: it is the year after the kapu were lifted and when heiau and idols were ordered destroyed.

PECKING

Gross pecking was noted at Kaʻūpūlehu and may be associated with attempts to eliminate certain motifs. As noted, the edges of some sails have superimposed anthropomorphic figures but a few sails have heavily pounded areas on the sail lines. It is likely that an image was here but was obliterated.[3] Whether the pounding was prehistoric or recent is unknown, for the pāhoehoe patinates rapidly. Why obliterate an image? Was it an effort to destroy the mana of an enemy or rival? The practice of effacing rock art images is not particularly rare. There are examples in Hawaiʻi (Paliuli, Puna, and Halape, Kaʻū) as well as in other parts of the world.

DISCUSSION

Kaʻūpūlehu's petroglyphs represent some of the finest images in the Hawaiian Islands; several motifs at this site are not found elsewhere in Hawaiʻi. We were impressed by the visual references to canoes, sailing, and fishing. Aside from sails, which comprise 25% of the total motifs, Kaʻūpūlehu has more fish, fishhooks, and fish-trap motifs than any other single site in the island, to our knowledge. The images exhibit enough differences from other island locales to suggest that this site was dedicated to special purposes, most likely dealing with status concerns, myths, and rituals, sailing canoes or perhaps a special school of instruction in the arts of sailing and navigation. Canoes themselves were status markers, and those belonging to a chief had special mana.

The site contains 435 units. However, quantity is not particularly germane here, for many of the designs are compounded, that is, part of something else. For example, the linked circle motif (see Figure 6.17), is counted as one petroglyph, but actually it is composed of many circles and lines and some of the circles are further elaborated into anthropomorphic figures.

Most of the motifs show considerable artistic and technical skill; nearly all were created with a fine sense of proportion and line, obviously by experts. In most cases, the quality of the pecking is excellent although we noted various degrees of skill. The few that are awkward and rough may date from fairly recent times.

In contrast to the historic lettering at Kaʻūpūlehu, some petroglyphs seem to be fairly ancient, such as the mysterious linked circle units. The bulk of the designs, however, probably date from AD 1600 onward. This estimate is based on the predominate triangle torso figure type and the fully-pecked akua figures, some of which echo the great carved figures from wood.

Some groupings of figures appear to be scenes and are most unusual in Hawaiian rock art; these include the sacrifice or burial scene and the chiefly figure with kāhili and long fishing line, reminiscent of the legend of Māui fishing up the islands. The kites, the great akua figures with feathered headdresses, and fish traps may be associated with legends. The presence of kites (identified with legends about Māui) suggests the possibility of a Māui cult.

Forty percent of the total are human figures of one kind or another but it is the quality of many of these images that is so extraordinary. The excellence of design, proportion, refined contour, and expressive power of these human images, as well as the sails and kites, suggest they were conceived and executed by masters. Status, kingship, and ritual are implied.

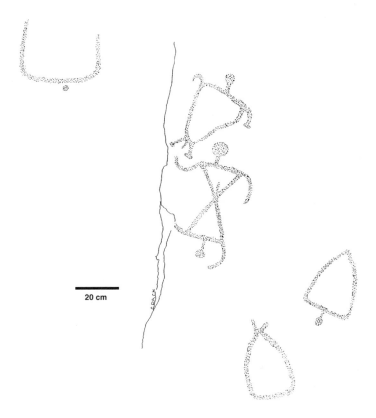

20 cm

Figure 6.20. Some figures appear to be unfinished, such as the two forms at lower right. The double triangle petroglyph may be an attempt to show coition. This panel is at the foot of the high lava flow that stopped in time to spare the site.

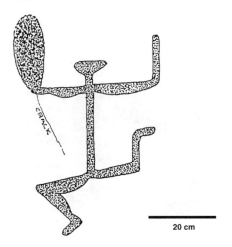

20 cm

Figure 6.21. A running stick figure has a muscled leg, a paddle-shaped hand and a flat head.

Section Descriptions: Ka'ūpūlehu

The site itself has four outlying groups of petroglyphs plus a center that has the most dense concentration and that was obviously the focus for petroglyph making. The outliers in the peripheral portions of the site are discussed first. See Figure 6.2 for a map of the site which shows the location of the sections.

Sections 1-12 and 14 (42 units): north end of the site.
This part of the site has few petroglyphs and these are scattered around without any apparent organization or relationship. The 'a'ā flow marks the boundary on the east, and on the north for Sections 8 and 9. Section 4 has a double figure, possibly showing copulation (Figure 6.20). Other motifs in this part of the site include sails and anthropomorphs, one with a paddle held overhead. Sections 8-9 have two interesting designs: one is a muscled open-base triangle torso figure and the other is turtle-like, a possible transitional form (see Figure 6.8). It has faint traces of fingers on the left hand. A running stick figure shows great animation (Figure 6.21). Famous runners appear in legends of Hawai'i; one is Keli'i-malolo of Maui who, according to legend, ran 90 miles without effort. Actively sprinting figures are known from other sites in the islands. The example at Ka'ūpūlehu is in the same tradition.

Sections 15 and 24 (21 units): east of the 'center' and associated with a small collapsed lava tube.

 Separated by some 25 meters from the central section, this grouping was found after some kiawe trees
were removed by resort personnel and the pāhoehoe
cleared of debris. This locus has a small collapsed lava
tube plus an extremely small and low cave with cupules
on its rim. These depressions are associated with seemingly random pecking which has chipped away the
edges. Cupules are rare at Kaʻūpūlehu, so these features
were noted with interest. One cupule, 9 cm in diameter,
is the largest; the others are smaller and some have been
broken off at the edges, leaving only half circular depressions. Two places on the edge have groups of cupules, one with six, the other five. It is possible that
pounding activity resulted in the cupules, rather than a
deliberate attempt to make rounded depressions. The
incidence of half cupules on edges was also noticed at
Puʻuloa (see the following chapter).

 As for motifs, Sections 15 and 24 have four motifs
that we suggest may represent fish traps and a collection
of nine fish. These are rare in Hawaiian rock art. Two of
the fish traps have a row of tiny dot-like cupules inside
the square forms; these might be interpreted as bait
(Figure 6.22).

Section 52 (4 units): far southeast portion of the site, isolated.
Three sails are located in this section, all of them are
small and poorly made.

Sections 13, 16-19; 25-26; 32 (42 units): west side of the site.
 The entry to the site was located through these sections. A fairly large concentration of figures is to the
south, partially hidden behind some kiawe trees. Papamū—game boards for playing kōnane a game similar
to checkers—are conspicuous. Five sails are interspersed
with anthropomorphic figures. Two very muscular triangle figures also are associated with a sail. These have
been damaged by what appears to be deliberate attempts
to disfigure them (Figure 6.23).

 As for other motifs, three petroglyphs depicting
human feet were recorded in this section; two are quite
graphic and another panel, nearby, contains what appears to be a stylized foot.

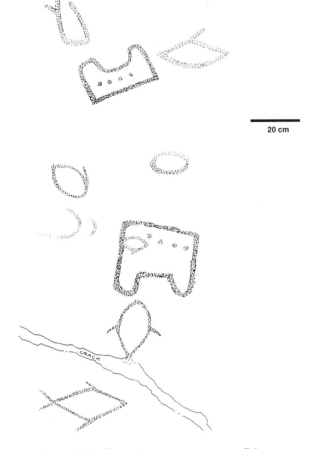

Figure 6.22. These shapes may represent fish traps, a
rarity in the rock art; they are accompanied by stylized fish
forms.

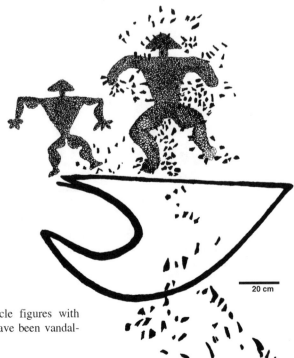

Figure 6.23. Two finely pecked muscle figures with
oddly shaped heads plus a crab-claw sail have been vandalized by gross pecking.

Fig. 6.23. p. 80

These muscled
f'gires could have
a heart line added
to torso.

Figure 6.24. A finely pecked anthropomorph with muscled legs at the center of the site near openings in the lava.

tions 20-23; 27-31; 33-51 (326 units): main part of the site and location of datum, on southern portion of the pāhoehoe flow. This fairly discrete central area of the site runs north/south along two small collapsed lava domes and extends to the south end of the site. It is here that the finest and largest petroglyphs are located (Figure 6.24). As smooth areas of pāhoehoe are present throughout the area, the center of the site was chosen by the ancient Hawaiians for reasons other than the availability of surfaces. This section may have been selected as a focus because of the collapsed lava bubbles and tilted surfaces, a pattern of behavior noted at other sites in Hawai'i. The incidence of petroglyphs decreases toward the southern end of this group. However, motifs crowd on or near the sloping surfaces and one long panel of sails runs most of the length of Section 45 (Figure 6.5). It is in these sections where we find the triangle torso figures with upraised paddles, concentrations of status figures with headdresses and fishing lines, finely pecked anthropomorphs, kites, and numerous papamū. The special features of Section 5 are described above in the main text.

FOOTNOTES

[1] Our recommendation, as part of a site conservation plan, was to reorient the entrance and install a walking ramp above the site in an effort to prevent foot traffic from impacting the petroglyphs. The new walking ramp opened in early 1998.

[2] One exception is a reconstruction of an Hawaiian kite by Henry (1998), who modeled his kite on the kite petroglyphs at Ka'ūpūlehu.

[3] We were told that some youngsters who lived here during the 1920s and 30s damaged the designs with hammers. One early resident, now in his 70s, recalled being involved in such activities (Lani Opunui-Anchesta, personal communication 1992).

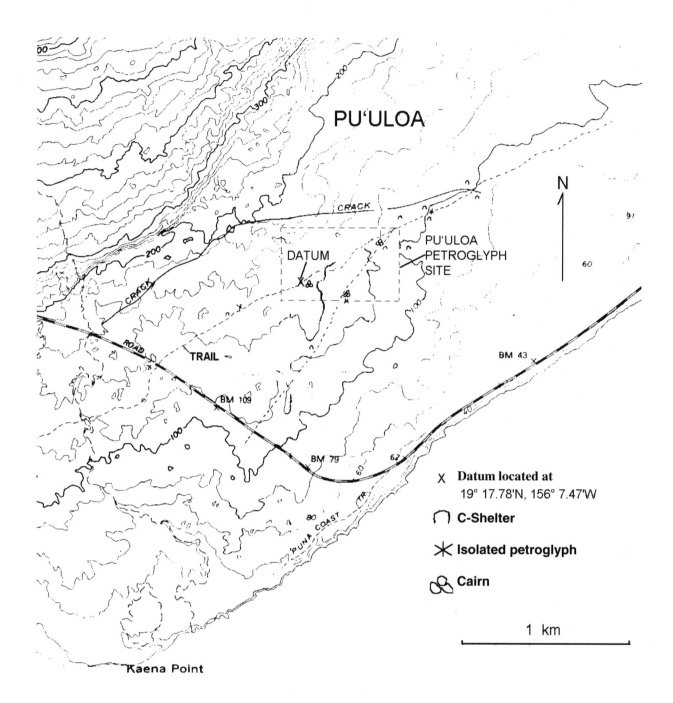

Figure 7.1. A map showing the location of the Pu'uloa petroglyph
site in Hawai'i Volcanoes National Park (from the USGS topological
map of 1982).

7

PUʻULOA: HAWAIʻI ISLAND, HAWAIʻI VOLCANOES NATIONAL PARK

Figure 7.2. The petroglyph area of Hawaiʻi Volcanoes National Park showing barren terrain. The viewing platform is visible on the left. View is from the puʻu, looking northwest.

Figure 7.3. View from the top of the puʻu, looking east. A stone cairn is in the foreground and another one can be seen below and beyond. The cloud of smoke and steam is from lava flowing into the sea.

Puʻuloa is located in Hawaiʻi Volcanoes National Park on the southeastern coast of the island of Hawaiʻi (Figures 3.1 and 7.1). This well-known petroglyph site is in the ʻahupuaʻa of Panau Nui, on the bleak and desolate windswept lower slopes of Kilauea Volcano. Aside from grasses and some scattered small plants, a few *ohia* trees provide the only break in the seemingly endless sweep of lava. There is no nearby water source. A less inviting spot is hard to imagine (Figure 7.2). Yet there is a hard grandeur to this area with its enormous black lava mountain on the north and deep blue ocean on the south. It is rather like "living on the edge", for steam and smoke from the current lava flow is visible from the site and sulfur fumes permeate the constant winds that sweep across the side of the mountain.

A few miles to the east, recent lava flows have covered over several other petroglyph sites on the slopes of Kilauea and it is possible that Puʻuloa—only two and one-half miles from the flow at the time of documentation in 1994-5—also will be lost if the trend continues.

The obvious focus of the site of Puʻuloa is a large pressure dome (puʻu) on the Kāne Nui o Hamo lava flow. It rises higher than the adjacent fields of pāhoehoe (Figure 7.3) thus providing a wide and un-obstructed view in all directions including south to the ocean.

Figure 7.4. A small shelter on the east side of the puʻu has cupules and other motifs worked into the vertical surface above the opening. The mound itself is covered with cupules and has several deep cracks. An ancient trail runs across the north end of the mound.

The puʻu was clearly the earlier, most intensively utilized part of the site and is literally covered with petroglyphs—most of them cupules. At the dome's peak is an *ahu:* a pile of stones of unknown antiquity. A low cave shelter is located on the eastern side of the dome (Figure 7.4) and there are large cracks crossing the dome. The name of the site, Puʻuloa, has been translated to mean "hill of long life" (Figure 7.5).

The inland fork of the old Hawaiian trail crosses the northern part of the dome and continues through the site (Figure 7.6). Petroglyphs are found below the mound to the east and north and extend along the trail to the northeast some 500 meters to where our Locus 1 was established. In addition to the petroglyphs included in this report, there are approximately 2000 other scattered elements, to the west and north of the puʻu and along the trail as it proceeds westward. These were recorded in 1997 (Stasack and Stasack personal communication). Thus our combined surveys include essentially all of the petroglyphs at the site.

Today the site is reached via a marked trail leading northeast from the

Figure 7.6. The ancient foot trail can still be seen today as it crosses through petroglyph-bearing surfaces, obscuring many motifs which have been worn and eroded by foot traffic.

Figure 7.5. The puʻu in the center background as seen from the east. Note the petroglyphs on the outcrop in the foreground.

Chain of Craters Road. It follows an ancient trail that originally ran through this area from Laeʻapuki to Keolakomo (Figure 7.7). Puʻuloa was not an occupation site. There are some temporary shelters ('C-shelters') near Locus 1, a few are located in a depressed area approximately 36 meters *mauka* (toward the mountain) from the puʻu, and an occasional shelter was noted nearby. Another trail runs inland from Kaena Point in the southwest and intersects the trail going east from Puʻuloa at a point near a few shelters, and just northeast of our Locus 1. The two trails combine and continue eastward; we were able to follow it as far as two kilometers beyond the viewing platform at Puʻuloa.

The trail system used by early Hawaiians served several functions. Some were destinations; others had ceremonial uses such as for the makahiki festival. The site at Puʻuloa appears to be clearly linked to the trail which runs through it, although Glidden (1995) suggests that Puʻuloa may also be located on an earlier ʻahupuaʻa boundary.

Early mention of this site comes from collections now in the Bishop Museum. One group of ten photographs, dated May 14, 1927, has a note accompanying the pictures stating ". . . near the sea coast, land of Panau in Puna, Hawaii. They are near a small rise with two ahu on it known locally as Puu Loa. This hill I am told is where the natives used to stop and rest when traveling from Puna to Kaū in the old days and is right on the old trail." The next set of photographs (chronologically) in this collection shows four pictures of chalked petroglyphs, which were taken by A.E. Hudson in 1931. Also in 1931, Rev. Albert Baker of Honolulu wrote an account of the site in *The Hawaiian Annual* (1931:62-67), following a visit to Puʻuloa. He comments: "It is the most mixed up field I have seen, with a great variety of symbols." He noted ". . . human figures, circles and concentric rings, dots, the usual phallic symbols, etc." Baker did not explain what he meant by "phallic symbols".[1]

Initial mapping of Puʻuloa in 1964 was by William Bonk of the University of Hawaiʻi at Hilo. This was a photo-mapping project for the Bishop Museum that produced a selection of ten maps of the petroglyphs (sixteen are listed but the other six apparently were not produced). According to Emory, Soehren and Ladd (1965:6-7), the recording was done:

> . . . by vertical photography . . . . Each photograph recorded the petroglyphs in an area covered by a five-foot square frame with a string grid marking off one-foot squares.

The report continues:

> . . . Bonk believed the Puuloa petroglyphs could be completely photographed and mapped within several weeks. However, the time and funds spent on this project far exceeded those originally estimated. From the middle of June to the end of July . . . the Puuloa area was surveyed and photographs taken . . . . Approximately 4,000 photographs were taken.

Despite these efforts, the entire site was not photographed. The present whereabouts of the negatives and photographs are unknown.

In 1966, on-site sketch maps were made of selected segments of the central part of the site by J. Halley Cox. They were used as a check against the drawings made from Bonk's photographs, which had not been field checked. Cox's drawings revealed considerable errors in the prior work, attributed to difficulties in interpreting the photographs and transferring them into drawings: ". . . significant omissions, discrepancies, and misinterpretations of the areas in question" (David Cox 1974:1). For example, the photographic method did not show details of configuration; width and size, and natural features in the rock were sometimes shown as petroglyphs.

Other problems with this survey were discovered when our scale drawings were compared to those prepared by Bonk. Some motifs had been misplaced or, in putting the grids together, some were offset several meters from their actual location. This made it impossible to do a direct comparison of our quadrants with those of earlier researchers.

David Cox's (1974) 1973 recording re-mapped the central part of Pu'uloa, using a grid system that partially overlaid the map by Bonk. Cox referred to Pu'uloa as the most impressive site in the state containing, in the first 0.3 hectare, at least 2300 motifs. He mentions tying into the original datum point (a spike) left by Bonk, but he does not say where it is/was placed. We were unable to relocate it.

J. Halley Cox (n.d.) mentions that, in 1973, a Mr. Kang of Honolulu made some trial silicone rubber molds of selected petroglyphs. How many were made and what became of them is unknown. Whether or not this silicone was left on the rocks is also an unknown. Today several petroglyphs exhibit such material, but this also could have been done by others attempting to make molds.

In an earlier account resulting from a trip made in 1824, Ellis (1917:203) made these observations:

> Along the southern coast, both on the east and west sides, we frequently saw a number of straight lines, semicircles, or concentric rings, with some rude imitations of the human figure, cut or carved in the compact rocks of lava. They did not appear to have been cut with an iron instrument, but with a stone hatchet, or a stone less frangible that the rock on which they were portrayed.
> On inquiry, we found that they had been made by former travelers, from a motive similar to that which induces a person to carve his initials on a stone or tree, or a traveler to record his name in an album, to inform his successors that he had been there.
> When there were a number of concentric circles with a dot or mark in the center, the dot signified a man, and the number of rings denoted the number in the party who had circumambulated the island.
> When there was a ring and a number of marks, it denoted the same; the number of marks showing of how many the party consisted; and the ring, that they had traveled completely around the island; but when there was only a semicircle, it denoted that they had returned after reaching the place where it was made.
> In some of the islands we have see the outline of a fish portrayed in the same manner, to denote that one of that specie or size had been taken near the spot; sometimes the dimensions of an exceedingly large fruit, etc., are marked in the same way.

One can only wonder what Ellis saw, or thought he saw. Depictions of fruit are, to our knowledge, unknown, and petroglyphs of fish are exceedingly rare (neither are found at Pu'uloa). And, looking carefully at his statement about the circumambulation, it defies analysis. How is it that in one case a ring represents the circumambulation and a person, and hence signifies the number in the party; and the dot represents a person, who by implication is the carver of the petroglyph? And in the second instance, that the ring represents only the circumambulation and the dots represent the members of his party? Ellis' account makes little sense. However, because he made these notations at an early date, they are repeated over and over in the literature and may have been the impetus for calling the petroglyphs 'doodles' or idle markings, for his "analysis" of their function suggests they are of little importance.

For example, based upon the account of Ellis, Emory, Soehren and Ladd (1965:9-10) decided petroglyphs:

> . . . served in the nature of signatures and the presence of names, some of them coupled with petroglyphs, after Hawaiians had learned writing further bears this out. Except for Ellis' information we would be quite at a loss to explain the circles and semi-circles. There is no reason to doubt the explanation given him that they were symbols which served to indicate a trip. . . ." And, "The appearance of the isolated form of the ancient Hawaiian sail presents a puzzle unless we regard it as a symbol denoting that the person who made it wished to indicate that he was a sailor or that he had come by sail on the way to reach this spot.[2]

The conclusion reached by Emory, Soehren and Ladd (ibid.) is that very many of the petroglyphs at Pu'uloa were made after European discovery and when travel was made easier by the introduction of horses.

But we have another early account to suggest a function for these petroglyphs. Cox and Stasack (1970:56) state:

> Puuloa is of particular significance because it is the only site for which a specific function has been recorded. Because it was still in use in the late 1800s, some of the older residents of Puna were able to relate some specific information abut the meaning of the symbols found there.

In 1914, anthropologist Martha Beckwith (n.d.) recorded the following in her field notes:

> Rode out to Puuloa on the line between Kealakomo and Apuki. Here is a large pahoehoe mound used as a depository for the umbilical cord at the birth of a child. A hole is made in the hard crust, the cord is put in and as stone is placed over it. In the morning the cord has disappeared; there is no trace of it. This insures long life for the child. Mrs. Kama, born in 1862, was a native of Kamoamoa. Her mother brought her cord there. She had 15 children and for each one at birth the visit was made to Puuloa. Another mound, on the southern boundary of Apuki, called Puumanawalea, was similarly used.

Beckwith's notes include sketches: a dot was 'the hole for a child'; a dot in a circle, 'the hole for a first born'; and a dot within two circles, 'the first born of an alii'. A plain circle was a 'calabash'; a zig-zag line was a 'mo'o' [lizard] and a circle with a long line was a 'puloulou' [kapu stick]; and so on. Beckwith went over these interpretations with Mrs. Kama who suggested that the informant *would say anything for the sake of pleasing.* (emphasis ours).

Another tale collected about Puʻuloa came from the son of Beckwith's informant, Sam Konanui:

> Puʻuloa means a long life, and that is why they chose Puʻuloa to deposit the piko of their children. "You make a puka (hole) by pounding with a stone, then in the puka you put the piko, then shove a stone in the place where the piko is placed. The reason for putting in that stone is to save the piko from the rats . . . ." Sam Konanui stated that *pikos* were apparently saved in a calabash, and then brought to Puʻuloa from all over the islands: "If they had ten children they would make ten pukas . . . .They made the holes round in a ring so they would know they belonged to one family." (Cox and Stasack 1970:56).

It also was said that a piko that remained undisturbed in its hole overnight, that would be a sign of a successful petition for a long and happy life; this is the opposite of the recollection by Mrs Kama, as cited in Beckwith's notes. Whichever, one can assume it was successful more often than not because of the great number of them. Other marks may have been made by tribute collectors, probably during the makahiki. Because of the diversity of images at Puʻuloa (and elsewhere) it is clear that there were many reasons for making the petroglyphs.

Whether intentionally or not, the piko hole became a birth record. By no means were they the equivalent of a census, however. Piko also were placed in crevices or man-made holes where the family thought they would do the most good for the child and, probably, the child's family. Thus they are found in various, but special locations on each island. The navel, being the vital link with the mother, became the link to the mana of wherever it was placed. At Puʻuloa, the family sought long life; those placed on Cook's ship, as mentioned earlier, would receive the blessings of Lono, with whom Cook was identified (Beaglehole 1967:1225).

Relying upon early accounts, such as those by missionaries and other visitors to the islands, is fraught with difficulties: Graves and Erkelens (1991:8-9) point out the problem of reliability when dealing with oral narratives or written sources. For one thing, errors may have been made when the information was first recorded, and those collecting the information were undoubtedly culturally biased. That which may have been true for one of the islands of Hawai'i might not be true for all the islands. Also, accounts recorded in historic times may not have applied to the pre-historic period. Therefore early accounts that describe uses or interpretations of petroglyphs must be carefully and critically evaluated. In our opinion, the interpretation of the cupules as repositories or symbols for the placement of an infant's umbilical stump is well within Polynesian tradition and has been recorded for Easter Island.[3] Calling the circles evidence for 'trips around the island', and so on, appear to be a guess made to Ellis by some early informant. As his comments have received wide distribution, this "interpretation" has been accepted by many. We think it an unlikely construct.

METHODS

Our documentation project at Pu'uloa began at the extreme eastern end of the petroglyph field and proceeded westward towards the pu'u. The petroglyph field was covered with a string grid in ten meter squares, oriented north-south/east-west (Figure 7.7). The grid began approximately 500 meters northeast of the pu'u and was constructed by sighting on the signpost on the northeast corner of the viewing platform which was chosen as the datum for the site.[4]

For convenience, the grid was divided into loci, providing a reference during the documentation process. Within each ten meter square, panels of petroglyphs were covered with twenty centimeter string grids and were drawn to scale on cross-section paper

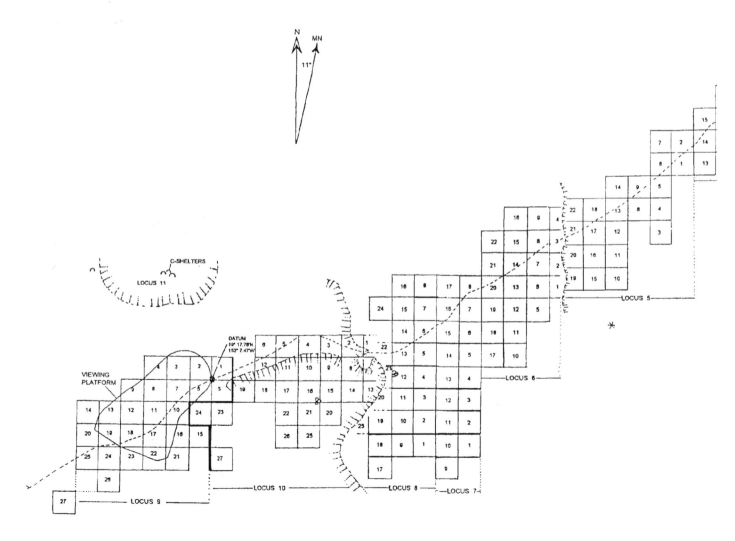

(Figure 7.8). Petroglyphs were recorded as full panels, that is, in context with other associated motifs. All elements were measured and notes made on relation to the trail, superposition, and other pertinent information.

The trail is the constant feature of this site. The incidence of petroglyphs is directly related to it and foot traffic over the centuries has made a clear path through the petroglyphs, some of which have been erased by it; others are barely visible.

By the end of our two-year project all petroglyphs to the east of the pu'u had been

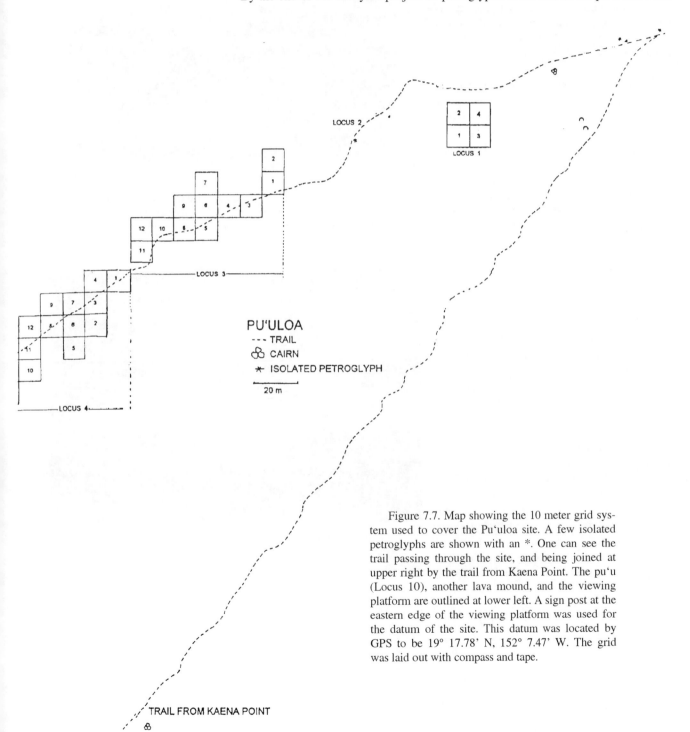

Figure 7.7. Map showing the 10 meter grid system used to cover the Pu'uloa site. A few isolated petroglyphs are shown with an *. One can see the trail passing through the site, and being joined at upper right by the trail from Kaena Point. The pu'u (Locus 10), another lava mound, and the viewing platform are outlined at lower left. A sign post at the eastern edge of the viewing platform was used for the datum of the site. This datum was located by GPS to be 19° 17.78' N, 152° 7.47' W. The grid was laid out with compass and tape.

mapped, as well as those petroglyphs within the confines of the viewing platform (Figures 7.7 and 7.9), and the pu'u itself.

Neither clearing nor excavation was done during this project. Although every effort was made to document each petroglyph in the areas studied, it is certain that a few may be hidden under accumulated overburden or in the grass, or are so eroded as to escape detection. Portions of the lava are breaking up and suffering from severe erosion and spalling which causes destruction of designs.

As noted at other sites in Hawai'i, natural formations in the lava were often utilized as part of, or as the setting for, the designs. A particular favorite seems to be small natural dome-like blisters which have one or more cupules pecked into the top. Pecked lines or rows of cupules along the spines of "ropes" of lava were also recorded. In some cases, natural inclusions in the lava were incorporated into the petroglyphs. Such features are called iconic congruence and are common in many parts of the world where natural forms in the rock either inspired the petroglyph or were found attractive by the ancient carvers.

DISCUSSION

Pu'uloa, with at least 23,566 petroglyphs, is clearly one of the outstanding petroglyph locales in Polynesia. The sheer numbers and density of units far exceeds other sites, providing certain evidence of the importance of the place in the lives of early Hawaiians. Activity in regard to petroglyph making was oriented toward the trail that passes through the site, and carving intensified with proximity to the pu'u.

At Pu'uloa, 84% of the petroglyphs are cupules (Figure 7.10) or have cupules in their design (such as cup and ring). Although cupules have been recorded in larger sizes and often quite deep, the vast majority are shallow and from 3 to 5 cm in diameter. These are hardly of sufficient size to hold anything. Many are on tilting surfaces, which further

Figure 7.8. This picture shows an east-west and a north-south line of the 10 meter grid and a smaller 20 cm grid being used to record petroglyphs to scale on cross-section paper.

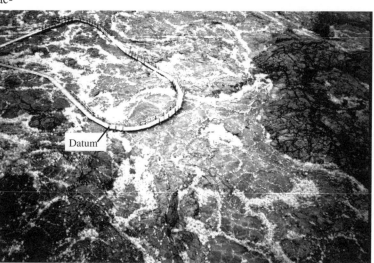

Figure 7.9. Aerial view of a portion of the pu'u (lower left corner) and the viewing platform. Locus 11 is in a low region to the right (north) of the platform (Photo: Don and Elaine Dvorak).

argues against their use a functional containers. More likely they had symbolic value. The recording of cupules on the vertical walls of the cracks that run through the pu'u is further indication that symbolism, not function, was the purpose of these tiny depressions. It may be that umbilical stumps were placed in the crevasse and a cupule made to signify that event.

Figure 7.10. Cupules and large cracks at the top of the pu'u. The petroglyphs are particularly dense on the edges of the cracks. Locus 10.

Anthropomorphic figures comprise only 1.9% of the total. Although all figure types (stick, triangle-bodied, and muscled figures) are found here (Figure 7.11), there are some local variations such as those with upward angled shoulders on some triangle torso figures (vs. the usual form: straight out from the torso). Many incomplete figures were noted, figures lacking one or more arms and legs or a head. Triangle torso figures outnumber stick figures (343 to 76 respectively). Forty-seven of the triangle torso figures are 'open body.' Few have sex indicated although some images do appear to refer to birth and/or family connections (Figure 7.12). Some motifs are hard to categorize, such as a figure with extra limbs surrounded by small cupules (Figure 7.13).

Figure 7.12. Some figures may depict birth or family connection. Locus 8.

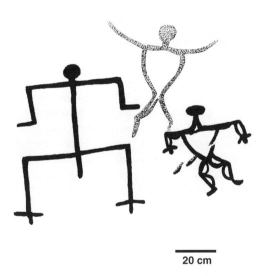

Figure 7.11. All three figure types are found at Pu'uloa but the triangle torso dominates.

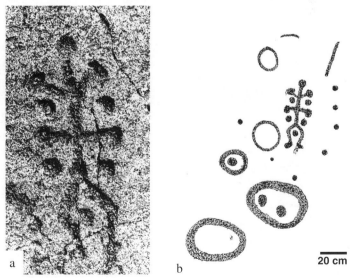

Figure 7.13. Photo a) and drawing b) of unusual human figure. Cupules surround or connect to the body, Might these be mana symbols, perhaps the image of a kahuna radiating power? Locus 6.

Figure 7.14. Triangle torso anthropomorphs, cupules, and an object resembling "barbells." Locus 8.

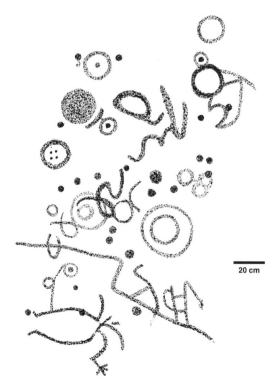

Figure 7.15. Some of the petroglyphs that appear to be attempts to depict cursive writing. This style has not been recorded elsewhere in the Islands. Locus 7.

Only one possible dog motif was found, although these are common in the petroglyphs on Lāna'i, O'ahu, Maui and Kaho'olawe. No papamū were recorded; at Pu'uloa, it appears that people were passing through and did not have time for amusement.

Zigzags are unusual in Hawaiian rock art, but seventeen were recorded at Pu'uloa. Another oddity is a motif that consists of two cupules connected by a line, resembling small bar-bells (Figure 7.14). The highest concentration of these objects is close to the pu'u. The 'bar-bell' form is suggestive of a gourd dance rattle, but there are so many of these at this site—225 examples—in an area hardly suited for dance performances, that it is possible they had a more familial meaning, such as a special link between two siblings (twins?), or something similar. An interesting variation is a motif of crossed lines and cupules at the ends.

The site has many historic referents: not only ships but also block lettering and attempts to show cursive writing (Figure 7.15).

Without doubt, Pu'uloa meant 'hill of long life' thus a visit to the site, and contact with it, apparently assured believers a long life. This idea is well within Hawaiian tradition. The placing of an umbilical stump was undoubtedly one of the reasons for the importance of the site, but not all of the depressions so served. According to Emory, Soehren and Ladd (1965:9):

> It must be true that Hawaiians did visit Puuloa to place umbilical cords there . . . . Some of the dots, or cup-marks may have been made to receive them, but it was usual to put such cords *into a natural deep crack or crevice.* [Emphasis ours]. Most of the dots are far too small to hold an umbilical cord, and some of them are in rows of shallow cup-marks on the face of vertical fissures in the Puuloa Lava dome . . . . As we are now certain that most of the petroglyphs were executed singly and that the many hundreds of dots are actually tally marks indicating the visit of an individual or of the number of people in a visiting group, a count of those on the maps would be of value in estimating the minimum number of Hawaiians who had stopped in the area.

J. Halley Cox (n.d.) suggests that one reason the pu'u became a special site is that it furnishes a view. If one is coming from Ka'u, it is from here that one catches the first view of Kalapana; if coming from the east, it provides a view of the old village of Kealakomo in the distance. Thus, 'revealed vistas' gave a special quality to the site.

According to Cox and Stasack (1970:68-70), cupules were only used once. They suggest that:

> The probable function of the piko tally marks at Puuloa and similar marks in other sites is fairly well established. Because of this and because of the great number of three particular kinds of these marks, a development from functionality to symbolism can be demonstrated. First, there is the simple piko hole, a circular depression in the pahoehoe lava which averages 2 inches in diameter and slightly less than 1 inch deep; second, the piko hole with a circle incised around it; finally, a great number of variations on the theme of a central dot with variously concentric circles, fragments of circular or U shapes, even such fragmented images as a series of dots which lie on the circumference of a circle, and bars or lines in series.

Kwiatkowski (1991:54), following the lead of Ellis, calls cupules at Puʻuloa 'tally marks,' suggesting that when dots are in a line, it indicates people marching in a single file; the numbers of dots describes the number of persons traveling together (ibid: 48). This is a repetition of the old (and, we believe, discredited) account by Ellis.

Cox (1971:171) suggests that the human figure is a form of self-portrait and probably developed out of the dot-circle (cup and ring) idea. Then, with increasing literacy, carvings became written names. However, dot-circles are found at late sites such as ʻAnaehoʻomalu and Puʻuloa, not early ones such as Puakō.

To discover the 'meaning' of the numerous circle motifs may be beyond our ability today. However, the concept of circle has many ramifications including Jungian theories of the symbol of the self. And, for Hawaiians, ". . . the circle evokes a being enclosed in on itself because it is complete and self-sufficient. Accordingly, circular things and things capable of circular movement are often considered divine . . . ." (Valeri 1985:89). It seems more productive to search for meaning in abstract theory rather than the mundane. Like ʻAnaehoʻomalu, a tendency was noted to outline designs in either enclosures, circles or squares (Figure 7.21).

One of the more interesting features at Puʻuloa is the variety of manufacture; some petroglyphs are deeply and carefully made, obviously by someone with skill and familiarity with petroglyph making. Others are crudely pecked, some seemingly half finished. Perhaps some were made by kahuna in the process of working magic and offering prayers. The less well-made examples may have been made by those who came to deposit the piko of their child.

Petroglyphs were not always located to be seen by individuals passing along the trail. Some motifs are pecked on surfaces that tilt away from the trail and can be viewed only if one leaves the path. In addition, some that are on tilted surfaces are visible only at certain times in the day when the light comes from an oblique angle. Such placement reinforces our idea that it was the act of petroglyph making which was of paramount importance.

It is clear that the puʻu was a sacred place. The large lava dome with its deep jagged cracks and spectacular view surely contained spiritual significance. Although this dome is far grander than the small rises seen at other sites, the concept of domes and openings in the earth probably was the same.

Vandalism, in the form of paint traces, chalk, and residue left behind from attempts to make castings, can be seen at the site, in two areas sections of petroglyph-bearing rock appear to have been removed. A few petroglyphs appear to be modern additions, as determined by the freshness of the cuts and the use of metal tools. Lava repatinates rapidly and it is thus difficult to identify those elements that have been added in recent years by visitors to the site.

The dates of the pāhoehoe lava flows that comprise this part of the volcano are AD 1200-1450 (Holcomb 1987:269; Ladefoged, et al., 1987:4). Puʻuloa's petroglyphs cannot be older than the lava flow. Cox and Stasack (1970:61) originally thought that Puʻuloa, along with Puakō, are the two oldest sites in the islands. However it now appears that the petroglyph site at Puakō has a greater claim to antiquity. Also, a later date for Puʻuloa would account for the majority of human figures as being depicted with triangular bodies. Excavations at Hilina Pali (Cleghorn 1980) provide strong evidence for this general date.[5]

In an early unpublished manuscript, J. Halley Cox (n.d.) proposed a time frame for Puʻuloa. His scenario (created before the lava flow was dated) had the central section of the puʻu approaching its present density of petroglyphs by AD 1000. By AD 1500, the entire north half of the hill was covered but the character of the petroglyphs had changed; now there were shallow dots, circles and lines replacing deep cups, rings and grooves. Dot groups became frequent, and some sails were carved. Human figures of the triangular shaped open body suggest a more sophisticated style that was developed elsewhere on the island. By the time of contact, usage was fairly heavy and the site was extended to the lower area on the north side along the trail. Pet-roglyph-making ended some eighty years later partially due to the introduction of Christianity.

In the light of our present knowledge of the lava flow, the time frame proposed by Cox must be compressed into a shorter (and later) period. Instead of allowing centuries for changes in the type of petroglyph being carved, it is likely that many of the different types of motifs were being carved at the same time.

An earthquake and tidal wave that struck the area in 1868 probably marked the end of the general use of Pu'uloa. Ka-lapana was abandoned and a number of other villages were obliterated. The few remaining families in the area may have still come here (J. Halley Cox n.d.) but due to the abandonment of the villages, travel along the trail must have decreased mark-edly.

The impact of volcanic activity is a fact of life in this part of Hawai'i. It continues, and is expected to do so, far into the future. Handy and Handy (1972:542) reported that Puna was once a rich agricultural region but lava flows in historic times have covered over much of its best land. Continuing flows have covered over many petroglyphs, heiau, and village sites. Other archaeological sites within this area—including the great site of Pu'uloa—are in the projected flow pattern and may be covered over at any time.

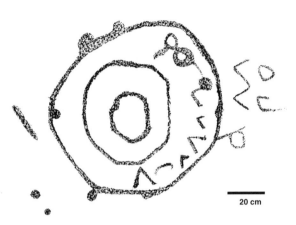

Figure 7.16. An unusual group combining circles and letter-like markings. Locus 3.

SITE DESCRIPTIONS: PU'ULOA

Locus 1 (4 sections, 14 units): a small raised mound of pāhoehoe (approximately 2 m high), south of the trail and 500 meters east of Datum 1. Documentation began here, the perceived start of the petroglyph area.

Locus 2 (1 section, 1 unit): 15 meters west of Locus 1, on an angled section of rock facing the trail. One roughly carved petroglyph appears to represent a cape with tie strings.

Locus 3 (12 sections, 340 units): on both sides of the trail. The north-east end of the site has a raised section of pāhoehoe with a few elements. The main part of Locus 3 is a large flat area of pāhoehoe just to the west.

Two missionary style letters (KE), plus some marks inside a large concentric ring motif that resembles letters (Figure 7.16) are, to-gether with a faint ship, the only historic motifs at this locus. The most prominent motif is a deeply carved "unidentified" figure with a square end and two leg-like extensions (Figure 7.17); nearby is a wavy form described as a sea-creature. What these might have represented is unclear. A few triangle torso figures with open bases were recorded as well as one figure with legs end-ing in a circle and one muscled arm.

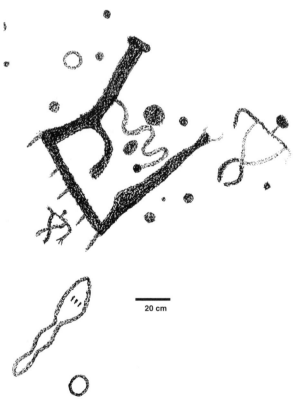

Figure 7.17. An unidentified figure associated with lines, cupules, and anthropomorphs; the wavy form (lower left) may be a sea creature. Locus 3.

10 cm

Figure 7.18. An open circle/ring motif at Locus 4.

<u>Locus 4</u> (15 sections, 239 units): on both sides of trail; petroglyphs on the south side of the trail are located on a raised section of pāhoehoe. This locus has few anthropomorphs but some interesting geometric designs including circle combinations, some with rays extending from their edges, and a set of open concentric rings (Figure 7.18). Among the geometric motifs are angular shapes, one a segmented rectangle. One of only two quadrupeds at Puʻuloa is located here: it resembles a goat or donkey (Figures 7.19).

<u>Locus 5</u> (22 sections, 935 units): on both sides of the trail, scattered on various levels of uneven pāhoehoe. Geometric motifs dominate, including cupules, enclosures (Figures 7.20 and 7.21) and a segmented rectangle. Two triangle torso figures are associated with lines of cupules (Figure 7.22).

10 cm

Figure 7.19. A rare quadruped, possibly a goat or donkey. Locus 4.

Figure 7.20. An enclosure with geometric motifs. Locus 5. The panel measures 106 x 59 cm.

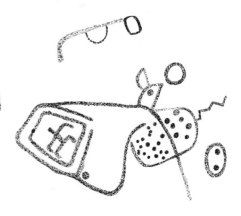

20 cm

Figure 7.21. Enclosures often contain clusters of cupules; one enclosure on this panel contains a stick figure. Note zigzag line. Locus 5 and 6.

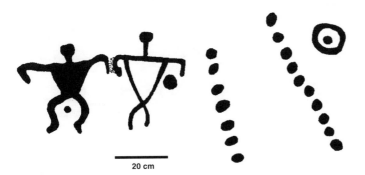

20 cm

Figure 7.22. Two triangle torso figures are associated with lines of cupules. The figure on the left is fully pecked and in a lively pose. It has a cupule in the crotch which may signify a female. The other figure is static with unpecked torso. Locus 5 and 6.

One panel that includes a rough attempt to depict an historic ship also has a petroglyph in the form of a capital "I" (Figure 7.23a). The most interesting panel at Locus 5 has a sail with ribbing, an historic ship (Figure 7.23b) and a heavily muscled anthropomorph (not shown). Sixteen meters south of Locus 5, quad 10, is a large phallic anthropomorph that is a modern attempt to emulate the ancient figures. It was made with a metal tool.

The pāhoehoe at the western end of Locus 5 drops down sharply into a valley-like area where Loci 6, 7 and 8 are located. The break in the terrain necessitated the addition of partial quadrants at this juncture.

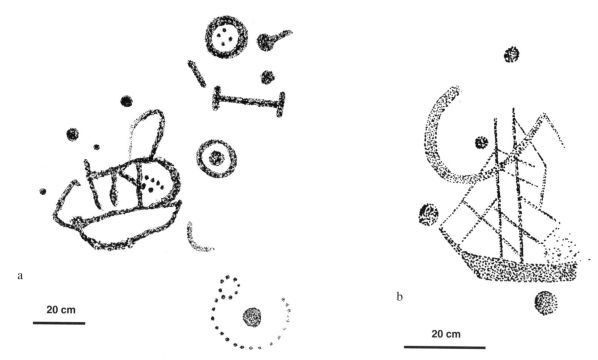

a

20 cm

b

20 cm

Figure 7.23 a) a rough depiction of a sailing ship, and a capital "I" form that may be an attempt to indicate "I", myself. b) a sailing ship has cupules and an unidentified sickle-shaped form. Note attempts to show rigging. Locus 5 and 6.

Locus 6 (22 sections, 996 units): Locus 6 has a low area on the east, but rises up to a higher plateau toward the south and west of the trail. The trail itself runs through the lower northern part of the locus. Motifs recorded in Locus 6 include human feet, geometric motifs, enclosures with cupules or figures inside (Figure 7.24), possible attempts at cursive writing (see Figure 7.15) and lines.

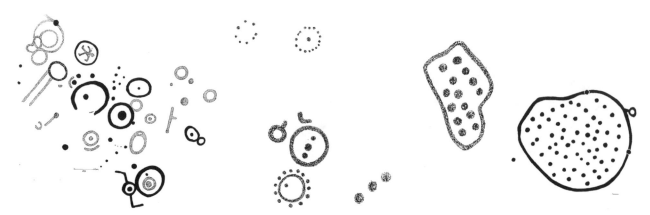

Figure 7.24 Enclosures are common at Pu'uloa where they surround groups of cupules or, sometimes, anthropomorphic figures. Some circles and enclosures are formed by cupules.

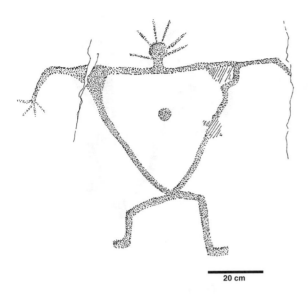

Figure 7.25. A finely pecked triangle torso figure

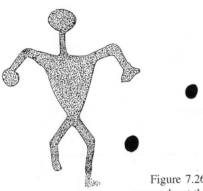

Figure 7.26. Several anthropomorphs at this site have raised elbows. Locus 7.

Other lines are distinct parts of panels. Sails are present but there are few anthropomorphs; one figure is surrounded by dots (see Figure 7.13). An imposing triangle torso figure with headdress is located on an angled portion of lava, directly visible from the trail (Figure 7.25). Other motifs recorded include zigzags as well as a cape.

Locus 7 (17 sections, 812 units): Loci 7 and 8 are on various levels, but mainly on flat surfaces as the pāhoehoe stretches out to the south of the trail. Some petroglyphs are 70 meters from the trail on the south, but few are located north of the trail. The crowded panels continue up to the base of the puʻu. Along the trail, the pāhoehoe dips and rises with some deeper depressions close to the base of the puʻu.

Locus 7 features circles, concentric circles and other geometric motifs including cupules. Anthropomorphs with triangle torsos are present, some with raised elbows (Figure 7:26), as well as sails and finely pecked oddities that defy categorization.

One elegant profile anthropomorph (Figure 7.27) is outstanding; the delicate pecking of the form is unusual at this site.

Close inspection of a motif that has been mistaken as a fish revealed a slight offset and actually consists of two triangular figures sharing the same shoulder line. (Figure 7.28). Another motif, a circle and lunar-shaped curves, is deeply and finely pecked and abraded. What this might have signified is unclear (Figure 7.29). It is associated with semicircles and cupules. A group of lines and cupules creates an unusual form, reminiscent of a profile figure, but is likely fortuitous (Figure 7.30).

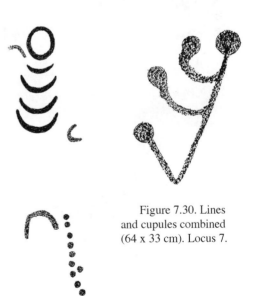

Figure 7.30. Lines and cupules combined (64 x 33 cm). Locus 7.

Figure 7.27. Profile figure. Note muscle on lower leg. Locus 7.

Figure 7.28. This motif appears at first sight to be a fish. Close inspection revealed something else. This panel measures (77 x 58 cm). Locus 7.

Figure 7.29. Curves, circles, and cupules are featured on this panel, measuring (195 x 50 cm). Locus 7.

Locus 8 (24 sections, 2546 units): closer to the pu'u, the petroglyph surfaces vary from level sections to irregular depressions and lava slumps. A cairn (ahu) of indeterminate age is located on one of the higher areas, directly below the pu'u. Most of the petroglyphs are south of the trail. A few scattered elements are located to the north.

Locus 8 has some fine examples of expressive anthropomorphs (Figure 7.31). Others here display a variety of form: one may be a birth image (Figure 7.32a); another is seemingly attached to a sail (Figure 7.32e. This section also has capes, sails, and rare examples of canoes with sails A number of triangle torso anthropomorphs are open at the bottom. These forms may indicate females, particularly when presented with smaller figures as if in giving birth or a larger figure associated with a smaller one (see Figure 7.32a). Some motifs are finely made and well designed. Lines with circle ends could be representations of kapu sticks (Figure 7.33) (poles with a gourd on top that were placed in sacred locations; they marked limits beyond which commoners could not go).

20 cm

Figure 7.31. An expressive and jaunty open base figure, Locus 8.

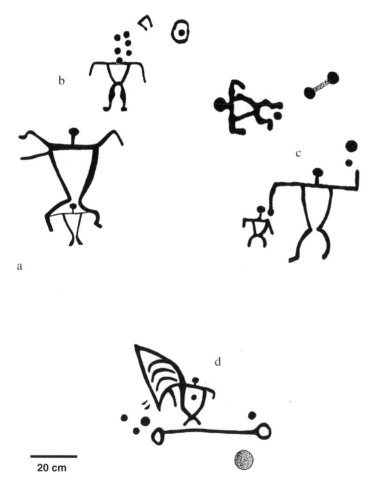

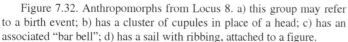

20 cm

Figure 7.32. Anthropomorphs from Locus 8. a) this group may refer to a birth event; b) has a cluster of cupules in place of a head; c) has an associated "bar bell"; d) has a sail with ribbing, attached to a figure.

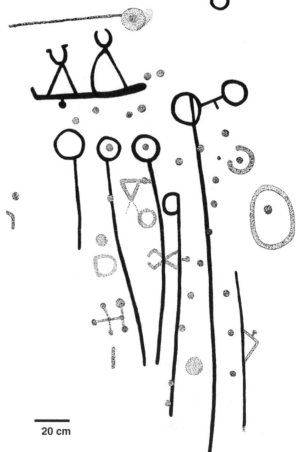

20 cm

Figure 7.33. Kapu sticks were placed to warn people away. These motifs may refer to such sticks. Note connected triangle torso figures, top.

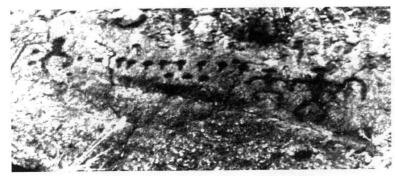

One angled panel in this locus has a row of cupules, some with tails, associated with a pair of triangle torso anthropomorphs (Figure 7.34). It is tempting to speculate that this may be a family group.

The main trail passes around the pu'u on the north and rises up to a higher elevation. It is in this area, west of the mound, that the viewing platform and Locus 9 are located. A faint secondary (?) trail runs across the pu'u itself, paralleling the other one. It is clearly visible on the east side but less so on the northwest portion of the mound. This secondary trail runs directly past the cairn, or ahu, located on the top of the mound.

Figure 7.34. Locus 8 panel, with two anthropomorphic figures and a row of cupules, some with tails. Might this represent a family group?

Locus 9 (27 sections, 4803 units): fairly level in parts, but some areas are irregular with depressions and mounds, sections of ropy lava, and jumbled slabs of pāhoehoe that offer vertical faces for some petroglyphs. The central part of Locus 9 has a wooden viewing ramp that runs around its perimeter. Traces of the trail can be seen running through the middle of the site. The ramp covers parts of some panels.

Locus 9 has interesting motifs, and some that are unique. One large figure appears to be a Lono representation although so much superimposition is present it is difficult to determine the original form (Figures 7.35).

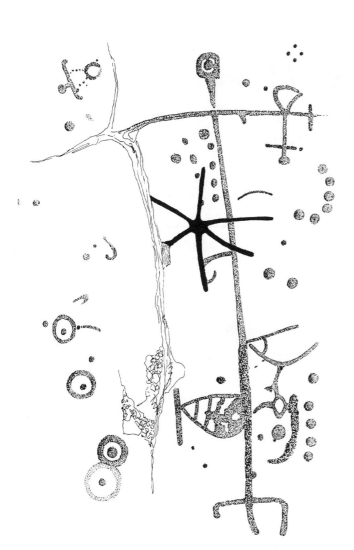

Figure 7.35. Large (267 cm) image at Locus 9 (drawing and photo) may be a Lono figure. Overlapping and possible sequences of carving are present. Note small sails near body of the figure. Note also the foreshortening of the Lono figure in the photo. This illustrates a difficulty when recording solely with photography.

There are a few individualized petroglyphs in Locus 9, such as anthropomorphs, but the majority are cupules and circular geometric designs. Human figures invariably have triangular torsos (Figures 7.36a, b). An interesting grouping combining circles, cupules and a human figure (Figure 7.37) suggests that the cupules were first carved and the figure added later by utilizing cupules for head and hands. Although speculative, two carvings bear some resemblance to vulvae (Figure 7.38).

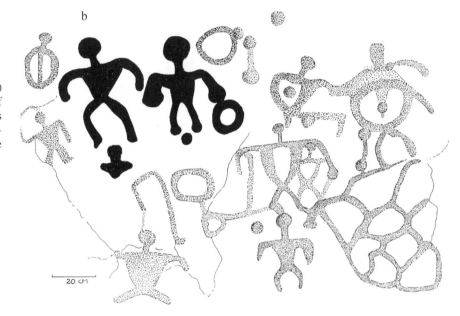

Figure 7.36 a) photo and b) drawing of a portion of a panel of anthropomorphs in Locus 9. This panel has been damaged by attempts to make rubbings; residue of paint can be seen on the panel.

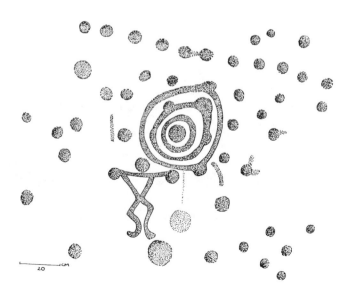

Figure 7.37. Cupules, concentric circles, and a figure that has cupules for hands and head.

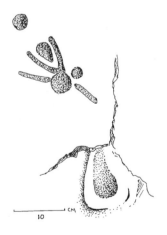

Figure 7.38. These motifs are two of only five vulva forms at Pu'uloa. Locus 9.

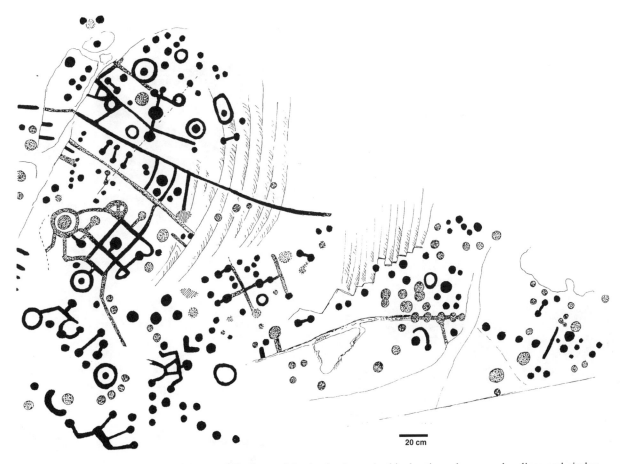

Figure 7.39 The complexity of the panels in Locus 9 is clearly shown in this drawing where cupules, lines and circles cover the available carving surfaces. Edge notching (see page 102), barbells, and other elements can be seen. The rough ropy parts of the lava were sometimes utilized as well as the smoother areas.

Locus 10 (25 sections, 12,844 units): the puʻu itself, a large lava dome with faint traces of a trail running across the top and deep cracks in many parts of the dome (Figure 7.40). A small cave is situated on the eastern side, at the same level as Locus 8 and a cairn is found on the top. The puʻu has little diversity in design elements. Cupules cluster significantly along the edges of the large cracks.

Figure 7.40. Great cracks split the puʻu and seemingly held significance as evidenced by intense carving of cupules along the edges.

Two previously unrecorded features were noted with
interest at the puʻu: Edge notching, which takes the
form of short straight lines, usually in groupings, that
run off the edges of panels or cracks (Figure 7.41);
and cupules placed on vertical walls of the large fis-
sures that run through the puʻu (Figure 7.42). The
density of carving that follows along the edges of the
cracks is noteworthy (Figure 7.43 a, b).

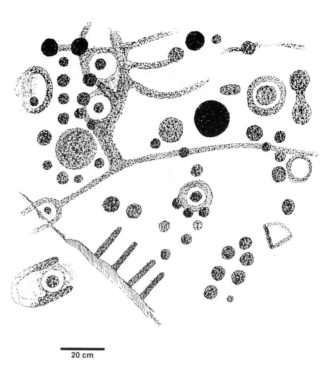

Figure 7.42. Cracks also have cupules worked into
vertical surfaces. The crevices are narrow so that the
carver had to have been lying on the ground and leaning
over the crack in order to carve the poho. Locus 10.

20 cm

Figure 7.41. Along with thousands of cupules on the
puʻu are short lines (edge notching) that run off from the
edges of the cracks.

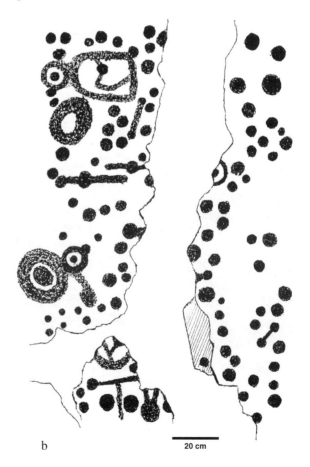

Figure 7.43 a) and b). Cupules and other elements cluster at the edges of cracks. As can be seen in the drawing,
many cupules run over the edges. Locus 10.

b   20 cm

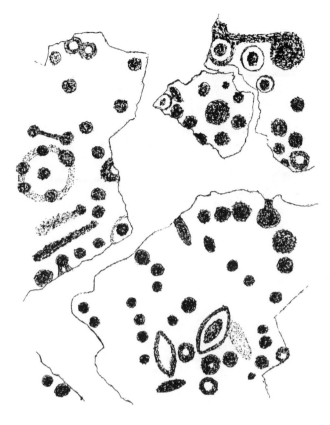

Not only lines but cupules or raised circles (doughnut-shaped, oval, and other variations) are half on, half off edges (Figure 7.44). Some other forms have phallic allusions (Figure 7.45).

Anthropomorphic images are few, and geometric motifs are clearly featured in this locus where virtually every available surface has been carved with cup and ring motifs, cupules, circles, and variations thereof (Figures 7.46 and 7.47, see also Chapter 12).

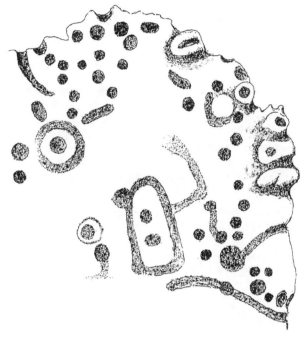

Figure 7.44. Ovals, barbells, lines, circles, and cupules cluster at the edges of cracks. This panel measures 142 x 126 cm. Locus 10.

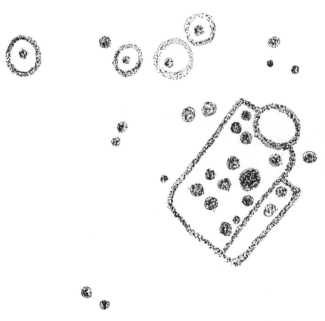

Figure 7.45. Some bas relief forms on the edges of cracks have phallic overtones. Note line running off the edge. This panel measures 126 x 126 cm. Locus 10.

Figure 7.46. The surface of the pu'u is covered with cupules and variations of circles. The cup and ring motif is notable. This panel measures 134 x 134 cm and features cupules surrounded by an enclosure. Locus 10.

Figure 7.47. Examples of the cup and ring motif, Locus 10.

Edges may be considered as the beginning or the end of something and are features noted in American Indian sites throughout western North America where they occur on both vertical and horizontal surfaces and often parallel each other. According to Steinbring and Granzberg (1986:209), the act of creating them is conditioned by the mystical boundary represented by the edge. What the edge notching might have signified to the Hawaiians is unknown. But the fact that lines, often in groupings, were designed to run off edges suggests that something in particular was intended.

The discovery of tiny cupules worked into the vertical walls of crevices was a surprise. These had to have taken special effort due to the narrow confines of the cracks. They are not immediately visible; often one has to lie down and peer into the crevices to see them. At times they are in vertical lines of three or four. Obviously these could not have held anything so they appear to strengthen our theory of symbolic content for cupules. Cupules play a major role at Pu'uloa. For a summation of distribution patterns, see Chapter 12.

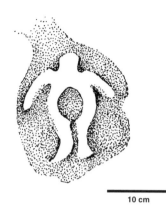

Figure 7.48. An unusual bas relief figure from the pu'u. Locus 10.

Another interesting discovery was that of a small anthropomorph carved in bas relief, located near the center of the pu'u (Figure 7.48). Few human figures are found in this section, and seldom is one carved with such care. The fact that the figure is very faint and eroded suggests some antiquity. As we noted at the other loci, cupules or other motifs are often enclosed and cupules frequently are on, or part of, the lines that form the enclosure (see Figure 7.46).

Locus 11 (incomplete, 1 section, 36 units recorded): north of the viewing platform and Locus 9 in a depressed area surrounded by mounds of lava. There are some cave shelters, some 'C-shaped shelters' and a smattering of petroglyphs. This section was neither mapped nor documented due to time constraints.

FOOTNOTES

[1] We distinguish between a disembodied phallus (considered to be a phallic symbol) and a line extending below a stick figure, the latter assumed to refer to an image of a male. Thus Baker's reference to the "usual phallic symbols" probably means that he observed some figures with lines that suggested phalli.

Stokes also mentions "phallic representations" for Ke'eku but a study of that site reveals no disembodied phalli. He probably also is referring to male stick figures. What we deem a phallic symbol is very rare in Hawaiian rock art; stick figures with penis lines are common.

[2] J. Halley Cox (1971:117) suggests that a representation of a crab-claw sail indicates pre-*haole* times for "... this type of sail disappeared almost simultaneously with the discovery of the islands in 1778".

[3] The piko concept has also been noted on Easter Island, which suggests considerable time frame for this practice, as wide dissemination indicates connections far back in Polynesia before the various groups split off from each other. On Easter, however, nothing has come down through the early ethnographies; the placing of an umbilical stump into a small natural bubble in the lava and covering with a stone was personally related by a member of a traditional native family. It was said that the practice was more widespread in earlier times but disappeared once women began to have their babies in the hospital. The difference is that the receptacle was a natural depression, not a man-made one.

[4] The location of the datum was 19°17.78' N, 152°7.47' W, measured with a Magellan GPS NAV 5000D programmed for the Old Hawaiian Datum, (Clark 1866) ellipsoid, used on the 1982 USGS map for the island of Hawai'i. The Magellan was also used to locate trails, shelters, and isolated petroglyphs.

[5] Excavations at Hilina Pali uncovered petroglyphs below the carbon-dated fill level. These included a preponderance of stick figures; above the fill level, triangular bodied figures were in the majority.

8

LĀNAʻI ISLAND

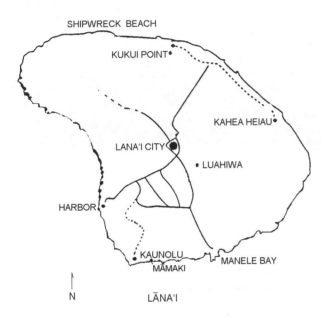

Figure 8.1. A map of Lānaʻi showing the location of petroglyph sites, the island's one town, and harbor.

Figure 8.2. View from Lānaʻi with Molokaʻi in the distance. Note eroded gulches in foreground. This portion of Lanai's coastline is known as Shipwreck Beach.

The pear-shaped island of Lānaʻi (Figure 8.1) is 13 km west of Maui and, like Kahoʻolawe, it lies in Maui's rain shadow (see page iv). Molokaʻi is 11 km to the north; Kahoʻolawe is 24 km to the southeast (Figure 8.2). This group of islands—including Maui—forms a partly sheltered sea. Lānaʻi originally had a forest of sandalwood, destroyed early on by an intensive trade with the Orient which depleted the islands of this valuable tree. Although both Lānaʻi and Kahoʻolawe suffer from lack of rainfall, Lānaʻi's mountain was replanted in recent years, dramatically increasing the island's moisture.

Lānaʻi is a mere 24 x 19 km (approximately 360 sq. km). In dry areas, red dirt is exposed and the lower slopes are eroded and bare (Figure 8.3). On the west, a large plateau terminates in steep cliffs; on the north and east sides, the island is cut by deep gulches. However, a shallow reef area extends out on the eastern side. In ancient times, large fish ponds were constructed here and these would have provided a good source of food. At a higher altitude, Lanai City is sheltered and cool due to a mature grove of Norfolk pines that are the result of a reforestation project by a New Zealand naturalist in the early 1900s. Since historic times, rapidly growing kiawe has formed a dense forest around the base of the island.

Originally a volcanic cone, the rich soil of Lānaʻi supported broad fields of pineapple but today the focus has changed; pineapples have been phased out and the island's economy is converting to tourism.

In 1779, Captain King (1785) of the Cook expedition noted that Lānaʻi seemed well inhabited and was told that the island "produced yams, sweet potatoes and tarrow". Cook himself did not see Lānaʻi but the *Resolution* and *Discovery*, sailing under Captain Clerke, passed the south and west coasts, close to Kaunolū point. Only 13 years later Menzies (1920), the surgeon on Vancouver's ship, commented upon the ". . . naked appearance of the island, which seemed thinly covered with shriveled grass in a scorched state. No hamlets or plantations were to be seen, no trees or bushes adorned the face of the country . . . . " The changes appear to be due to havoc resulting from raids and warfare. During these years, Kalani'opu'u, accompanied by Kamehameha, defeated the warriors of Lāna'i, slaughtering soldiers and inhabitants. The land was devastated; Charles Wilkes (1861), the stern Captain of the 1838-1842 U.S. Exploring Expedition, wrote that Lāna'i was "destitute of cattle, water and wood."

According to tradition, Lāna'i originally was inhabited by evil spirits which prevented it from being occupied by humans. It is said that around AD 1400, Kaulula'āu, a mischievous son of the Maui chief Kaka'alaneo, was sent there in exile. Being resourceful and shrewd, Kaulula'āu outwitted the demons and ghosts and thereafter Lāna'i was safe for others to settle (Emory 1924:11-12). Despite what legend tells us, it is difficult to accept that this island was uninhabited for the hundreds of years during which time the other is-

Figure 8.3. The eroded and barren landscape of Lāna'i. This section of the island is called "Garden of the Gods."

lands had settlements, for Lāna'i 's east coast is a relatively easy and short trip by canoe from Maui, Moloka'i, and Kaho'olawe, and is visible from all three. It would have been the logical stopover for trips from O'ahu to any of these other islands, or beyond to the island of Hawai'i.

An early legend describes the gods Kāne and Kanaloa, along with their younger brother, Kane'āpua, as living at Kaunolū, on the south coast of Lāna'i. It is said that, at times, they changed into the form of birds. Kāne'āpua's cousin was Halulu, the bird monster, who lived in a cave to which it carried men to be devoured. The bird concept will be explored later in this chapter.

Emory (1924:122-3) affirms that Lāna'i was an out-district of Maui, only poorer and more sparsely populated. He located evidence of occupation including 489 house sites and arrived at a conservative estimate of 630 sites. There were dwellings and heiau in every part of the island.

Lāna'i has several petroglyph sites. However, due to time constraints, only four were documented: Luahiwa, Kaunolū, Kukui Point (or Poaiwa) and Keōmoku. Emory (1924) mentions some petroglyph boulders that could not be relocated by us, and surely more examples are to be found at the lower altitudes, in areas now obscured by kiawe trees and detritus. We lacked sufficient time to record a site at Māmaki. However, documentation of the primary sites, which undoubtedly contain a major portion of the island's boulder art, was completed.

In contrast to Hawai'i Island, Lāna'i's petroglyphs are found on basalt boulders and these intractable surfaces result in shallow and faint petroglyphs, some barely bruised into the boulder face. These are quite different in appearance from motifs found on pāhoehoe.

In our study of Lāna'i's petroglyphs, we had access to some of Emory's photographs from 1921. These were helpful in several instances at Luahiwa and Kaunolū (Emory did not see the site at Kukui Point). However, Emory chalked nearly all his figures prior to taking photographs. These images were not always accurately chalked. We also had access to photographs taken by Ed Stasack in the 1960s which proved useful for comparative purposes.

LUAHIWA

Luahiwa is located on the central plateau overlooking the Palawai Basin, near the center of the island. The site is on a steep hillside of at least 30° slope (Figure 8.4a and 8.4b). The petroglyphs are located on boulders scattered over the hillside. A short but very steep cliff below the lower boulders drops into a modern ditch before rising up to an artificially raised roadbed. The ditch and roadbed were made in the 1930s to prevent runoff from the hill onto the cultivated fields below. Today severe erosion threatens these lower boulders. Some are perched precariously on the edge of the eroded area.

A rain heiau was the main feature of this area and this shrine undoubtedly brought in considerable traffic including a proportionate number of petroglyph makers. The rain heiau, as described and photographed by Emory in 1924 (Figure 8.5), has not been relocated. But it did exist as his photograph clearly shows. In regard to the heiau, Emory (ibid.: 69) states:

Figure 8.4 a) Luahiwa as it looked in the 1920s, photo by Kenneth Emory, Courtesy of the Bishop Museum (#CP5145A). b) Luahiwa in 1988 showing heavy grass cover and eroded area in foreground. The large boulder, center, is Emory's Boulder #8. Note the eroded area just below this boulder which is labeled ditch in Figure 8.6.

At the head of the ravine which rises among the petroglyph bowlders at Luahiwa several massive bowlders come together, forming the back of a circular terrace eight feet deep with perpendicular wall, 5 feet high and 12 feet long. This was called the heiau of Luahiwa and was used for regulating the rain; it was particularly powerful because the rain clouds pass close above it.

The heiau was still in use into historic times. Emory (ibid.) adds: "Keli'ihananui, who lives at Lalakoa, two miles away, stated that his father used this heiau." The boulder in question may have tumbled downhill when the lower ditch was created in the 1930s. Several boulders can be seen lying on the edge of the fields below and we attempted to view these but found no visible petroglyphs. It may be that the surfaces with petroglyphs (if there are any) are face down. The location of the rain heiau presents a problem. Emory's sketch (Figure 15, page 96)[1] only shows boulders numbered 1-15, but in the text describing boulder #12, he adds:

About 30 feet southwest of this bowlder is a stone with dog figure and several indistinct figures; west, stones with several faint triangular figures; and north on a stone at corner of Luahiwa shrine for causing rain, 3 triangular horseback riders cut upon other figures in soft boulder.

His motif description of the horseback riders and photograph matches one face of boulder #15. If this is correct, then the rain heiau would have been at that location. However, the early photograph (see Figure 8.5) that lists the image as "Stone in corner of Luahiwa shrine . . . . " shows a cluster of large boulders, one with petroglyphs clearly visible. But this is not boulder #15. Nor does it match any of the boulders that we recorded. At this time, the problem appears unsolvable without further field study including an examination of the boulders now lying below the site, or a search for a nearby site with a matching boulder, in the chance that the photograph may have been mislabeled.

Luahiwa's boulders are scattered between the lower road and the upper road (Figure 8.6). Surveying on the hillside was difficult due to the high, dense and sticky molasses grass. The grass cover is a fairly recent development, as earlier photographs by Emory show the hillside as relatively bare (compare Figures 8.4a and b).

Emory noted 15 boulders with petroglyphs. Most of Luahiwa's boulders are massive and usually have petroglyphs on all faces; indeed some panels are literally covered with designs, superimposed one upon the other.

Figure 8.5. The rain heiau, photograph taken by Emory in the 1920s. Courtesy of the Bishop Museum (#CP5153).

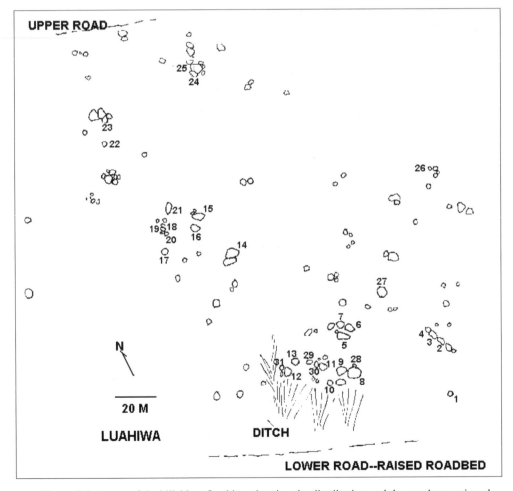

Figure 8.6. A map of the hillside at Luahiwa showing the distribution and the numbers assigned to the boulders.

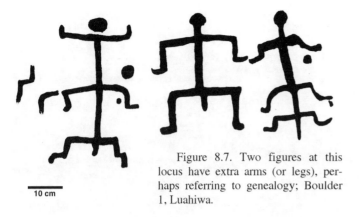

Figure 8.7. Two figures at this locus have extra arms (or legs), perhaps referring to genealogy; Boulder 1, Luahiwa.

10 cm

During our survey 17 more petroglyph boulders were added to Emory's original count but Emory's boulder numbers were maintained where possible.

One of the most distinguishing features at Luahiwa is the way in which figures are crowded together on some panels. Often we see figures which appear to have extra arms and legs or are connected to others, sharing limbs or torso lines (Figures 8.7 and 8.9). Dog images, most of which sport curly tails, are featured (12% of the total). Some are connected to anthropomorphs or are 'lined up' in a row (Figure 8.8). The human figure types range from basic stick types to elaborate muscled men holding clubs aloft, or with arms outstretched in a wing-like pose. Some are quite lively, with gestures (such as one hand placed on head), or with objects in hand, and a few are shown on horseback (Figure 8.9). Stick figures outnumber triangular-bodied figures, 36% v. 25%.

Figure 8.8. A panel of dogs from Boulder 4. Several seem to be barking. Note headless humans. This panel measures 121 x 74 cm.

Figure 8.9. A crowded panel of figures on Boulder 5. This panel measures 288 x 163 cm.

Several of the larger boulders in the lower central area contain a mass of petroglyphs (Figure 8.10), one over the other, and are very difficult to see. Undoubtedly the count for Luahiwa's petroglyphs is low due to problems involved with sorting out images on heavily superimposed panels. Judging from the height of some of the carvings, there may have been a scaffolding used to carve the motifs near the tops of the largest boulders, although erosion surely has lowered ground level.

Based on several factors, Luahiwa appears to have been in use for a fairly long period of time: Stylistically the stick figures appear more ancient than those at Kukui Point on the north side of the island, while the men on horseback obviously were made in the historic period. The density of petroglyphs suggests use over a long period of time.

Figure 8.10. A jumble of superimposed forms make some of Luahiwa's panels difficult to document. Some units on this panel on Boulder 13 have been chalked and scraped by visitors to the site. Photograph taken in 1960 by Edward Stasack.

The few cupules present are on vertical surfaces which negates their use as piko containers. There are more images (at least 571) on Luahiwa's 32 hillside boulders than are found at the other individual sites on Lāna'i and so many motifs are superimposed that it appears the boulders may have been re-used because of their sacred qualities.

This site, easily accessible from Lanai City and open to the public, is being changed dramatically by visitors who feel compelled to recarve the images or to vandalize the petroglyphs by adding chalk or crayon, destroying irreplaceable information about the ancient designs. (Figure 8.11).

Figure 8.11. Boulder 14, Luahiwa. Photograph on the left was taken in 1960 by Edward Stasack. The photograph on the right was taken in 1988.

KAHE'A HEIAU, KEOMOKU

Kahe'a Heiau is on the eastern side of the island at sea level (see Figure 8.1). The petroglyphs at this site are located on massive boulders forming part of the foundation and wall of a sacrificial heiau with a 'strangling stone' (Emory 1924:65). Spilled blood was considered impure, thus strangling was the preferred method of sacrifice. It was of interest that locals warned us to watch out for ghosts while working at this site.

The boulders with petroglyphs face southeast into a dry gully. Near the heiau are the remains of an historic well and some old windmill machinery. In 1988 the area was covered with a tangled mass of kiawe trees. Petroglyphs are concentrated in one area and form a unique panel of figures that includes an image of a pig (Figure 8.12).

As background for this unusual motif on the heiau wall, pig sacrifice was an important part of the consecration of a *luakini* heiau (sacrifice shrine), according to Valeri (1985:288ff). Numerous pigs were killed during the many nights of ritual that prepared the shrine for its ultimate use: for example, on the fourth evening, the king kills a pig by dashing it against the ground and then offering it to the god along with prayers. On the fifth morning, four pigs are cooked in the oven; by evening, 40 pigs are cooked and a man is killed, along with a pig. By the evening of the 7th day, 400 pigs are sacrificed (ibid.:309ff) — along with some human victims. There are intricate rituals involved with the sanctification of a luakini heiau (for more detailed information, see Valeri 1985) but the point is made that pig sacrifice is an integral part of the ceremonies, and pigs are considered to be symbolically potent enough for a luakini sacrifice. Pigs might also be powerful 'aumakua (ibid:29), or could represent the nature deity *kamapua'a*, who is the rain-making form of the god Lono and a ribald figure in Hawaiian mythology (Knipe 1989:126). It seems that the image of a pig on the heiau might be expected; however, this is the only site where one has been documented thus far.

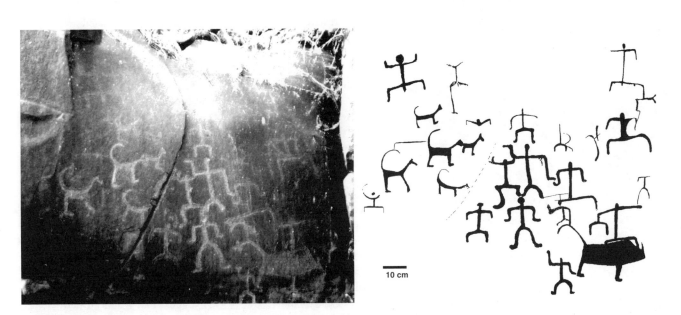

Figure 8.12. Kahe'a heiau; photo and drawing of panel on heiau wall with figures of humans, dogs, and a pig. This is the only known pig motif in Hawaiian rock art and may refer to sacrifices made at this luakini heiau.

Figure 8.14. Kaun-olū's breathtaking location is on the edge of a cliff overlooking the ocean. The ruins of the heiau are on the point of land that juts out (center right). This was Kamehameha's favorite vacation place. Kāne'āpua rock, which also has ruins on top, is the wedge-shaped sea stack at center left.

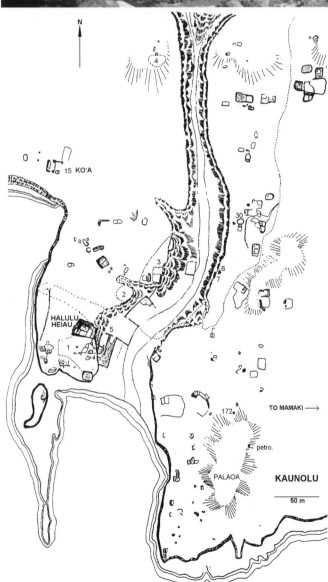

Figure 8.13. Map of Kaunolū (after Emory).

KAUNOLŪ

Kaunolū undoubtedly was reached from the sea in earlier days; it certainly would have been the easiest means of access. Today one crosses the dusty plateau from Lanai City and drives to the edge of the cliff, a distance of approximately 11 km (See Figure 8.1). Orienting oneself by a lighthouse beacon on the ocean's edge, the descent begins. A jeep trail, by comparison, would seem a super-highway. A two-mile bone-jolting ride down the mountain brings one to the remains of a village with marked walking trails.

The site (Figure 8.13), is divided by a deep ravine that terminates at a rocky beach. In the past, canoes landed here and the remains of an ancient canoe shed are still visible. Kāne'āpua Boulder, an eroded sea stack just offshore, looms like a beached ship. Its top contains ruins of a fishing shrine (*ko'a*) (Figure 8.14). On a promontory across the ravine is Kaunolū's heiau—the most impressive structure on Lāna'i. It is in a commanding location, surrounded on three sides by cliffs. The walls are thickest and highest (2.5 m) on the inland side (the side unprotected by cliffs). The width of the walls on the top is 5 meters. The heiau, according to Dixon et al. (1995:244-5), had three phases of construction and may originally have been a *heiau lono* (fertility temple). Later it became a sanctuary for violators of kapu and was still in use between 1778 and 1810. Dixon et al. (ibid.: 251) interpret elements of the archaeological site at Kaunolū as evidence of influence from Maui, including a more rigid kapu system which excluded Lāna'i residents after the subjugation of the island by Kamehameha I.

Gosser and Dixon (1998) suggest that Kaunolū had two settlement systems, based upon a study of the patterns of habitation sites.

In addition to the heiau and canoe shed, Kaunolū has a fish shrine, house sites (including the remains of Kamehameha's royal residence), a good water source (now dry), breathtaking vistas, and excellent ulua fishing. Ulua was a significant game and food item, important enough to be used as an offering at luakini temples; it was forbidden to women (Malo 1951:29).

Directly south of the heiau and continuing to the cliff edge is a group of house sites, perhaps for priests. A stone pavement on the valley floor may have been connected with the heiau. The site and structures of Kaunolū have been described by Emory (1924), Dunbar (1987), and Dixon et al. (1995).

Petroglyphs are scattered around the site of Kaunolū, on both sides of the gulch as well as on the walls of the ravine. Emory divided the sites on the west side of the gulch into four loci: Areas 1-4. Area 1 is close to the heiau; Area 2 is on the edge of the gully, inland and northeast from the heiau (Figure 8.15); Area 3 is also on the edge of the gully, associated with house foundations; and Area 4 is further up on the side of the mountain. Emory's site 15, the fishing shrine, also has petroglyphs (Figure 8.16).

The majority of the house ruins are found on the east side of the gully. Some petroglyphs are also found on this side, mainly at Emory's Site 30. A few scattered units are located between Site 30 and Palaoa Hill. Where possible, our numbering system follows Emory's map of the site.

The entire site has changed considerably since Emory worked here in the 1920s. The recent heavy growth of kiawe has turned the ravine into a jungle of thorn trees that form an impossible tangle of branches and prevents access to most of the gully's cliffs (Figure 8.15). Kiawe trees are impacting the site itself. The ancient paved trail to Māmaki has disappeared.

Emory's journal (Bishop Museum Archives, Ms. Sc. Emory Group 12, Box 8, File 4) has the following entry concerning his work at Kaunolū:

> Lunch was a hearty meal. Then Heck [Hector Munroe] and I went upon the west bank with our stone-working tools and dressed down one petroglyph stone for transportal. When Hector left at 4, I accompanied him down to show him a game stone which perhaps could be removed. On the way back I hammered out a petroglyph of my own, a record of my presence to this famous spot—as I believe others have. The metallic blows filled the glade with a merry sound and started Boynton drilling a picture of himself into the cliff opposite camp.

Unfortunately, they did not sign their attempts to make petroglyphs so we are not sure which were created by them. However, there are some marginal-looking motifs on the cliff walls that appear to be of questionable authenticity; these may be Emory's and Boynton's work. Adding onto petroglyph sites appears to have been a common practice in earlier days of recording, and sadly, the practice continues. Because stone patinates rapidly, within a few years new additions appear to be ancient, thus skewing the prehistoric record forever.

Kaunolū is a special place of mana, myth and history. The ambiance is that of a stimulating and visually beautiful retreat. It is here that Kamahameha came for rest and relaxation, although Kaunolū certainly predates his reign (Dunbar 1987:19). When he first visited Kaunolū he proclaimed it as the landing place of the original ancestors of his genealogical line (Beckwith 1970:11). It is likely that political councils were held here that

Figure 8.15. View looking inland from Emory's Area 1. A corner of Halulu Heiau is visible top left and a faint pāpamu is in the foreground. The trees in the center left are growing up from the ravine.

Figure 8.16. Fishing shrine (koʻa) at Kaunolū. Petroglyphs are associated with this shrine.

Figure 8.17. One of two beautifully stylized birdmen from a panel in Area 3. Several similar figures are located nearby. These images are very faint (see Figure 8.42).

affected the power structure of the islands and, in ancient times, this site was the place for restoring mind, body, and energy. Ali'i of the highest rank were in temporary residence and they brought with them the appropriate entourage or priests, political advisors, craftsmen, servants, relatives, lovers, guards and seers.

Near the heiau of Halulu, named for a giant mythological bird-man, there are petroglyphs of muscled figures with spread-out, wing-like arms (Figure 8.17). We assume that the petroglyphs had some association with the sanctuary. There is precedent for this at Pu'uhonua O Hōnaunau on the Big Island, where there is a petroglyph of an anthropomorph is found near the great walled refuge where kapu violators could find safety.

Petroglyphs of muscled men are found on other islands, but few are the equal of Kaunolū's graceful bird-like anthropomorphs. These may be symbolic 'descendants' of the mythological Halulu. Many other muscled anthropomorphs have bird-like characteristics, suggesting a connection to the myths concerning the heiau and the site itself (Figure 8.23).

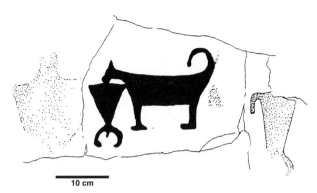

Figure 8.18. An anthropomorph's head becomes the head of a dog in this unusual combination that may suggest an 'aumakua. Traces of triangle torso figures are on each side; both are extremely faint and one has partially exfoliated. Area 3.

Our total at Kaunolū is 276 units, compared to Emory's count of 60 petroglyphs. With the inclusion of Palaoa and the few units at Māmaki, the total is 307. Triangle torso forms outnumber stick figures by 2 to 1; dogs comprise 3.4% of the total. In one instance, man and dog are combined as if the dog represents an 'aumakua (Figure 8.18). Other combinations are of interest: a large muscled figure with two tiny figures under the arms and one with another small figure on its elbow see Figures 8.45 and 8.46). A few are joined together in a classic example of a family grouping. Another one appears to be a mo'o, with multiple legs. Although the majority of petroglyph figures from Lāna'i are generally consistent with what is considered the traditional Hawaiian-style figure, Kaunolū 's muscled figures appear to be a later development and some are carved with considerable artistic skill.

Our recording at Kaunolū located all of the petroglyphs shown in Emory's 1924 book, with one exception: the motif in his Plate IXA eluded us. One of the problems we had at Kaunolū was correlating the petroglyphs with various motifs which had been chalked by Emory, for his photographs show the highlighted and enhanced image, as interpreted by the one doing the chalking. If deeply pecked, the forms are easy to see but those which are lightly bruised and repatinated resemble a Rorschach test: the faint traces blend into natural forms in the boulder and can be interpreted in several ways, all dependent upon ambient lighting. It appears that the majority of petroglyphs photographed by Emory have not suffered much from natural weathering. One of the few unchalked images (ibid.:Plate XE) appears the same today. It seems that little damage has occurred from natural causes; changes are due to human activity.

KUKUI POINT-POAIWA

Lāna'i's Kukui Point site (also known as Poaiwa) is located on the north side of the island near Shipwreck Beach (see Figure 8.1). Shipwreck Beach, as the name suggests, is famed for the numbers of vessels that foundered on the offshore reefs. The earliest reported wreck was the American ship *London* which went aground in 1826 (Emory 1924:7); today at low tide the tips of masts from various sailboats appear, rusted anchors litter the beach, and a large Liberty ship from World War II slowly corrodes in the waters of the reef.

The petroglyph site is located 200 yards inland (Figure 8.19), on the banks of an intermittent stream in an area of dense kiawe. The site consists of a large outcrop of reddish-brown basalt and some detached boulders (Figure 8.20). The main massive outcrop is roughly triangular and measures approximately eleven meters across. At ground level, the

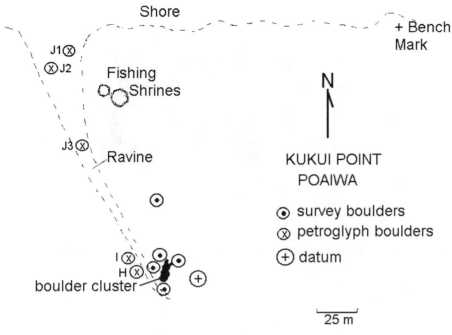

Figure 8.19. Map of the Kukui Point Site (see also Figure 8.49 for detailed map).

west side is 4.7 meters high; the east side is 2.3 m high. Thirty-three of the boulders in this cluster contain petroglyphs, many on all available sides (see Figure 8.49). This site is advertised in local guide books and brochures and it receives a fair amount of unrestricted visitation. The result is that the site has been severely impacted by vandals.

Kukui-Poaiwa also may have been used as an ancient quarry, judging from the chunks of stone that have been chipped away from the edges of some boulders and the lithic scatter in the area. In some instances, chipping has partly eliminated petroglyphs. A nearby fishing shrine has heavy lithic scatter as well as shells and coral fragments.

It is possible that more petroglyphs remain to be discovered in the vicinity because the dense basalt is difficult to impact, and designs are faint . Kiawe trees form a barrier all along the dry wash.

Two hundred forty-six petroglyphs were recorded at Kukui Point-Poaiwa, including 19 images of dogs. Seventy-five percent of the total are human figures of one kind or another, with triangle torso anthropomorphs far outnumbering stick figures. Designs tend to be small and shallow and several are barely bruised, while others are heavily, but unevenly re-pecked. Few elements are clear-cut or deeply pecked, as we see at Lua-hiwa.

It is difficult to glean much information about Kukui Point-Poaiwa. As this site is easily accessible, it has suffered much damage. Crayon, chalk, and other materials have been added to some units but the majority of real damage is from scratching and reworking the motifs. Indeed, many of them may not have any great claim to antiquity. Some clearly authentic elements have been re-pecked in recent years to make them more visible for photography. This was determined by comparing the boulders as they appeared in 1988 against photographs taken in the 1960s by Edward Stasack.

Directly below panel 14 on the north side of the boulder cluster we found a small detached stone (33 x 50 cm) with a tiny carved face. It was left *in situ*, but turned face down. A few months later it was decided to collect this artifact to protect it from vandals but it had already been stolen. (Mikilano Ho, personal communication).

This site, like Kaunolū, also has images of figures with wing-like arms or with wings emanating from their shoulders, or plumes springing from the head.

Figure 8.20. The boulder cluster at Kukui Point. Panel 1 is at the lower left center. Nearly every surface of rock has been defaced by vandals.

Some appear to be in flight (Figure 8.21). Clearly, there is considerable latitude in interpreting these figures. Many are very subtle. However, taken as a whole, it does appear that bird symbolism was intended. We have already mentioned anthropomorphs with feathered headdresses as possibly representing legendary figures. Because feathers were sacred, we can assume that these images referred to supernatural entities.

Figure 8.21. Detail of birdmen from Kukui Point. The appendages on the heads appear to represent feathered headdresses. This panel is 98 x79 cm.

DISCUSSION

We recorded 1151 units at four sites on Lāna'i, an estimated 85% of the total (Emory's count was 216 for the island). Lāna'i's boulder art sites surely are wahi pana, exhibiting all the attributes of storied places. All have special features and exciting images, and most have breathtaking vistas. Three of the four are associated with heiau; the fourth has a fish shrine in association. This seems to indicate sacredness and power in specific spots. Almost all varieties of anthropomorphic images can be found here including stick figures, triangle torso figures, and muscled figures. Many images are of dogs and some of these are connected to human figures. Whether these connected units refer to an 'aumakua is unknown, but this is a distinct possibility.

That which is absent is significant: there are few cupules on flat surfaces (to hold a piko) and circles or other geometric motifs as are found at some sites on the island of Hawai'i are rare. Only two human feet and three turtles were recorded. A dearth of crab-claw sails is notable as is the lack of images of ceremonial regalia. Sites display interesting differences: Luahiwa stands out for the intensity of carving and superposition of motifs. This is not the case at the other sites where motifs tend to be isolated and free-floating. The pig motif at Kahe'a Heiau is unique in the islands.

Many of the images in Lāna'i have bird-like overtones. Some have wing-like arms and legs that suggest tails of frigate birds, or have plumes extending from the head that imply feathers. In Hawaiian myths, birds are potential gods or spiritual beings. Migratory birds were messengers for high chiefs who sent them ahead as scouts or to carry messages while some were intended to be bearers of messages to the heavens. Both the great gods and subordinate deities appear in bird form and some were special guardians; for example, the *elepaio* bird (flycatcher) was worshipped by canoe makers, and *kiwa'a,* the pilot bird, conducted navigators into landing places.

Of particular interest to Lāna'i is the legendary man-eating bird called Halulu, which is said to take human form. At Kaunolū, the heiau of Halulu was the most important shrine on the island and the mythical landing place for this bird-man (Beckwith 1970:90-92). Many species of birds appear in myth as kin, family guardians or totems, or servants of gods. The god himself might appear on earth in bird form and be worshipped under the name of that particular manifestation (ibid:92). Hawaiian legends refer to a child born from an egg who hatches into a many-colored bird and becomes, through the power of a bird ancestress, a *kapua* (supernatural being), with power to take the form of a bird or a beautiful girl (ibid.:428). Flying humans are mentioned Hawaiian myths and the cock-like crests on helmets—also seen on sculpture—show bird connections.

The Hawaiian god of fertility, Lono, was represented by a long wood post with a figure of a bird at the top where a crosspiece was decorated with feathered wreaths and imitation bones of the *ka'upu* bird (Beckwith 1970:34).

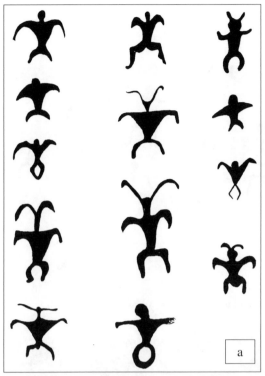

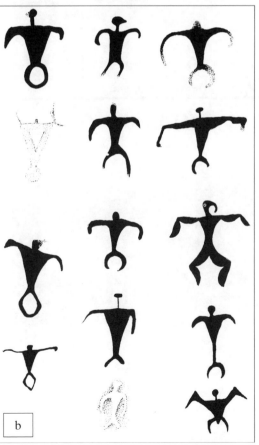

Throughout Polynesia (and beyond) we find legends concerning birds. In Rotuna two sisters who conceived miraculously by a great god incarnate in a frigate bird are described (Williamson 1924, II:282). In the Marquesas Islands it was forbidden to kill frigate birds (ibid.:291). Native pastors sent messages from island to island via frigates (Beckwith 1970:91). Even today fishermen of the Caroline Islands use pet frigate birds to locate schools of tuna (Gillett 1987:46). The importance of birds to the Easter Islanders is attested to by the extraordinary birdman motif that permeates the boulder art of that island.

Thus it is not unusual to find bird imagery on the island of Lāna'i (Figure 8.23a and b). What is puzzling is why such images are not more prevalent throughout all the islands. A few have been noted at Moanalua on O'ahu, and a profile birdman-like petroglyph can be seen at Puakō on the island of Hawai'i. We assume that the difference lies in Lāna'i's rich mythology of Halulu. This legendary bird provided feathers "made out of particles of water from the dazzling orb of the sun" according to Kamakau (1870) or, more prosaically, plumes from the frigate bird (Beckwith 1970:92). Only on nearby Kaho'olawe is there a similar situation with many motifs containing bird characteristics.

In general, Lāna'i's images have more in common with the petroglyphs at Kaho'olawe and Maui than with those on the Big Island. This may be due to the type of available surfaces. Dense basalt is harder to work than pāhoehoe, thus images tend to be small and shallow. Some of the elegant images may date from Kamehameha's time and reflect status and kingship. However, the sheer numbers of images bespeaks of ritual activity, all the more puzzling because of Lāna'i's estimated small population and marginal position in the hierarchy of the islands. Future archaeology on this tiny island will perhaps reveal a more intensive occupation that is now generally accepted.

The change from agriculture to tourism is likely to result in further deterioration to the petroglyph sites, particularly Poiawa-Kukui Point and Luahiwa, both easily accessible to visitors. Alternatively, the sites could be turned into archaeological parks with interpretative brochures and walkways, which would greatly enhance visitor enjoyment. Left alone, the sites may continue to be impacted by those who feel impelled to recarve the designs or otherwise damage them.

The site of Luahiwa faces another problem: the man-made ditch below the large petroglyph boulders has destabilized the lower portion of the site. Without stabilization, further erosion likely will cause the boulders to tumble downhill.

Figure 8.23. a) Birdman images from Kukui Point and b) from Kaunolū. Note the many figures with plumes or suggestions of headdresses and wing-like arms. Several have legs that resemble the tails of frigate birds.

SITE DESCRIPTIONS: LUAHIWA

Boulders are listed below, in the order found in the field. Thus some are not in numerical order so that we could retain the original numbers given by Emory (see Figure 8.6). The plate numbers refer to Emory's 1924 book.

Boulder 1 (Emory's 1, Plate VIIA), (3 units): Small boulder on the lower east end of site. Three stick figure anthropomorphs, one of which has an extra set of limbs (see Figure 8.7).

Boulder 2 (Emory's 2, Plate VIIB), (22 units): One of three contiguous boulders with petroglyphs, east side of site, uphill from Boulder 1. This panel has a delightful collection of stick figures, many with one arm up and suggesting action poses. A few on an adjoining panel are ungainly. One figure has a circle in mid torso (Figure 8.23).

Boulder 3 (Emory's 3), (30 units): One of three contiguous boulders with petroglyphs, west of Boulder 2. A collection of anthropomorphic images, dogs (see Figure 8.8), and an angular form.

Boulder 4 (Emory's 4), (6 units): One of three contiguous boulders with petroglyphs, west of Boulder 3. This panel includes a running stick figure, a fat-bellied figure, and a stylized anthropomorph which may not be aboriginal (based on style alone).

Boulder 5 (Emory's 5, Plate VIID), (68 units): A very large oval-shaped boulder to the west of Boulders 2-4. Part of a cluster of three boulders. Petroglyphs are found on three faces; a natural depression on top of the boulder resembles a vulva form. Motifs include stick figures (some with an extra set of limbs), dogs and, on the southwest face, dense superposition. Some anthropomorphs on this panel have triangular torsos and one seems to be wearing a cowboy hat (Figure 8.24; see also Figure 8.9).

Boulder 6 (Emory's 6), (4 units): A large boulder adjacent to Boulder 5. Stick figures including one with a tail and lizard-like attributes (Figure 8.25).

Figure 8.23. A panel of lively anthropomorphs, one with a circle torso. Boulder 2. This panel measures 127 x 50 cm.

Figure 8.24. A densely carved boulder with both stick figures and triangle torso bodies. The figure at the upper right seems to be wearing a hat. Boulder 5. Photograph taken in 1960 by Edward Stasack.

Figure 8.25. A lizard-like form with fingers. Boulder 6 (32 x 20 cm).

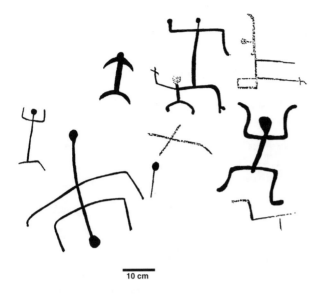

Figure 8.26. Panel high up on the top of Boulder 8, and out of view from the ground.

Figure 8.27. A figure with a long torso is associated with dogs on Boulder 8. Note detached head and muscled legs.

Boulder 7 (Emory's 7), (9 units): Partially buried boulder near Boulder 5. Motifs include a dog and several anthropomorphs with fat rounded bodies and fingers.

Boulder 8 (Emory's 8, Pl. VIIH), (at least 77 units): Southeast from above group, this 4 meter high boulder stands out because of its size. Petroglyphs are found on all faces of the boulder including the top, completely out of sight of viewers on the ground (Figure 8.26). We had to climb the boulder to photograph them. All are stick figure types, some are joined together and one has extra limbs.

The east face (described as the south face by Emory) is densely carved, particularly the lower portion which has much superposition of stick figures (plus some modern efforts to mimic the petroglyphs). One figure on this face of the boulder is a thin triangular anthropomorph 110 cm long, associated with dogs (Figure 8.27). High on this face is a stick figure with six sets of legs. The west face has triangle torso figures.

Boulder 9 (Emory's 9), (12 units): Directly to the west of Boulder 8. Emory noted only four figures here. There are tiny cupules on a vertical face and a multi-legged stick figure.

Boulder 10 (Emory's 10, Plate VIIF), (2 units): west of Boulders 8 and 9. An armless and headless triangle-bodied figure with muscled legs and a penis. A single dog is above the figure. (Figure 8.28). It is unusual to see fully pecked muscled legs with a torso in simple outline.

Boulder 28, 3 units. A small boulder at the base of Boulder 8. Not on Emory's list. A small panel at ground level has a flat-headed active figure; others here include what appears to be a double stick figure, possibly unfinished or eroded.

Figure 8.28. A headless figure with muscled legs, and a dog. Boulder 10.

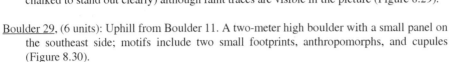

Boulder 11 (Emory's 11, Plate VIIE), (4 units): One panel has a long set of stick figures, some multi-legged and with 'shelf' hands and feet. A 'barking' dog is located near the first figure in this line. A very faint triangle torso anthropomorph just above the line of stick figures was recorded which is not shown in Emory's photograph (the other images he chalked to stand out clearly) although faint traces are visible in the picture (Figure 8.29).

Boulder 29, (6 units): Uphill from Boulder 11. A two-meter high boulder with a small panel on the southeast side; motifs include two small footprints, anthropomorphs, and cupules (Figure 8.30).

Boulder 30, (1 unit). Adjacent to Boulder 11 on the west. One stick figure with additional limbs.

Boulder 12 (Emory's 12, Plate VIIC, VIIIA-D), (at least 122 units): A huge boulder to the northwest. Boulders 12-13 form the boundary of a court-like area. Boulder 12 was extremely challenging to record; Emory (1924:96) refers to the great four meter high southwest face as a "maze". This face of the boulder is literally covered with petroglyphs upon petroglyphs—from extremely large muscled figures to tiny dogs (Figure 8.31). The east face has easier access; it contains a collection of human and dog figures including a man on horseback, and two turtles.

Figure 8.29. A multi-legged figure with a barking dog. Boulder 11. Panel measures 103 x 40 cm.

Figure 8.30. Footprints pecked out (intaglio) and small anthropomorph. Boulder 29. This panel measures 65 x 39 cm.

Figure 8.31. The heavily carved southwest face of Boulder 12.

Figure 8.32. The north side of Boulder 12. Two large muscled figures over other images plus lettering. This panel measures 124 x 82 cm.

The north side contains a variety of figures; particularly notable are two very large and finely pecked muscled triangular figures superimposed by the letters KAI (Figure 8.32). One hundred twenty-two figures were recorded on this boulder; there may be more. The southwest face is particularly challenging; one needs a long ladder and several days to recheck all the numerous carvings that have turned it into a maze of lines.

<u>Boulder 13</u> (Emory's 13, Plate VIIIE), (30 units): East of Boulder 12, in the same central part of the site. The west face of this boulder has an elaborate panel (Figure 8.33) of men, dogs, and men on horseback. As it is easily accessible, it has suffered from vandalism and modern-day recarving. Among the 30 motifs here, a large dog with a curly tail stands out; it is attached by a long line to an anthropomorph. Another dog with a curly tail has been modified in recent times by the addition of antlers (Emory's 1924 photograph shows the figure prior to vandalism).

Figure 8.33. Petroglyphs of men and dogs with much superposition and vandalism. Boulder 13, Luahiwa. The dog on the right has had antlers added in recent years. This panel measures 230 x 210 cm.

Boulder 31, (3 units): A small boulder next to Boulder 12. Apparently overlooked by Emory. The panel contains very elegant muscled anthropomorphs, one with a club raised above his head and one with great outstretched arms that are wing-like (Figure 8.34). These figures are on a par with the best at Kaunolū, another site on Lāna'i (see below).

Boulder 14 (Emory's 14, Plate VIIG), (34 units): Northeast of Boulder 12, at the top of a water-cut ravine. This petroglyph panel, photographed earlier by Emory, has been recarved in recent years (see Figure 8.11). In the 1920s, the petroglyphs chalked by Emory included a simple canoe shape, a dog, and some other lines and figures (Emory 1924). It now has been elaborated upon with, among other elements, an outrigger. Emory noted specifically that no outrigger was present in 1921 (ibid.:114). Local informants suggested that this act of vandalism occurred between 1968 and 1974, but we noted new additions to this panel during our visit in 1988; documentation of this panel began on a Saturday; when we returned the following Mon-

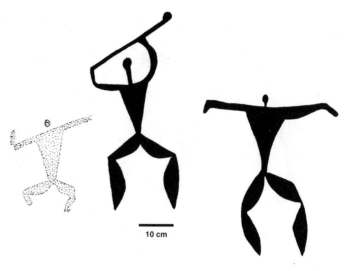

Figure 8.34. Boulder #31. Two beautifully stylized anthropomorphs with muscled legs.

day, one anthropomorph had been recarved into a turtle (see Figure 8.35 lower left) and several other figures altered. Undoubtedly this panel originally contained many more petroglyphs than Emory noted, but in light of modern-day additions, it is difficult to separate out the two. The boulder patinates quickly and within a short time, the new markings blend in and appear to be of the same time-depth as the earlier, original petroglyphs.

Figure 8.35. Drawing of the panel on Boulder 14 as shown in the photographs, Figure 8.11. The photo insert and drawing below (left) show how vandals replaced a figure with a turtle. A recent geometric design can be seen to the right of the turtle. This panel measures 355 x 181 cm. and continues over onto page 123.

the turtle, left, has replaced the tall anthropomorph, right

Boulder 15 (Emory's 15, Plate VIIIF-G), (29 units): North of Boulder 14. A massive boulder with panels of petroglyphs on three sides. The west side includes two figures on horseback (Figure 8.36); all other motifs are of humans and dogs plus one 'teardrop' geometric element. Boulder 15 is the last number given by Emory for this site, although he mentions that "Near top of slopes a large bowlder has a few linear figures. Other bowlders in vicinity are without trace of petroglyphs." (Emory 1924:97).

Boulder 16, (3 units): Adjacent to Boulder 15. Three anthropomorphic figures together with many recent scratches and markings.

Boulder 17, (3 units): West of 15-16: we counted three cupules.

Boulder 18, 19 and 20, (10 units on all three boulders): These are located in a cluster of small boulders and the three boulders contain a variety of small anthropomorphs, mostly stick figures (Figures 8.37, 8.38).

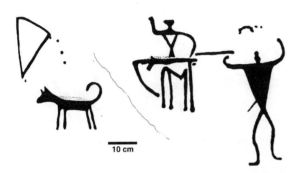

Figure 8.36. This panel on Boulder #15 includes men on horseback and dogs. Note the prominent fingers on the upper anthropomorphs and the knee joints on the upper horse.

Figure 8.37. A group of stick figures and some random pecking on Boulder 18.

Figure 8.35 continued.

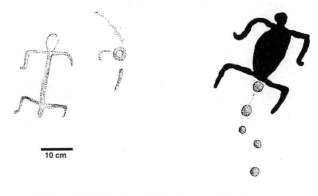

Figure 8.38. Boulder 20 in the same boulder group as Boulder 18. The figure on the right is associated with cupules on a sloping surface.

Figure 8.39. Boulder 27. Dogs and humans are featured on this boulder. Note the faint triangle torso under the large dog. This panel measures 230 x 110 cm.

Boulder 21, (3 units): East from Boulder 20. Three small anthropomorphs.

Boulders 22-23, (26 units including both boulders): Boulder 23 is a large boulder that is part of a massive grouping of boulders, Boulder 22 is located slightly west. These boulders contain crudely made figures on rough irregular surfaces.

Boulders 24-25, (20 units): Part of a very large group of boulders, near the upper trail. Two small panels have cupules; the major panel, which is undulating and rough, has a mixture of human and dog forms. All the anthropomorphs are stick figures.

Boulder 26, (3 units): This boulder is above the cluster of Boulders 2-4 and contains three anthropomorphs.

Boulder 27, (25 units): East of Boulders 5-7. Large oblong boulder, 3 m high. Petroglyphs are found on the south and west faces and feature at least 14 dogs, plus a few human figures (Figure 8.39).

KAHE'A HEIAU

This small site was documented by placing a string grid over the panels and drawing the petroglyphs to scale. A series of slides also were taken. Kahe'a's panel is one of the most elegantly carved on the island and, in 1988, was in good condition. It is rare to find petroglyphs on the stones of an heiau. Only one other comes to mind: that of Kamo'oali'i, in the Ka'ū District of the Big Island.

There are 28 petroglyphs at this locus, including 3 whose forms are unidentified, 7 dogs, 16 stick figures, and 1 triangle torso anthropomorph, and what appears to be a boar (see Figure 8.12). Several of the stick figures are connected to each other, a pattern noted at Luahiwa.

Figure 8.40. Kaunolū, Area 1. Petroglyph was chalked by vandals.

Figure 8.41. Boulder cluster Area 1 near heiau. Petroglyphs are seen at upper and lower left.

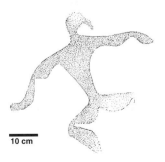

10 cm

Figure 8.42. Muscled figures at Area 3.

KAUNOLŪ

Area 1 (Emory 1924:Plate IXA-H), (71 units): Bounded by the cliff edge on the south, the gully on the east, and the heiau on the north. A considerable number of rocks in this area contain petroglyphs (Figure 8.40). Some are associated with ruins of house terraces and foundations (Figure 8.41). Papamū are located near the southeast corner of the heiau. This area, which receives the majority of visitation due to the proximity of the heiau, has suffered the most from graffiti, including what appears to be modern efforts to make petroglyphs.

Images range from well-made triangular bodied anthropomorphs to stylized goats. The goats, which Emory also recorded, are made with incised lines, probably with a metal tool (ibid.:Plate IXI). One panel has 'edge notching'. This is shown in Emory (Plate IXE); we were able to see this panel clearly and it seems to have changed little although it had been heavily colored in with crayon. A figure with a forked penis (?) also appears the same as shown in Emory, although the secondary figure on the panel is very much fainter in 1988 (ibid.:Plate IXC). Our panel 11 (ibid.:Plate IXG), a bas relief figure with bird-like arms was created by pecking around the form. Erosion is severe and the image is extremely faint.

Our panel 27 (see ibid.:Plate IXB) appeared basically the same as when Emory photographed it, with a few exceptions. Erosion has occurred. Although we could pick out the general figure shapes, much of the detail has weathered away.

Muscled anthropomorphs are much in evidence at Area 1, as are triangle figures with circles or partial circles instead of legs (ibid.:Plate IXF). The latter figures have outstretched arms that give a bird-like impression.

Area 2 (Emory 1924:Plate XA), (32 units): North and inland from Area 1, on the edge of the gulch. The images here are much less clear and not well made. The majority are triangle torso anthropomorphs. A panel with a phallic figure appears to be in similar condition in 1988 as in 1923 when recorded by Emory; this is one of the few petroglyphs that Emory photographed without first chalking. Thus it was possible to make a real comparison with its condition over time. There are several triangle torso figures with outstretched wing-like arms, and with legs that nearly form a circle, similar to those in Area 1.

Area 3 (Emory 1924:Plate XB-G), (66 units): Northeast and bounded on two sides by a bend in the gulch. This locus has scattered petroglyphs. Panel 5 has a triangle torso phallic anthropomorph that is partially over the head of a large dog with a curly tail (see Figure 8.18). Two other partial anthropomorphs are located nearby.

In the same area are several other triangle torso figures with muscled legs and wide arms. These are the famous birdman figures shown by Emory (ibid.:Plate XF). This panel has three muscled triangle figures with widely stretched arms and what could be interpreted as plumes or beaks. A fourth partial form is located below, with a possible secondary form emerging from the upper arm. All of these are lightly pecked or bruised with little depth, making them very difficult to see (Figure 8.42).

<u>Area 4</u> (43 units): North and inland. Stick figures are dominant motifs. One particularly fine example is shown in Emory (Pl. XI A). This grouping has at least four figures connected together (Figure 8.44). Others here have multiple legs. It would appear from the figure style that the petroglyphs in this area were earlier than those lower down on the slopes.

The remaining petroglyph sites are out of the area designations made by Emory.

<u>Site 5</u> (5 units): East of the heiau, a small group of figures on the west side of the gulch wall. All anthropomorphs, two of them connected.

<u>Site 6</u> Kanemakua (Emory 1924, Pl. X H), (11 units): On east side of gulch, near the top. On an outcrop looking out over the gulch, there are large figures facing west. Emory shows four or five petroglyphs in his photograph. Due to its inaccessible position on the cliff wall and the present entanglement of kiawe trees, we were unable to directly access the panel but had to sketch it from a distance. The major figure is a muscled anthropomorph with two tiny figures under each arm. (Figure 8.45).

<u>Site 7</u> (11 units): On east side of gully on vertical faces of the cliff, to the south of Kanemakua. A series of panels with anthropomorphic figures, one of them particularly interesting in that it has a second figure on its left shoulder and another element on the right shoulder. It may have some sort of headdress (Figure 8.46).

<u>Site 15</u> (13 units): A fish shrine west of gulch, above Kolokolo sea cave (see Figure 8.16). Anthropomorphs are scattered around on various small boulders in the vicinity of the fish shrine. Emory did not record any petroglyphs in this area. The figures are not well made, and many are incomplete. There is one triangle-bodied anthropomorph with muscles.

Figure 8.44. Connected figures from Area 4.

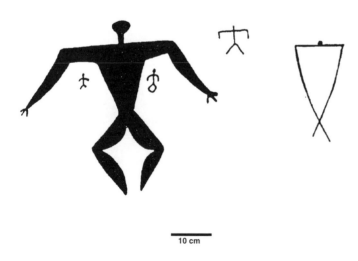

Figure 8.45. East side of the ravine near the top is a large anthropomorph with two small ones placed below the arms. The simple line figures on the right appear to be more recent.

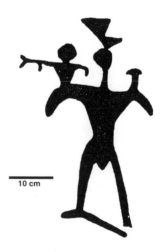

Figure 8.46. Another petroglyph group on the ravine wall with tiny figures coming out of the elbow of the larger one and a strange extension from the head.

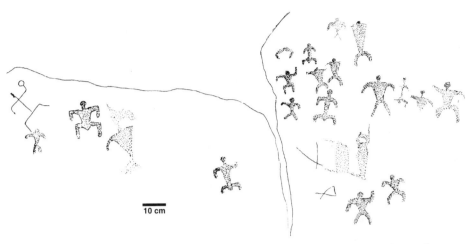

10 cm

Figure 8.47. East bank, clusters of small faint figures; The smallest complete anthropomorph we recorded measures 7.5 x 6.0 cm. Some appear to have been altered in recent years,
and the panel also includes modern scratching.

Site 30 (Emory 1924, Pl. XI-G), (24 units): East bank of gulch, at top. Associated with an enclosure and tower. Emory (1924:103) noted: "A rock tower (Site 30, Pl.11) covered with small bruised figures." Some of these figures are very small. Panels face north and contain a cluster of faint figures. Most are triangle torso and some shapes are unclear (Figure 8.47). Emory chalked 20 or 21 figures. Some lines now seen on the rock appear to be modern additions.

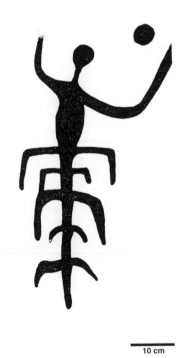

10 cm

Figure 8.48. A figure from Māmaki with multiple legs and a cupule.

Site 172, 1-2 (Emory 1924, Pl.X-D), (17 units): Palaoa, south of the village at Kaunolū and toward the present lighthouse. Two loci were documented: one, west of the present road, is shown in Emory's 1924 photograph. This panel is severely eroded and contains some recent additions in the form of modern stick figures made with metal tools.

The second locus in the area is a large boulder on east of road, and overlooking the west coast has two figures, not recorded by Emory (no site number given). One is a stick figure anthropomorph with shelf-like feet and an indeterminate figure with a wedge shaped body and lightly pecked extremities.

MĀMAKI

Site 173, Māmaki (Emory 1924:Pl. XI D), (13 units): A flat area with many large boulders 3/4 mile east from Kaunolū. Due to time constraints it was not possible to fully document the site. A quick survey at Māmaki noted 28 boulders with 56 figures. One is a very interesting multiple-legged figure (Figure 8.48). Only those actually recorded have been placed into the data base. Several of the figures have distinct bird-like attributes.

KUKUI POINT

A map of the boulder cluster at Kukui Point is shown in Figure 8.49. Beginning at the east side at northeast corner of the rock outcrop, boulders are numbered counter-clockwise around the boulder cluster. Individual rocks have from one to six panels each. On the west, south and north sides of the outcrop are peripheral boulders (Rocks B through I) that also have petroglyphs. Other boulders are located across the ravine to the south and a massive rock in the middle of the creek bed contains a single large cupule (not given a designation). Boulder D on the pathway into the site contains petroglyphs, 22 cupules and a painted sign: "Do Not Deface". Rock J is an outlier, near the fish shrine. See Figure 8.19.

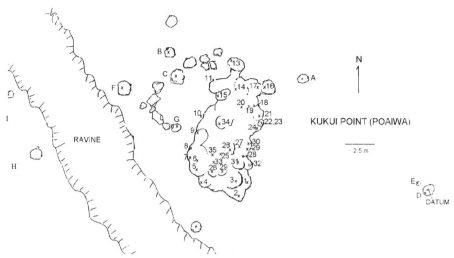

Figure 8.49. Map of the boulder cluster at Kukui Point. The numbers and lettered boulders indicate petroglyph panels.

Most of Kukui-Poaiwa's motifs are fully repatinated and very difficult to see. They are shallow, and some are either unfinished or are so faint as to be indecipherable. Modern graffiti and attempts to enhance the petroglyphs by scraping them has done irreparable damage. It is difficult to discern the old from the new due to the rapid rate of patination.

East Face of boulder cluster, Panels 1 to 3, (30 units): Several vertical panels with figure groupings including stick figures, triangle torso figures, and dogs. A few of the figures exhibit heavy pounding. Whether this was part of the original petroglyph or later attempts to reinforce the images is unknown. The peck marks all show the same degree of patination (Figure 8.50). Some anthropomorphs have unusually shaped heads, either mushroom-like or flat on the top. One has antennae sprouting from the head (Figure 8.51).

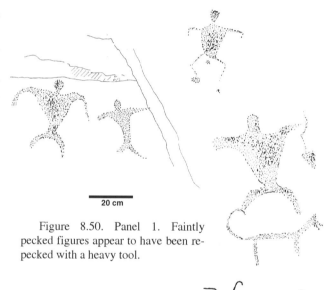

Figure 8.50. Panel 1. Faintly pecked figures appear to have been re-pecked with a heavy tool.

South Face of boulder cluster, Panels 4-7, 28-29, (44 units for rocks 4-7 and 29 units for rocks 28-29): This 'downhill' side of the rock outcrop faces inland toward the dry creek bed. Panels of figures are arranged all along this side, from eye level to the top boulders. At the base of this side of the outcrop is a low step-like stone with a clearly notched edge, like a sawtooth formation. What this might have signified is unclear. The petroglyphs are very rough and have been scratched by vandals.

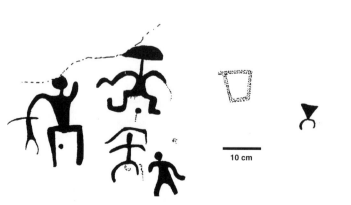

Figure 8.51. Panel 3 has figures with oddly shaped heads.

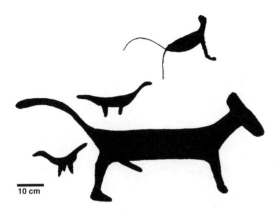

Figure 8.52. A large phallic dog and other figures on Panel 9.

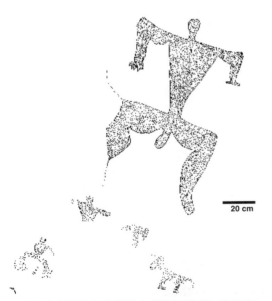

Figure 8.53. Phallic and muscled figure on Boulder I in creek area.

<u>West Face of boulder cluster,</u> Panels 9-15, 33-35, (40 units for rocks 9-15; 7 for panels 33 and 35). Several panels on this side of the outcrop include recent vandalism in the form of names, and other markings. A few of the petroglyphs appear to have had some re-carving in recent times and a few exhibit scratching. The motifs continue to the top of the outcrop. One panel is notable for an image of a large phallic dog (Figure 8.52). Associated on this panel are anthropomorphs with circles in the mid-section and modern graffiti.

<u>North Face of boulder cluster,</u> Panels 16-22, (27 units): All available surfaces have some anthropomorphic elements pecked or bruised into them. One panel from this site, illustrated in Cox and Stasack 1970 (Figure 43), could not be relocated.

<u>Top area of boulder cluster,</u> Panels 28-30, (31 units): The top part of the outcrop apparently is popular with visitors who climb up and mark small poorly made anthropomorphs on the rocks, and on the petroglyphs.

<u>Boulder A,</u> Survey point. No petroglyphs.

<u>Boulder B,</u> (9 units): A large flat boulder to the west of the outcrop. One of the finest panels at this site, it has two fine triangle torso figures with long plumes coming from their heads. (See Figure 8.21). Nearby is another muscled figure holding a spear or club overhead.

<u>Boulder C,</u> (6 units): Some figures are extremely faint and unidentifiable. The most interesting is a bird-like figure with antennae and widespread arms.

<u>Boulder D,</u> (26 units): At entry to site, and local datum. Cupules and anthropomorphs; the latter are faint and poorly made.

<u>Boulder E,</u> (1 unit): A small, well carved triangle torso figure on a low boulder, near Boulder D.

<u>Boulder F,</u> (6 units): Large boulder with a panel of anthropomorphs or partial anthropomorphs; petroglyphs are on sloping underside panel. Some of these appear to have been re-pecked recently.

<u>Boulder G,</u> (1 unit): A free standing boulder west of the boulder cluster; one small poorly made human figure.

<u>Boulder H,</u> (2 units): Large boulder, across gully from main outcrop on edge of dry creek bed. One incomplete triangle torso figure and a cupule on the vertical face.

<u>Boulder I,</u> (6 units): Large boulder, across and on far side of dry creek bed. The major figure is a large phallic muscled anthropomorph with fingers on the left hand. Other images include a dog, partial figures, and some unidentified markings (Figure 8.53).

<u>Boulder J,</u> (3 units): Outlier site, near fish shrine and north of the boulder cluster, all human figures. Two figures are located on one boulder.

FOOTNOTES

[1] It appears that Emory's site sketch was drawn from the photograph; see Fig.8.4; numbers written on the picture refer to boulder numbers given in description of this group of petroglyphs. It is a good match to his sketch. The photo shows only those boulders he drew, suggesting that the missing heiau stones may have been out of sight from the lower part of the site.

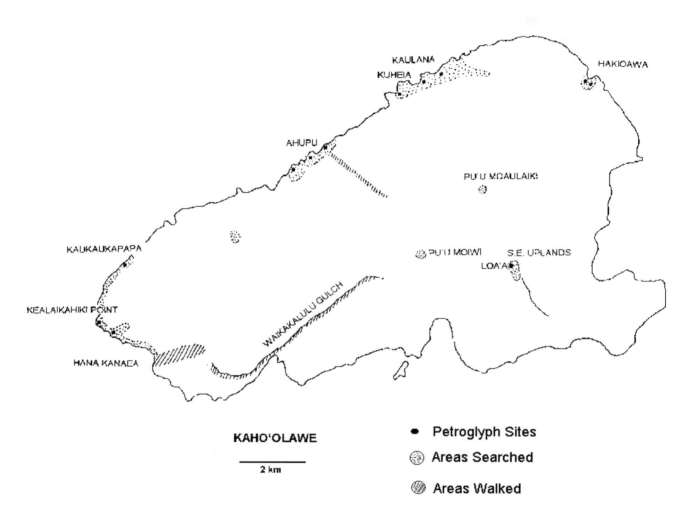

Figure 9.1. A map of Kahoʻolawe Island.

9

KAHOʻOLAWE ISLAND

The tiny barren island of Kahoʻolawe is an eroded volcano with steep cliffs on the southern and eastern coasts and stream-cut gulches radiating out from its central plateau (Figure 9.1). Lying in the rain shadow of Maui, 18 km to the northeast, Kahoʻolawe is a mere 116 square km and the smallest of the eight major Hawaiian islands. It seems to be an island of red dirt (Figure 9.2). Aside from the ubiquitous kiawe at lower altitudes, little vegetation is to be seen except where recent efforts at reforestation have established a tenuous toe-hold for a few native trees. Constant winds, little rainfall and decades of hungry goats (introduced shortly after contact) have made an indelible impression on the fragile ecosystem. Before that time, the island had a dry land forest or scrub park land—a savanna of grass, shrubs and small trees. In the upland areas there was open dry-land forest, pili grass and low shrubs. The west end was almost all pili grass. The vegetation held the soil and allowed rainfall to penetrate. Thus the loss of plant cover not only resulted in erosion, but also caused depletion of the ground water supply (Hommon 1982).

Remains of former settlements are found in nearly all parts of the island, despite its small size and relative impoverishment. This is probably due to the excellent fishing in the waters around the island and, at one time, there may have been considerable agricultural wealth. A large stone adze quarry, Puʻu Moiwi, was actively utilized by ancient Hawaiians. Sources of fine basalt and volcanic glass were in short supply on most Hawaiian islands and the size of the quarries on Kahoʻolawe suggest that they probably supplied this trade item to other islands, such as Maui, in exchange for food.

In historic times, most early visitors to Hawaiʻi passed by Kahoʻolawe but did not land, so our early accounts are from ships sailing past and making long-distance judgments. However, in 1819 Jacques Arago (Reeve 1992:26), artist on the French corvette *Uranie*, observed the island with a different eye. He wrote:

Figure 9.2. A typical view of inland Kahoʻolawe showing the eroded landscape.

Taouroe [Kahoʻolawe] arose before the corvette, reddish on the sides, black at her base, copper at her summit; Taouroe, island of rock, embattled, notched at the peak in pointed ridges, similar to a decrepit wall of lava chiseled by the centuries. Who, then, has touched this ground barren of any greenery, who then has tried to scale these formidable ramparts on which the waves thunder and crash with such violence? No one. And yet the long and perilous reefs surround Taouroe, as if the crags had to fear the conquest of man, as if they wanted to defend against all greediness the wealth that is hidden perhaps in its sides. Taouroe will be eternally uninhabited, for life there is impossible.

Criminals from the other islands in Hawaiʻi were shipped to a penal colony at Kaulana on the north coast of Kahoʻolawe from 1826 to 1859. A census in 1866 reported twenty people living on the island and employed in ranching, and plans were made to import from 10,000 to 20,000 sheep. Both efforts failed, likely due to a lack of water. Overgrazing caused major erosion; as Stearns (1940:147) noted, "Here in the short span of 152 years the soil accumulation of a million or more years was blown away forever and the former green little island became a bare bald forbidding land".

In 1910 the island was declared a Forest Reserve. Some of the animals were removed and attempts were made to rid the island of goats. Then, in 1941 the island was taken over by the military and, for some 45 years, it was used as a target for practice bombing. Declared an archaeological district in 1981 and placed on the National Register of Historic Places, the government has returned the island to the Hawaiian people. A surprising amount of archaeological research has been done, and a clean-up project to remove debris left behind from years of target practice is on-going.

Fairly well-preserved archaeological remains are found on Kahoʻolawe, similar to those found throughout the islands (Kirch 1985:144) for, despite disruption caused by the military, the island has not been impacted by plantation agriculture or tourism.

Kahoʻolawe is mentioned in traditional myths and legends, in which the island is associated with a number of Hawaiian gods, including Kanaloa, the god of the sea. In fact, the ancient name for the island was Kanaloa. Kahoʻolawe also is linked to the shark god, Kamohoailiʻi, brother of the fire goddess, Pele. Oral traditions (Reeve n.d.) describe the hill at Moaulaiki as the site of a school for astronomy and navigation. Atop this hill is a large boulder on a pedestal which rings when struck. Nearby is an adze quarry, the second-largest in all the islands.

In 1875, King David Kalakaua made a retreat to Kahoʻolawe for religious purification, as was reported in *Ka Lahui Hawaiʻi*, the Hawaiian language newspaper.

Figure 9.3. Dense groves of kiawe trees at low elevations made mapping and recording difficult. Kaukaukapapa, Site 135.

Kahoʻolawe's rock art has been mentioned in various earlier surveys that were carried out over a period of years (Hommon 1980 a, b). Our project, which was to systematically relocate and document all the known petroglyphs, was brought about as the result of a visit to the island by Hawaiian scholar, Rubellite Kawena Johnson, who visited some of the petroglyph sites. Upon comparing the results of earlier surveys with that which could be seen on the rocks, it appeared that erosion had attacked many sites.

Figure 9.4. The Site at Hakioawa (485D). Maui and the islet of Molokini are in the background.

The numbers of petroglyphs identified and recorded by us did not always match the information provided on earlier site forms. In some instances, we located more petroglyphs than had been recognized previously; at other times, we found that natural features had been misconstrued as petroglyphs. At least one boulder cluster has been destroyed by target practice; we do not know if it contained any petroglyphs.

Because petroglyphs are located on large, dense basalt boulders similar to those on Lāna'i, motifs are not deeply pecked. Indeed, some are so lightly pecked into the surface that they are hard to see. The difficulties encountered in recording were compounded by dense growths of kiawe trees, making mapping and documenting an arduous and prickly process (Figure 9.3).

Kaho'olawe is a rugged island with few jeep trails. Transport around the island for the documentation project was not easy; two of the sites had to be accessed by helicopter. To reach Hakioawa required a steep hike for no jeep trails exist in that part of the island. Because of danger from unexploded ordinance, it was necessary to have an ordinance person with us in the field. Some sections of the island were off-limits, preventing systematic exploration.

As part of the Kaho'olawe Island petroglyph project, 13 dates were obtained by radiocarbon analyses with accelerator mass spectrometry (AMS). This part of the study was conducted by Dr. Ron Dorn of Arizona State University. Dating results are discussed in Appendix A.

DISCUSSION

The motifs on Kaho'olawe most closely resemble those on Maui and Lāna'i. This may be due to the surfaces upon which they were executed: dense boulders as opposed to pāhoehoe. However, all these islands are easily accessible by canoe and one must assume that there had been considerable travel back and forth in the early days which could account for the similarities. Kaho'olawe's chert quarry would have led to a certain amount of trade with other islands.

Two of Kaho'olawe's sites stand out: Hakioawa, (Figure 9.4) on the northeast coast opposite Maui; and Loa'a, on the inland plateau. Hakioawa is notable because of its complexity. This was a major settlement on the island with some 182 individual features. Two streams form a valley with a central ridge where house terraces, heiau and fishing shrines are located. The site once had potable water. The majority of the petroglyphs are found on boulders on the central ridge, but one cluster is located along the face of a ridge along a stream bed. A notable petroglyph from Hakioawa is a large fishhook motif (Figure 9.5).

Loa'a is located on the southwestern slope of Pu'u Moaulanui at an elevation of 350 meters. Today the area is totally denuded with only a few scattered kiawe trees. Loa'a consists of a cluster of boulders with figures, cupules, and traces of temporary camp sites. The site stands apart by virtue of the designs carved on its rocks, its remoteness, and distance from water.

All the other known petroglyph sites are on the west and northwest coasts of the island and tend to be located where stream-cut ravines open out to sea. We found three petroglyph sites that had not been reported previously: Kaulana, Kealaikahiki, and an unnamed site east of Kealaikahiki. Added to these are others on the western coast: Kuheia, three sites at Ahupū, two sites at Ahupuiki, Makaalae, and Kaukau-

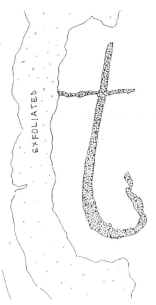

Figure 9.5. A large fish hook (32 x 10 cm) motif from Hakioawa. This is the only fish hook representation found on the Kaho'olawe.

kapapa. Many of these contain historic motifs of goats (Figure 9.6)

The total petroglyph count for the Kaho'olawe petroglyph project (82 petroglyph loci and 423 units) may be low, for unexplored areas of the island may contain petroglyphs, and it was not possible to relocate a few sites noted in earlier surveys. One of the more frustrating aspects of this project was trying to correlate earlier drawings and reports with what was found at the sites. It is difficult to see eroded motifs on heavily patinated rocks, often covered with lichen and moss or hidden in poor light beneath kiawe trees. Many rock surfaces are pitted, irregular, and suffer from spalling. Several times we found ourselves surrounding a rock, agonizing over whether or not we could see a faint figure or were 'reading' more into the rock than was actually there.

One of the keys to locating petroglyphs is to have a mental template of what might be there, determined by past experience. Thus when references were made to tiny petroglyphs (as recorded by Streck in 1980) that were said to measure 3 x 0.05 cm, suspicions were aroused. Motifs of such minute size are out of the norm for the islands. In these instances we determined that natural features in the rock were mistaken for petroglyphs.

Vandalism in the form of gunfire has drastically affected many panels on the west coast. The delightful little figures on the rocks were irresistible targets for vandals (Figure 9.7). The damage continues in that the impact of a bullet breaks the "crust" on rocks, enabling moisture to penetrate and thus exfoliation increases.

Considering that Kaho'olawe is only a little smaller than nearby Lāna'i, the difference in number of petroglyphs between these two islands is conspicuous. It is said that both islands suffered from degraded environments and had small populations; however, it appears that Lāna'i must have had a more desirable environment in earlier times and thus supported more inhabitants and, consequently, expanded ritual activity.

Kaho'olawe's petroglyphs may span a long period of time—from prehistoric through the early years of this century, the latter times clearly seen in the goat images and lettering. Seventy-one per cent of the petroglyphs represent human figures, with stick figures outnumbering the triangle torso anthropomorphs. Petroglyphs tend to be small and shallow, found near settlements, and display individualized types among some of the anthropomorphs. Some of the most outstanding images are of bird-like humans with great outstretched wing-like arms, similar to those on nearby Lāna'i.

Dates obtained from petroglyphs have far-reaching implications. If these dates are substantiated, we will have an additional tool to help comprehend the petroglyphs, evaluate their contexts, and

Figure 9.6. Images of goats are found at sites on the west side of the island. Goats were brought to Hawai'i by Capt. Vancouver; the first were gifts to Kamehameha. This panel, from Site 121G in the gulch west of Ahupū Iki, measures 30 x 30 cm.

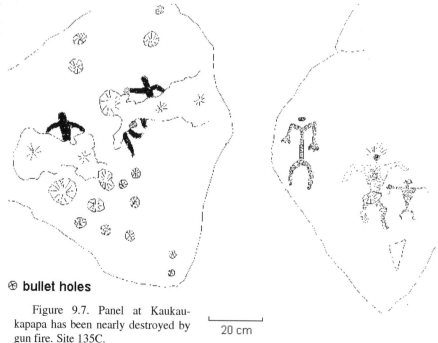

⊗ **bullet holes**

Figure 9.7. Panel at Kaukaukapapa has been nearly destroyed by gun fire. Site 135C.

20 cm

place them into the archaeological matrix of the islands. If this type of dating can be done on other islands, we will be able to hypothesize sequences in the marginal, late-settled islands such as Kahoʻolawe and also will have a base reference for petroglyphs executed elsewhere in the islands. Furthermore, actual dates open up a new field of study for petroglyphs which subsequently will be looked upon as more important components of the archaeological record.

The dating of some of Kahoʻolawe's petroglyphs was made somewhat more secure by the island's isolation for the past 45 years. Petroglyphs that have been scraped, repecked, chalked, or otherwise contaminated are not good candidates for this type of analysis. It may be difficult to find petroglyphs on other islands that have not been impacted previously.

SITE DESCRIPTIONS
HAKIOAWA

Hakioawa (Figure 9.8) appears to have been the major settlement on Kahoʻolawe during the late prehistoric period. The valley was formed by two streams that join at the beach. Today the area supports a moderate growth of kiawe trees. Between the two streams lies a central ridge, on which are 41 archaeological sites including house terraces and religious temples. The majority of the petroglyphs at Hakioawa are situated along the ridge. Motifs are pecked, abraded, or incised into the basalt boulders that are scattered around the area. There are no historic elements present in the rock art at this site.

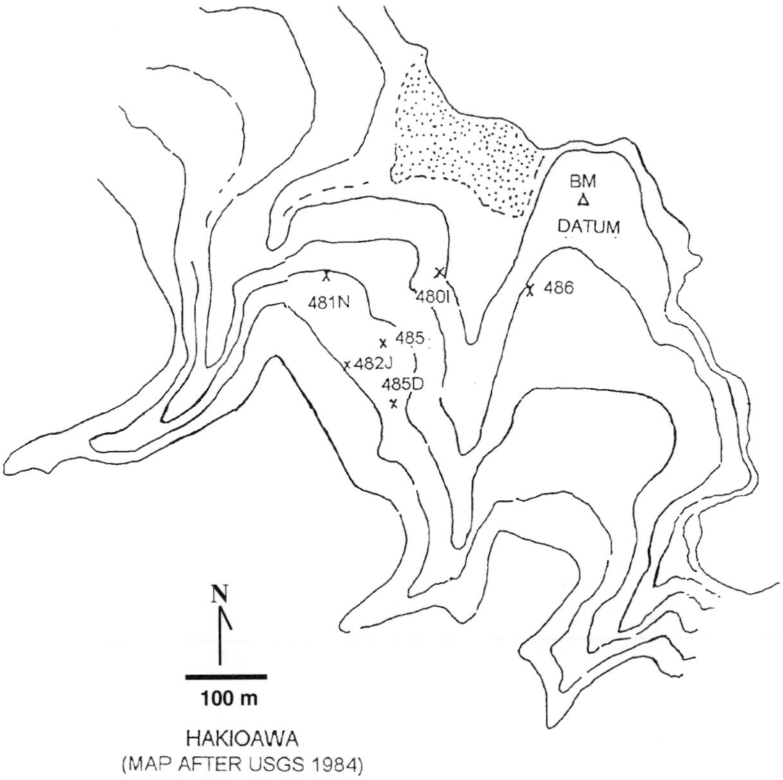

N

100 m

HAKIOAWA
(MAP AFTER USGS 1984)

Figure 9.8.

Site 480, central ridge; a complex including cairns, habitation terraces and petroglyphs (Hommon 1980a). Hommon described petroglyphs at Sites 480G and 480H; however, despite a search, these were not relocated. The vegetation has grown in the years since the earlier survey, thus making it difficult to find sites hidden in brush and amongst kiawe trees.

Site 481N, central ridge (4 panels, 6 units): Five motifs plus a panel of incised lines and random pecking. Four boulders containing petroglyphs are on a slightly sloping area, and stretched out over some 35 meters. The previous survey by Hommon (ibid.) recorded one petroglyph at this site.
Panel 1, a phallic stick figure.
Panel 2, a rare fishhook motif (see Figure 9.5), unique on Kahoʻolawe. Roughly pecked, it is of the type used for deep sea fishing. The surface of this rock is exfoliating on one edge and the design is being impacted by erosion.
Panel 3, a group of incised lines over some pecking; there is no clear indication of what these signify. The (22 x 40 cm) panel was recorded as one unit. The face of this boulder has natural creases, and part of the pecking crosses one of these.
Panel 4, two T figures and a cupule. One T figure is square and symmetrical; the second is more fluid in form. Recent scratches are evident on this rock.

Site 481N central ridge, (5 units): A basalt dike with one boulder containing petroglyphs. According to the previous survey, the site contains 12 features, including two rocks with petroglyphs; one said to have three figures, the other "may have" two others. We were unable to locate a second boulder with petroglyphs, but the panel we did find contains five stick figure petroglyphs.

Panel 1, a figure with a line for a head and legs that disappear into an eroded area; a phallic stick figure with wide arms; a central stick figure with short curved legs; a stick figure with an object in one hand; and a running figure. Some of these appear to be interacting (Figure 9.9)

Site 482J central ridge, (1 unit): A complex about 15 meters southeast of a large grinding stone with a shrine, habitation terraces, midden and 1 petroglyph. The site has an excellent overview of the surrounding area. The Hommon survey cites a petroglyph but the accompanying drawing shows two figures. Only one was seen.

Panel 1, a stick figure with rounded legs and raised elbows.

Site 485C central ridge, (1 group of incised lines and pecking, associated with habitation terraces): The earlier report cited another boulder with petroglyphs but close inspection of the area revealed that natural features in the rock must have been mistaken for motifs.

Panel 1 was documented by mylar tracing. Among many seemingly random lines on the panel is a stick figure with pecking for the head as well as a possible canoe shape. The overall distribution of the lines suggests they were made at different times, in an incremental process (Figure 9.10).

Site 485D central ridge, (4 panels, 30 units). A basalt dike on a hillside with an overview of the area; three boulders and four panels with petroglyphs. Described in the Hommon report (1980) as two rocks with petroglyphs, one with scratched incisions. Three rocks were recorded and many figures but no incisions were found. We assume that this site was confused with Site 485C.

Panel 1, on a rock located 8 meters east of the others, contained 2 active stick figures; one is in a running posture, the other has a line for a head and one arm raised.

Panel 2, (3 units): roughly pecked figures on the top of the west side (Figure 9.11). These are not in the earlier report by Hommon (1980a); covered with lichen, they probably were not observed. Panels 2 and 3 are on the same large horizontally-oriented boulder.

Panel 3, (25 units). This is one of the more interesting panels in the area in that it has a grouping of figures in several styles and superposition, which is fairly rare on the island (Figure 9.12). Hommon's report (ibid.) noted 8 figures on this vertical panel.

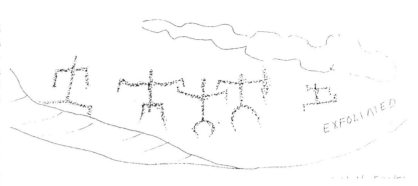

Figure 9.9. Hakioawa Site 481N; line of stick figures that seem to be interacting. The figure far right is in a running posture.

Figure 9.10. Hakioawa Site 385C. A small boulder with numerous incised lines plus peck marks. A possible stick figure is located at lower left, and curved lines suggest a canoe shape, lower right. The panel measures 74 x 57 cm.

Figure 9.11. Hakioawa Site 485D, Panel 2. Crudely pecked figures appear ancient. They were almost hidden beneath lichens. This panel measures 102 x 32 cm.

There actually may be more petroglyphs on this panel than we were able to record; we did not include some very faint pecking that could be remnants of figures. Those on the upper part of the rock appear to be older due to heavy patination and lichen growth in the grooves of the figures. Units include a curved line, stick figures, and triangular bodied anthropomorphs. Some are incomplete and several are joined and/or overlapping.

Panel 4 (one incomplete triangle torso figure) faces west and is on a vertical surface.

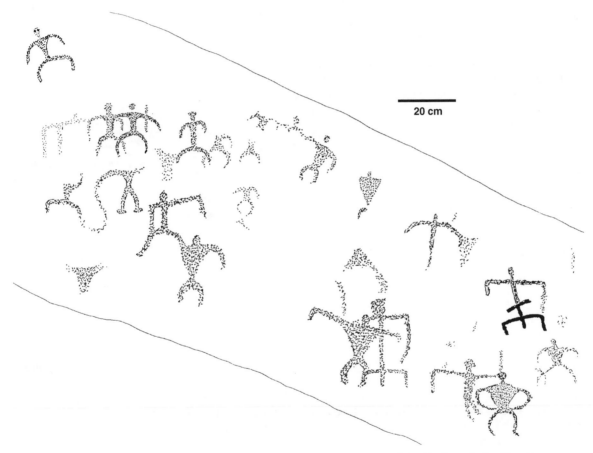

Figure 9.12. Hakioawa Site 485D, Panel 1. At least 25 images are pecked into this face of a boulder. Some are superimposed over others and a few are joined.

Site 486, slope of southern ridge, (6 panels, 19 units): This site has a midden scatter and habitation terraces. Unlike the other petroglyph sites which lie along Hakioawa's central ridge, this site rests on the slope of the valley's southern ridge and is located on a bedrock ledge above the stream bed. There are six panels.

Panel 1, one stick figure with shelf-like hands and feet, in lively poses, and one dog.

Panel 2, one stick figure with shelf like feet, and one dog. Panel 1 is located directly above panel 2. Both dogs are shown with 2 legs each and tails that angle backwards, rather than curled forward.

Panel 3, on boulder 20 meters to the left of panel 2. Panel includes one stick figure and three triangle torso figures, one of which is superimposed over the leg of the stick figure. Faint
traces suggest another anthropomorph was here.

Panel 4, on adjacent boulder; one triangle torso figure with wing-like elements. Arms are
long and wavy (Figure 9.13a).

Panel 5, 1 meter to the left of panel 4, with four stick figures which form a separate group
and two triangle torso anthropomorphs which are angular with bird-like arms.

Panel 6, on a boulder 1.3 meters to the left of panel 5, includes four (or five?) stick figures,
two joined. One 'double' figure is unusual (Figure 9.13b)

According to the earlier study by Hommon (1980), Hakioawa has at least 29 petroglyphs; our count is 65 despite the fact that we were unable to relocate some sites.
This number (65) does not include the numerous incised lines on two boulders; each of
those panels was counted as one unit.

The figure types vary from simple T-figures to stick figures to triangle torso anthropomorphs, some with muscles. Compared to sites near Ahupū on the other side of
the island, there are few dogs, and no goat images. Notable designs are the fishhook,
figures with bird attributes, and connected figures which may represent family kinship.
Stylistically, the designs are similar to those of Lāna'i and Maui.

Figure 9.13a. Hakioawa Site 486-4.
A triangle torso figure with bird-like
wings (24 x 12 cm).

Figure 9.13b Hakioawa Site
486-6. A panel of stick figures;
three attached. Note graceful pose
of central figure, perhaps with
ears (55 x 32 cm).

KAULANA

Site 444 (1 unit): Kaulana's bay, on the northwestern coast, is north and west of Hakioawa. The
bay has a good sandy beach inland of a wide gulch. In the 1800s, a government penal colony was established here. Our survey of this area located only one petroglyph on a large
boulder approximately 35 meters from the valley floor.

Panel 1, a phallic triangle torso figure, with a line for a head, arms stretched out.

KUHEIA

Kuheia bay is just west of Kaulana. A former ranch headquarters was located here
in the late 1800s. It's primary purpose was ranching sheep, goats, and cattle. A number
of historic inscriptions were recorded by Tomonari-Tuggle and Carter (1984). These
leftovers from the early ranching days consist of names and dates.

Site 175: no petroglyphs, only historic names and dates.

Site 128A (3 units): is just west of Site 175. It consists of a large boulder located at the foot of the
gulch's eastern ridge, inland of the beach. A fishing shrine is located upslope.

Panel 1, two dogs, one with a curly tail, as well as lettering in the form of three sets of initials.

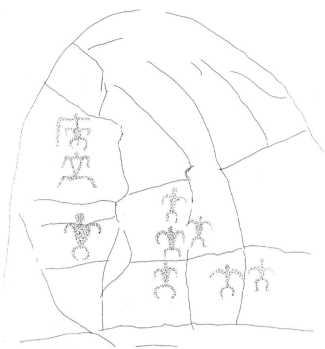

Figure 9.14. Kuheia Site 128D, Panel 3. A panel of triangle torso figures, most with rounded arms and legs. This panel measures 150 x 150 cm.

<u>Site 128D</u> (18 units). Located further inland from the above Site 128A, on the east slope of the gulch. Three stone faced terraces against a bedrock cliff contain five panels, many damaged by gunfire.

Panel 1a, triangle torso anthropomorph with rounded legs and arms, damaged by gunfire.

Panel 1b, stick figure with rounded legs, damaged by gunfire.

Panel 2, two triangle torso figures, on adjacent surfaces. One has arms up and out, birdlike.

Panel 3, cluster of ten triangle torso figures, most with curved arms and legs (Figure 9.14).

Panel 4, three triangle torso anthropomorphs.

Panel 5, one triangle torso figure plus traces, damaged by gunfire.

AHUPŪ

Ahupū Bay (Figure 9.15) is the next site to the west of Kuheia. Historic names are carved along the coastal area from northeast to southwest. Ahupū Bay has a beach and a gulch running inland with a fresh water source.

<u>Site 113</u>, feature AM: the small bay just east of Ahupū Gulch, close to water's edge. Historic names are carved in the rock. One of these (KELIIKIPI) has been identified in the 1866 census (Reeve n.d.).

<u>Site 673</u> (2 units). On top of the eastern headland of Ahupū bay. Both units are fragments of Hawaiian names.

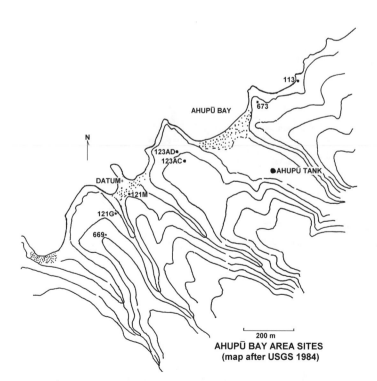

Figures 9.15. Map of the Ahupū area showing the location of petroglyph sites.

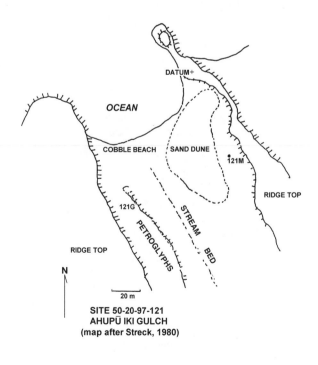

Figure 9.16. Map of Ahupū Iki Gulch showing the location of petroglyph sites.

AHUPŪ RIDGE

Site 123 designates all of the coastal settlements at Ahupū Gulch. It contains habitation terraces and platforms, enclosures, shrines, historic ranching structures, and a considerable growth of kiawe trees. Two areas of petroglyphs on the ridge to the west of the gulch were discovered that were not recorded by Hommon (1980). Hommon's Feature L is described as a petroglyph site with five figures; we located the shelter as described but found no petroglyphs.

Site 123 AC (6 panels, 15 units): a boulder cluster on the ridge west of Ahupū gulch.
Panel 1, Hawaiian names as well as graffiti.
Panel 2, an elaborate panel with four or five stick figures linked together, damaged by gunfire, and a separate stick figure and a triangle-bodied anthropomorph (Figure 9.17).
Panel 3, a single stick figure anthropomorph.
Panel 4, Hawaiian lettering.
Panel 5, one stick figure, curved arms and legs.
Panel 6, one triangle torso figure with widely curved legs.

Site 123 AD (3 units): a large boulder on ridge closer to sea and overlooking Ahupū bay. Lettering (some in copperplate style), and modern incised graffiti of boats.

AHUPŪ IKI GULCH

Ahupū Iki Gulch is in a narrow sheltered bay and gulch immediately west of Ahupū Ridge (see Figure 9.16). The site is located inland of a cobble beach, sand dune, and dry stream bed. Evidence of occupation comes from habitation terraces, shelters, and midden scatters; historical remains include a corral from the ranching period.
The early survey forms (Streck 1980) cited 378 petroglyphs on 35 rock faces. Considerably fewer were found and discrepancies were noted between Streck's drawings and descriptions and what was seen on the rocks. Gun fire bullet marks have disfigured many elements and have caused subsequent exfoliation.
Petroglyphs were located at two places within the gulch. The major concentration is along a bedrock cliff at the western edge of the stream bed, designated as Feature G in the original survey. A second cluster of units was found on the walls of a rock shelter on the eastern slope of the bay (Feature M). Designs include human figures and quadrupeds which appear, for the most part, to represent goats.

Site 121G (20 panels, 94 units): A series of boulders. Three panels are on horizontal surfaces, the remainder on vertical faces. Virtually all have been damaged by gunfire.
Panel 1 (6 units). Panel faces the ocean. At least 4 images of goats, one stick figure which has been superimposed by a goat image. Bullet marks dot the panel. Some random pecking is visible.
Panel 2 (12 units). Human figures, goats or dogs, and lines. Superposition figures include a stick figure over a triangle torso figure and a goat covering human and possibly a dog figure. Two bullet marks are visible (Figure 9.18).

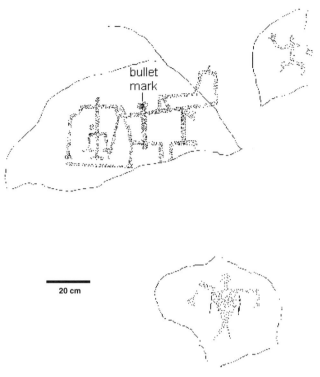

Figure 9.17. Ahupū Ridge Site 123, Panel 2. An interesting group of stick figures joined together. A bullet hole has defaced the head of the central figure, upper group.

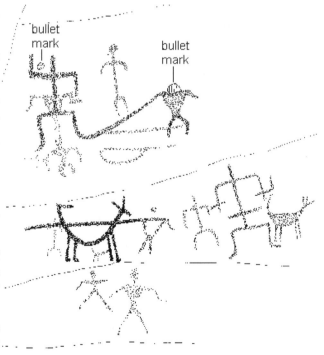

Figure 9.18. Ahupū Iki Site 121G, Panel 2 (114 x 110 cm). A goat is superimposed over human and dog figures.

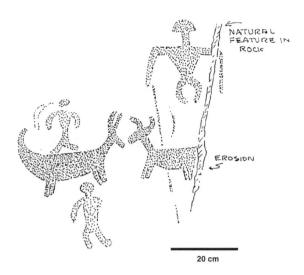

Figure 9.19. Ahupū Iki Site 121G, Panel 8. Goats and human figures. Note faint trace of triangle torso on right, below a smaller figure with mushroom shaped head.

Figure 9.20. Ahupū Iki Site 121G, Panel 9 (95 x 63 cm). Dogs and anthropomorphs, one with long curved legs and a flat head. The two cupule-like figures are bullet marks.

Panel 3 (7 units): All anthropomorphs. Some are very faint and have been superimposed by later figures or are joined. Two of the anthropomorphs have detached heads, and several are flat-headed. Bullet marks have damaged the panel.

Panel 4 (3 units): A goat superimposed with a partial anthropomorph and a short curved line.

Panel 5 and 5a (3 units): Anthropomorphic, one is triangle torso plus a partial stick figure (due to exfoliation). Bullet marks have damaged the panel.

Panel 6 (1 unit): A stick figure with shelf feet and random pecking associated.

Panel 7 (1 unit): A partial triangle torso figure.

Panel 8 and 8a (6 units): Three are of goats or dogs. One triangle torso figure has a mushroom shaped head and is placed over a triangle shape that may have been the start of another figure (Figure 9.19).

Panel 9 (6 units): Two dogs; one long-legged stick figure with a flat head, and three other anthropomorphs. Bullet marks were also noted (Figure 9.20).

Panel 10 and 10a (4 units): Three are zoomorphs and two likely are goats.

Panel 11 (1 unit): A single stick figure, placed in a concave section of rock.

Panel 12 and 12a (3 units): Two are goats facing each other, nose to nose (Figure 9.21, see also Figure 9.6).

Panel 13 (1 unit): A dog with a backward curving tail.

Panel 14 (1 unit): A single very symmetrical phallic stick figure, in concave area of the rock.

Panel 15 (1 unit): A dog with shelf feet plus a curving line.

Panel 16 (1 unit): A triangle torso figure with muscled arms and legs; the head incorporates a natural bubble in the rock.

Panel 17 (2 units): Faint triangle-figures.

Panel 18 (1 unit): a stick figure.

Panel 19 (1 unit): a triangle torso figure with muscled legs and wide stretched arms.

Panel 20 a-e (11 units): on four sides of the rock. Panel 20a has two figures, one may be a stylized turtle; 20b is the top of the rock, two stick figures; 20c is the east side, two partial figures; 20d has active muscled figures, and one has bird-like characteristics and a detached head; 20e is the south side, with one muscled triangle torso figure with a flat wedge shaped head. Bullet marks have damaged this panel.

Figurte 9.21. Ahupū Iki Site 121G, Panel 12. Two charmingly depicted goats, nose to nose (Photograph, Rowland Reve). See drawing on page 131.

<u>Site 121M</u> (5 units): site is located across the gulch at an overhang shelter. Streck (1980) described this site as possessing five bedrock faces with at least 15 petroglyphs. His figure list includes a dog, an animal, turtle and eight human figures plus four enigmatic figures. As no drawings were included, there is no way of knowing whether we located and documented the same site, interpreted it differently or have found a different locus. Two panels were located. One is at the back of an overhang.
Panel 1, three stick figures and incised lines, random (?) peck marks and some incomplete figures. Two incised figures have triangle torsos. There are many undecipherable markings on this panel, and it may be the one described by Streck.
Panel 2, two triangle figures, one with muscled legs and a long neck.

There is a distinct quality to the petroglyphs at Ahupū Iki and Ahupū, including detached or wedge-shaped heads or flat, narrow heads. Some have bird attributes. All the petroglyphs of goats found on Kahoʻolawe come from Ahupū Iki and obviously date from ranching times. Three human figures have goats superimposed and others have these two elements closely associated. Dog images are fairly common at both sites. Some motifs are so similar in style that they suggest the same hand. Two petroglyphs from this site were dated by Dorn (see Appendix A).

Streck's survey (1980) described his site 121J as having 10 faces of rock with 109 petroglyphs. Despite extensive searching, no trace of petroglyphs was found at this locus. Natural features which appear to match Streck's 'petroglyphs' were noted, and we assume these were mistaken for petroglyphs. Two other loci, Site 121K and 121L are described as having petroglyphs in association with habitations. These were not found. Measurements given for some of the missing petroglyphs are "2 x 0.5 cm". There is no precedent for such tiny motifs in Hawaiian rock art. It is unlikely that so many could have eroded from the rock surface while leaving others nearby. As far as we know, only five panels were drawn in Streck's report, so there is little comparative information.

Ahupū Iki West

<u>Site 669</u> (7 units) west of Site 121: A cluster of small, possibly temporary settlements at a boulder outcrop on a flat ridge, approximately 240 meters inland from the coast.

<u>Site 669C</u> (3 units):
Panel 1, stick figure with extra legs or two figures joined together on the flat upper surface of a large boulder. This may represent a moʻo figure.
Panel 2, an adjacent boulder with a triangle torso figure with arms and head, but no legs.

<u>Site 669F</u> (4 units): This site was discovered in our survey and designated as 669F.
Panel 1, one roughly pecked stick figure, bullet mark.
Panel 2, three roughly-pecked stick anthropomorphs. The surface of the rock is rough and weathered and the motifs are heavily patinated. Two of the figures have wedge shaped heads and one is open bodied.

Kaukaukapapa

<u>Site135C, D, and E</u> (119 units):
Kaukaukapapa is approximately 1000 meters north of Kealaikahiki Point on the northwest side of the island (Figure 9:22). Situated on a low rocky

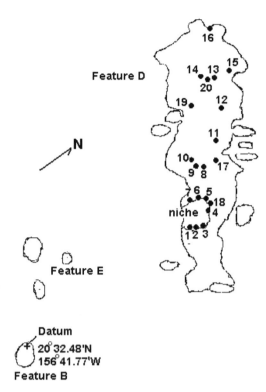

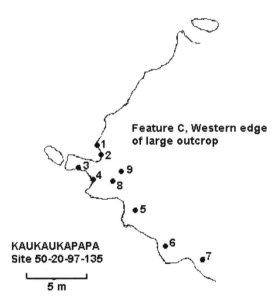

Figure 9.22. Map of Kaukaukapapa showing boulder clusters and other loci.

headland at the eastern end of Kaukaukapapa beach is a cluster of occupation sites, a fishing shrine and petroglyphs. A sample of basaltic glass from this site was dated to AD 1241±43 (Hommon 1980).

Anthropomorphs are the most common element with slightly more stick figures than triangle torso types. There are two dog images. Some recent vandalism shows an incised spaceman and rocket ship.

Site 135C (26 units): a massive outcrop of boulders including 9 loci, all at the west edge of the outcrop. Shelters are found among the boulders. Some panels have been used for target practice. The original survey form (Barrera 1977) cited 15 petroglyphs at this locus.

Panel 1, three fragments of figures amongst 22 bullet marks.

Panel 2a, b: a) One stick figure with detached head, 2 triangle torso figures (one with a rayed headdress) and a triangle that may have been a start for another figure. Damaged by gunfire. b) on east face of boulder, one headless figure.

Panel 3, small boulder separate from boulder cluster. Badly defaced by gunfire. One triangle torso figure and a faint curved line remains. (Figure 9.23)

Panel 4, two faint human figures.

Panel 5, one possible figure. Rock in very poor condition.

Panel 6, one stick figure with widely curved legs and detached head, and a partial figure.

Panel 7, three human figures, one with fingers on one hand.

Panel 8, two units, one is a compound or two figures joined together; the other is a fat bodied anthropomorph with short legs.

Panel 9, three human figures and one dog. Two of the anthropomorphs are incised.

Site 135D (61 units): a large outcrop of boulders, with panels facing in varying directions. Twenty panels were documented here, some in elevated niches in the rocks.

Panel 1, east end of outcrop, around a naturally-raised niche. Pecking and incising. Two very minimal figures plus incised lines. These are poorly executed.

Panel 2, east side of boulder; five animated stick figures in lively poses. One appears to be running, one is in a dance posture; another has long wavy arms (Figure 9.24). Panel is damaged by gunfire. One figure has very long arms, and another has a detached head.

Panel 3, two faint triangle torso figures, one with very short curved legs, incised lines; and one figure with incised fingernails.

Panel 4, inside a south-facing shelter. Incised lines in a grid, probably from an earlier period are superimposed by a spaceman, rocket, and other modern elements.

Panel 5, on west face of a boulder, two heavily pecked figures, one phallic.

Panel 6, on side of boulder with grinding slick on top surface; two figures, one a dog.

Panel 7, one stick figure with curving legs.

Panel 8, on top of boulder; three faint stick figures, one with extra line in torso.

Panel 9, six stick figures plus incised lines and bullet marks. One figure is in an unusual horizontal position. (Figure 9.25).

Panel 10, on side of boulder, pecked and incised partial trian-

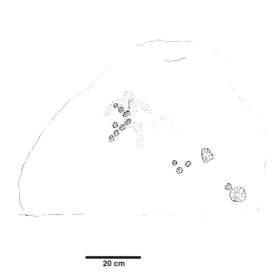

Figure 9.23. Kaukaukapapa Site 135C, Panel 3. Gunfire has severely damaged the figure on Panel 3.

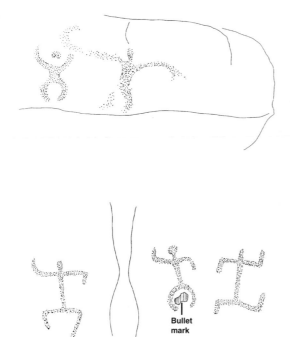

Figure 9.24. Kaukaukapapa Site 135D, Panel 2 (71 x 51 cm). A collection of lively figures. The figure upper right has unusually long arms.

gle torso figures.

Panel 11, one stick figure with a curved line for a head.

Panel 12, one stick figure.

Panel 13, a cluster of eight small figures, half of them are stick figure types.

Panel 14, one roughly pecked phallic anthropomorph.

Panel 15, three anthropomorphic figures, all headless. Bullet marks.

Panel 16, the westernmost locus in the outcrop, consisting of two boulders, one on top of the other and several faces. Ten figures including incised lines cover much of the panel. Some of the figures themselves are incised.

Panel 17, one stick figure with long legs and a possible plume.

Panel 18, two simple stick figures with lines for heads, located on vertical face.

Panel 19, two partial triangle torso figures plus an incised square motif.

Panel 20, two triangle torso figures, one with detached head.

<u>Site 135E</u> (32 units): three large boulders lying just west of Locus C and close to a stone fishing shrine which appears to have been the focus for this site. Five panels. The larger boulder has been used as a base for a small shelter. These motifs appear to be the most ancient at this site; they are not only faint but covered with lichens and patina.

Panel 1, a cluster of seven figures on large boulder; three are identifiable as anthropomorphs; the other elements appear to be partial figures and lines.

Panel 2, 3 stick figures, one armless; 2 triangle torso figures. Some incising.

Panel 3, 12 human figures on a vertical face, four have triangle torsos. Some have long legs, some are headless.

Panel 4, small rock with 3 figures. One may be a turtle.

Panel 5, a cluster of 5 figures plus incising. Both stick and triangle torso figures, plus some figure elements. One stick figure has an extra set of legs. Kaukaukapapa's images focus on anthropomorphs, with slightly more stick figures than triangle-bodied forms. Considering that the incised panels were counted as one unit, the actual count for this site is higher than the 119 units cited. There are two dogs, but no images of goats.

KEALAIKAHIKI

<u>Site 137, 142</u> (2 units plus inscriptions): is approximately 60 meters from Kealaikahiki Point and consists of a boulder outcrop with small shelters. Two panels were located, one with lettering.

Panel 1, in a slight recess, visible as one approaches the outcrop. One motif is a bird-man like figure, made by both pecking and abrading. It has been damaged by bullets.

Panel 2, Hawaiian letters (backwards and upside down) read La Luna Hakukai.

<u>Site 142</u> is located on the shore of a sandy bay just southeast of Kealaikahiki Point. The site is a large dune deposit with scattered shelters. The boulder cluster may have been used for temporary shelter. Two of the boulders are located close together forming a small crawl space. Within this space a single petroglyph has been carved. The figure is that of a bird-like human with out-swept arms and legs resembling the tail of a frigate bird (Figure 9.26).

Figure 9.25. Kaukaukapapa Site 135D, Panel 9 (102 x 55 cm). The figure lower right is unusual because almost horizontal position.

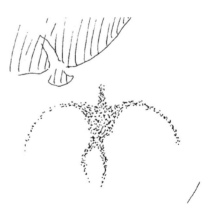

Figure 9.26. Kealaikahiki Site 142. This figure (20 x 13 cm) has bird-like form and suggests a frigate bird.

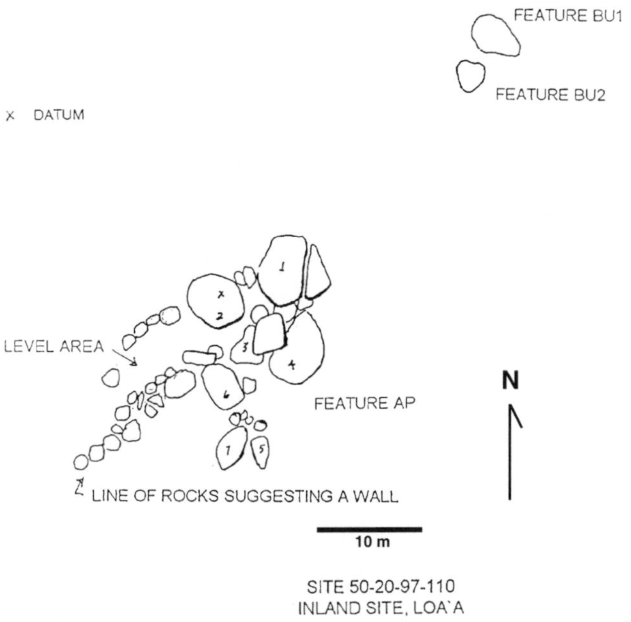

LOAʻA

<u>Site 110</u> (91 units): Loaʻa is located on the southwestern slope of Puʻu Moaulanui and is a recent discovery; its original name is unknown. The site, at an elevation of 350 meters, is spread out over a sloping stretch of hardpan, devoid of vegetation except for a few hardy kiawe trees. There is no nearby water source and it is a long distance from the nearest settlement, Hakioawa. The site includes some 72 features, many of which appear to have been temporary occupations. Petroglyphs on massive boulders constitute three of the designated features (Figure 9.27). With erosion and thus removal of the overlaying soil, fire-cracked rock, midden, and lithic scatter lying on the hardpan have been exposed. Boulders stand out starkly against the bare red surface. Flakes of basaltic glass recovered from here by the 1976-80 surveys yielded a date of AD 1486±43.

The original documentation of Loaʻa was under the direction of Hommon (1980) who reported at least 75 petroglyphs on 14 faces of 7 boulders, named Feature AP. Whenever possible we used the boulder and panel designations of Hommon. A total of 91 units was documented but few match those illustrated in Hommon. This includes two petroglyph boulders not in the earlier survey, Features BU1 and BU2. Located 25 meters to the northeast of Hommon's Feature AP, both are on the edge of an erosion gully and are in danger of collapsing downslope. During recording, the presence of what may be a short stone alignment running west from the main boulder cluster was noted. The terrace of this alignment is small and shows no outward signs of occupation, but the possibility exists that the terrace and boulders once served as a site for a small shrine.

Feature AP

Boulder 1 (2 units): A large boulder on north end of the cluster, two stick figures, one incomplete. Hommon's (1980) report listed seven anthropomorphs on this panel. Only two were found, neither of which matched his drawing.

Boulder 2 (10 units): A large boulder just west of Boulder 1, four panels including ten figures and traces. Panel 2a: one incomplete stick figure; Panel 2b: two faint human figures and one unusual anthropomorph with a divided triangle head and shelf hands (Figure 9.28). Hommon (ibid.) noted six other figures on this panel, none of which could be relocated; Panel 2c: two figures, one stick figure with extra limbs; and a triangle torso figure with bird-like arms. Panel 2d: top surface of the boulder; it has a stick figure with extra legs, a T-shaped figure, and two other elements, perhaps incomplete. Hommon reported 8 figures here, only one of which matches our records.

Boulder 3 (4 units): A boulder located south of Boulders 1 and 2. Panel 3a: one stick figure with an extra line in torso and shelf feet and hands. Panel 3b: a running figure with one arm raised; an incomplete stick figure, and a stick figure with one arm raised. This panel is very eroded. Hommon showed these figures as being connected, our

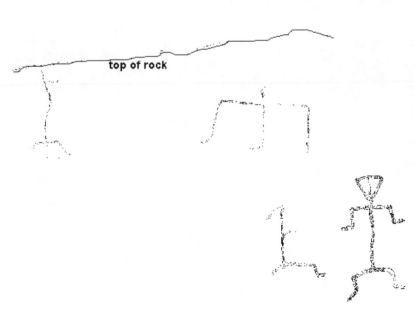

Figure 9.27. Map of Loaʻa Site showing location of petroglyph panels.

Figure 9.28. Loaʻa Site 110, Panel 2b. Triangle headed stick figure (30 x 16 cm) , is one of several at this site.

observation was that they were not.

Boulder 4 (25 units): A large boulder resting on the top of other boulders forming a niche that is difficult to access; Panel 4a: two figures, a stick figure with extra limbs and triangle head and one 'unidentified' unit.

Panel 4b (5 units): Outside the niche, with stick and triangle-figures, one in a running pose. The triangle torso figures are incomplete; and Panel 4c (ten units): stick figures, some active as well as phallic, and one cupule and a line (Figure 9.29).

Boulder 5 (5 units): On a smaller rock at south edge of cluster are five stick figures, some are phallic and/or in lively poses. One anthropomorph has a split head.

Boulder 6 (3 units): A large boulder south of Boulder 3, two stick anthropomorphs plus a cupule. One is an active running figure.

Boulder 7 (1 unit): A medium-sized boulder on the south of the rock cluster, next to Boulder 5. One phallic stick figure with raised arm plus possible other traces. Hommon's report listed numerous figures on this rock. The irregularities in the rock do suggest figures; the rough surface is dimpled with many natural bumps and depressions that may have been mistaken for petroglyphs. Hommon's report shows a photograph of this boulder with chalked images but the only one that we could see that was correctly chalked is the one we recorded.

Feature BU1 (44 units): A large flat stone, horizontally oriented and resting on a natural pedestal, 12 figures and long lines and 32 cupules. The stone resonates with a bell-like peal when tapped. Lines run the length of this surface and cupules have been carved around the perimeter; some are quite deep and large, ranging in size from 3 cm to 15 cm and up to a depth of 3.5 cm. The figures are mostly oriented in the same direction and four are triangle forms. One has bow-shaped arms and lines protruding from the head; another figure has one bow shaped arm. One stick figure has a wedge shaped head. This boulder is unique on Kahoʻolawe, and indeed, unequaled in the Hawaiian islands, as far as we are aware (Figure 9.30a, 9.30b).

Feature BU2 (1 unit): A smaller rock, a few meters south of BU1 with one phallic stick figure, arms are raised and fingers displayed.

Fifty-two percent of the motifs at Loaʻa are human figures; only seven of these have triangle torsos. There are no historic elements such as lettering or images

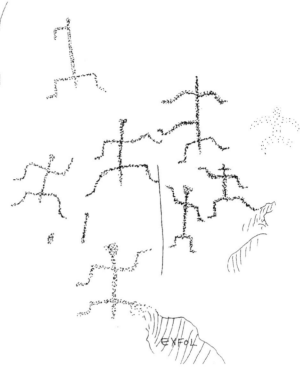

Figure 9.29. Loaʻa Site 110, Panel 4c (95 x 83 cm). A cluster of active stick figures with triangular or wedge-shaped heads.

Figure 9.30a, Loaʻa Site 110, Feature BU1. The large horizontal boulder situated on a natural pedestal has petroglyphs on the top surface and large cupules around the outer edge.

of goats as there are at other sites. The distinctive features of the stick figures include oddly formed triangular heads and headdresses. Many of the anthropomorphs are in active poses, as if running or dancing, and have stylistic unity.

The petroglyphs discovered recently on the large, horizontal boulder (Feature BU1) that rests on a natural pedestal are most interesting particularly in conjunction with the bell-like qualities of the boulder. Although other ringing rocks are known from the various islands, this is unique in Hawai'i because of the petroglyphs that cover its top surface. Many of the large cupules on the face of this rock could have been containers; we were present after a brief shower and nearly half of them held water.

It must have required great effort to create these large cupules in such dense rock; they appear to have been refined by abrasion although erosion over the years may have contributed to the smoothing process.

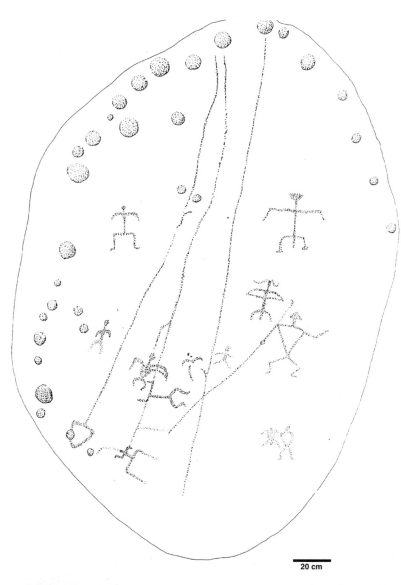

20 cm

Figure 9.30b. Drawing of Loa'a Site 110, Feature BU1 shows cupules around the outer edge and long lines with figures on the inner surface. Some of the figures have unusual head forms and two have arms that appear to be wings (a feature noted also at Ka'ūpūlehu on Hawai'i Island).

10

HAWAIIAN CONNECTIONS

Many are the strange things to be learned about Hawaii. However diligently the foreigner seeks he cannot find out all. He gets a fragment here and there and goes home.

—Kepelino's *Traditions of Hawaii* 1932

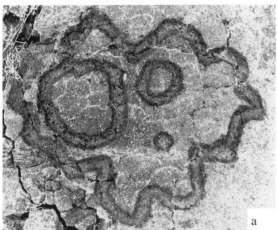

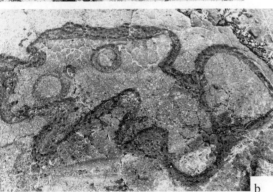

Figure 10.1a, b. Pohue Bay "sea creatures" are unusual forms, not seen elsewhere in the islands.

Petroglyph sites on Hawai'i Island, Lāna'i and Kaho'olawe have been documented and described, however, there are other sites in the Hawaiian Islands; indeed, there are many more on Hawai'i Island that are not included in this study. Are inter-island variations found in Hawaiian rock art? The answer is both yes and no.

The rock type greatly affects the quality of the motifs. Differences have been noted between petroglyphs on pāhoehoe and those made on dense basalt boulders. The latter usually were created by faint pecking. The surface of pāhoehoe, however, breaks more easily and lends itself to deeply pecked designs. On Kaua'i, O'ahu, and Moloka'i there are—aside from basalt boulders and pāhoehoe—sandstone ledges located on or near the ocean's edge, some of these have petroglyphs.

Before moving on to the other islands, it is important to note that the island of Hawai'i has at least seventy petroglyph sites (Cox and Stasack 1970:7), all located on the south and west sides of the island where there is an abundance of pāhoehoe and little vegetation. Only six sites have been described in this book. None are reported for the eastern side of that island but some were noted on the northern tip, near Hawi (Mahina Leitel, personal communication 1989). Cox and Stasack (1970:81-7) cited at least 22,600 petroglyphs on the Big Island but this count, as we know now, is quite low. For example, 85 units were listed for Ka'ūpūlehu (vs. our updated count of 435), and over 23,000 have been documented at Pu'uloa alone. It is not possible to adequately estimate just what the total might be for Hawai'i Island but the numbers surely will be very high.

We have pointed out unusual, and often one-of-a-kind motifs, particularly at the site of Ka'ūpūlehu with its kites, fish traps, kāhili and a burial scene. Pu'uloa contains some rarities also. The other sites exhibit some heterogeneity, but it is variety that tends to be based upon general motifs: stick figures, triangle torso figures, sails, circles and variations thereof, and cupules. One form that we find provocative is that of a human figure in profile, sometimes with a bird-like head. This configuration, seen at Puakō, Pu'uloa, and Keauhou Cave (Ka'ū) is discussed below.

Most of the unrecorded sites on the Big Island have been at least viewed by us, and the only one that appears to have different motifs is Pohue Bay, near South Point, at the southern tip of the island. This site has some strange amoeba-like forms that might be described as sea creatures of some sort (Figure 10.1a, b). What these may have represented is unknown.

MOLOKAʻI

The island of Molokaʻi apparently was not of major political importance amongst the islands but it was known for its connections with sorcery and kahuna. It is said that a potent school of supernaturalism was here, instilling fear in the people of the other islands. Despite this, Molokaʻi was conquered by Oʻahu and then by Maui. In 1790 Kamehameha conquered the island, destroying the fields and plantations of the inhabitants. He re-conquered it in 1795.

Molokaʻi has some amazing heiau including two major luakini temples dedicated to the god of war. Island wide, there were 87 temples and 21 shrines; one of these is the largest heiau known anywhere on the islands.[1]

Documentation of the numerous archaeological sites of the island began over 100 years ago. One researcher, Catherine Summers (1971), visited most of these sites in 1951 and gathered together all the known information. In this survey nine petroglyph sites are reported for the island. One of those was subsequently destroyed by development and another has not been relocated. Cox and Stasack (1970:7) list five sites on Molokaʻi. At least 500 units are estimated for Molokaʻi, including those mentioned in Cox and Stasack (ibid.). Probably this is a low estimate. Most published notations describe the sites as having "several" or simply "petroglyphs." One outstanding petroglyph site at Moʻomomi, described below, still is undocumented.

The two sites we visited have been damaged: Palaʻau and Moʻomomi. Palaʻau has been vandalized with carved names and initials cut into the petroglyph boulders (one of the worst examples of damage we have seen), and Moʻomomi has sustained damage from cattle walking across its surface and from general erosion. Palaʻau is on a high ridge on the north side of Molokaʻi, approximately in the middle of the island. The petroglyph boulders are near the famed phallic stone, Kauleonanahoa, on the brow of Nanahoa hill (Figure 10.2). Prior to reforestation with ironwood (*casuarina equisetifolia*), the phallic stone could be seen for miles on the skyline (Summers 1971:28). This stone is inclined upward at a 45° angle and rises about five feet from the ground. It may have had some artificial shaping. Legends describe its powers: women wishing to conceive would spend the night at the base of the stone and leave offerings. Several small rocks with carvings that appear to represent vulvae were found here and are now in the Bishop museum (Figure 10.3). Summers (ibid:30) reported "more than 24" petroglyphs located on nearby boulders. Only thirteen of them were relocated due to the extensive vandalism (Figure 10.4) and the diffi-

Figure 10.2. The famed phallic stone, Kauleonanahoa, on the brow of Nanahoa Hill, Molokaʻi.

Figure 10.3. A drawing of one of several stones found near Kauleonanahoa. These appear to be naturally shaped rocks with a vulvae form pecked into one surface. This example measures 13 x7.2 cm.

Figure 10.4. Vandalized petroglyph boulders at Nanahoa Hill. Layers of carved names and initials obscure the ancient petroglyphs.

Figure 10.5. The site at Moʻomomi, Molokaʻi. An extensive and very eroded formation of sandstone has petroglyphs of human footprints.

culties presented by heavy tree cover. All are stick figure anthropomorphs, with the exception of four straight grooves.

The second site, Kalaina wāwae (foot prints), Kaluakoʻi, is on the north coast at Moʻomomi, on an extensive sandstone slope about one-half mile from the beach (Figure 10.5). A shelter near Moʻomomi was excavated and dated at AD 1408± (Kirch 1985:125). This site is remarkable in that Stokes (1910:62-65) estimated more than 500 footprints pecked into the sandstone, with the footprints frequently shown in pairs. This is a staggering number. Time constraints limited our visit to this site but, in a few minutes, 52 carvings of footprints were located, all but one pecked out (intaglio); the exception was in outline form. Of those we noted, most were in pairs and ranged in size from 'baby' to adult footprints; the largest was 23 cm long. Some of the footprints had toes indicated and a few small cupules were in association (Figure 10.6 a,b). Given the ease in which these petroglyphs were found, there is little doubt that the site contains an astonishing number of footprints. This major concentration of petroglyphs is deserving of detailed study.

A legend is associated with the Moʻomomi site: it tells of a prophetess[2] named Kalaina who lived nearby. One day she made two footprints in the stone and called the people to show them her work, saying "See what I have done. Bye and bye people will come from the sea with flat feet like these." In following years, visitors from other parts of Molokaʻi and other islands made their marks here also (Stokes 1910:62-5).

Vulvae pecked on small rocks (not reported elsewhere for Hawaiʻi) and many pairs of foot motifs suggest that Molokaʻi's petroglyph sites are atypical for the islands in general. Although petroglyphs of footprints are found at many sites around the islands, such a concentration seems extraordinary. Although dog figures have not been reported, the remainder of the motifs on Molokaʻi fit well into the aesthetic for the other islands of Hawaiʻi. Perhaps the odd features in the rock art of Molokaʻi have some connection with the island's ancient reputation for sorcery and magic.

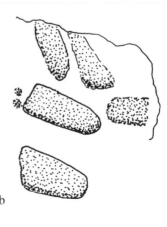

Figure 10.6 a) Photo of a pair of footprints at Moʻomomi and b) a drawing of one of the many groups of footprints at this site. Note the toes. Foot sizes measured range from 6 x 15 to 9 x 23 cm. Most are pecked out in intaglio.

KAUA'I

The island of Kaua'i is the greatest distance from the rest of the major Hawaiian islands and has some variations in material culture. The form of poi pounder is a notable example. According to Cox and Stasack (1970:89) Kaua'i Island has nine petroglyph sites and approximately 220 petroglyphs.[3] Since that publication, another site has been found deep in Waimea's canyon. To our knowledge, it has not been documented; it is on the face of a cliff and contains a few red painted figures as well as petroglyphs. One of these is a late-type muscled figure (Figure 10.7). Red pictographs have been reported also from the island of Maui so the paintings, although unusual, are not unique. .

Several of Kaua'i's sites are on sandstone ledges at the shoreline and are often covered by sand. They were said to be visible only after heavy storms (Bennett 1931:90). According to Farley (1898) the beach at Koloa has subsided at least six feet since the petroglyphs were made. Other petroglyphs are found on boulders or cliff faces, and one site, at Lihue, is said to have been destroyed by construction of a pier. Bennett's (1931:91) report has line drawings taken from Judd and Stokes who sketched some of the forms in earlier days. Many are the familiar stick figures; one shows a triangle-figure. Oddities are figures with chevron lines along the torso, looking rather like fish skeletons. Some of the images have triangle-shaped heads, and one canoe is pictured.

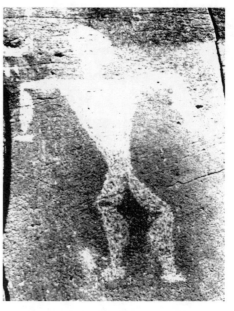

Figure 10.7. Kaua'i: Waimea Canyon muscled anthropomorph; this site has some painted elements as well.

The best known petroglyph site is located on boulders that lie in the mouth of the Wailua River (Figure 10.8). The site is connected with a legend, a heiau, and a dance; no other petroglyph site has this distinction. The location of Hikina'akalā Heiau and the petroglyph site, called Pae-ma-hu-o-Wailua or *paeki'i*, picture rocks, is one of the most famous in the Hawaiian islands (Kikuchi 1994).

Figure 10.8. Kaua'i; the Wailua River petroglyph site is found on the boulders at the mouth of the river.

The legends relate to the boulders themselves, but the dance refers to both petroglyphs and carved wooden images that formerly stood nearby. One of the legends describes Kapo, the half-sister of Pele, who caused men to be pounded to death by the surf and then changed their bodies into boulders to remind people of her powers. The other describes the rocks as being the eight brothers of Māui who looked back to see the beauty of Hina-ke-kaa and were turned into stones at the mouth of the Wailua River.

The thirty-six boulders, which are often under water, are approximately 50 or 60 feet from the shoreline. In this large cluster, only eight of the rocks are known to contain petroglyphs, however, changes in the water level and the river bed may have obscured more images. Sixteen of the petroglyphs are stick figures, some with extra legs, four are circles (Figure 10.9). There are no triangle torso anthro-

Figure 10.9. Petroglyphs on a Wailua River boulder (from Kikuchi 1994).

Figure 10.10. Plaque with profile figure, formerly in the Kaua'i Museum. It was found in a field on the island during plowing (Photograph: E. N. Ferdon).

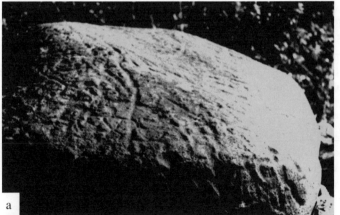

Figure 10.11 a) Photograph of a boulder in the Moanalua Valley, O'ahu. Birdman figures predomate. b) Drawing from Barrow (1998:350) of some chalked petroglyphs on this boulder.

pomorphs.

A short distance to the south is the location of Hikinaakalā Heiau; these petroglyph boulders are said to have formed a part of the wall of the City of Refuge before the river course changed. Did the legend or the petroglyphs came first?

The most provocative motifs at the Wailua River site are those of human figures in profile, and one of only three known spiral forms in the entire Hawaiian Island chain.[4] Kikuchi (1984) notes that the profile figures ('kneeling prayer figures') may be one of the more ancient motifs to be found in the islands. A small portable plaque with the same type of figure was found in a field on Kaua'i (Kikuchi 1984). Formerly it was in the collection of the Kaua'i Museum but is now missing and presumed stolen from the Museum (Figure 10.10).

Aside from the profile figures and the spiral, the other petroglyphs are stick figures, some with extra limbs, and circular elements. There is one fish-like form. Associated with the petroglyphs are grinding or honing facets and some of these are over the petroglyphs, thus eradicating a portion of the figures.

Other than the rare spiral and the uncommon profile figures, there is little here to suggest isolation from the rest of the Hawaiian Islands, or unusual influences. The presence of stick figures as well as triangle torso anthropomorphs suggests activity here from early through late times. The Wailua River area motifs contain the earlier style while the Waimea Canyon area has later syle motifs such as the muscled anthropomorphs, copperplate letters and painted figures. As with Moloka'i, images of dogs in the rock art of this island have not been reported.

O'AHU

Cox and Stasack (1970:97) mention 150 petroglyphs from ten sites in O'ahu. Four of the sites are on sandstone ledges at the edge of the ocean, and other sites are found in inland valleys. Seven of the sites include dogs and human figures. Nuuanu Valley, in Honolulu, contains panels of dogs and men but its ease of access and proximity to the city has resulted in a distressing amount of vandalism. A site in the Moanalua Valley, 'Oahu, has a large boulder with various figure types, from cupules and simple stick figures to bird-men. The latter are square bodied anthropomorphs with bird beaks and arms that have wing-like characteristics. A long serpentine line curves up and over the boulder (Figure 10.11a, b).

Moanalua Valley also is the original location for a boulder that was excavated around the turn of the century. Now in the Bishop Museum, the boulder was found on the east side of the valley in an area that had been uninhabited from the middle of the last century until around 1891. The rock is called Pu'u O Ma'o and contains two extraordinary figures, deeply carved in bas relief. (Figure 10.12a, b). These squatting figures resemble the birdman figures of Easter Island, despite their lack of beaks (the heads are human-like) (see Stokes 1908). If there is an enigma in Hawaiian rock art, it surely resides in this relief carving. The stone figures do have a resemblance to those that act as end supports for large

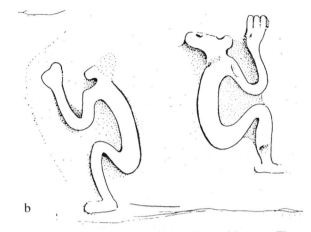

Figure 10.12 a) photograph, and b) drawing of the Moanalua Valley petroglyph boulder, now in the Bishop Museum. The faces are human, not bird-like. These figures are close in feeling to Hawaiian wood carvings. The panel measures 41 x 30 cm.

Hawaiian wood bowls, but there is only one precedent for any such developed stone sculpture, the small carved plaque plowed up on Kaua'i (Figure 10.10). It is hard to imagine what tools may have been used for the Moanalua bas relief boulder, yet petroglyphs from the Marquesas and Easter Island were carved onto basalt with equal facility. The style resembles the crouching or praying figures from Puakō and Pu'uloa. The sweeping curvilinear forms and deep relief suggest the carvings were made by a master. This level of excellence was achieved in the rock art only in the periods after AD 1600, with the advent of the triangular bodies and well-defined muscles. Thus the boulder might have been carved as early as AD 1600 and as late as the 19th century, although Stokes (1908) did not see any modern tool marks (nor could we after examination of the boulder). The figures on the Bishop Museum boulder are stylistically close to wood sculpture but this does not help us to pinpoint when they were made.

As for the technique of bas relief, we have already mentioned a few petroglyphs in shallow relief at Puakō, one at Pu'uloa, and on Lāna'i. Although these have little depth, it is clear that the intent was to raise the figure above the matrix of the rock (see Figure 7.48).

MAUI

Approximately 450 petroglyphs have been noted at eighteen sites on Maui (Cox and Stasack 1970:92-3). Six of these sites also contain pictographs. This estimate may be a low, as some reports do not specify exact numbers. Dog images are present at some nine of the 18 sites. One site, Papakea, contains human footprints. Maui's petroglyphs are found on a variety of surfaces from cliff faces to boulders, to one site located on pāhoehoe. Maui's sites appear to be popular attractions, much to their detriment, and vandalism has been heavy. The island's rock art sites are in need of thorough documentation.

NIIHAU

This small dot of land 17 miles east of Kaua'i is said to have one petroglyph which has not been described (Cox and Stasack 1970:7).

DISCUSSION

It appears that the ancient rock carvers of Hawaiʻi were depicting things of the spirit, the family or legend, and not that which nourished the body alone. This is clear, not only from the distribution of certain images, but also by the presence or absence of certain design motifs. For example, why are there no representations in Hawaiian rock art of plant life, and why so few of fish? As we will see in the next chapter, other Polynesian islands selected different images for rock art subjects.

POWER OF LANDSCAPE

There is the question of why certain places were selected for petroglyph sites, while others nearby—and seemingly (to our eyes) having equal attributes—lack them. There may have been a connection between openings in the earth's crust (lava mounds, cracks, or caves) that drew the attention of petroglyph makers. The lava dome at Puʻuloa, where the piko of the newborn was deposited, the smaller domes at Kaʻūpūlehu with their clusters of petroglyphs, the collapsed lava tube at ʻAnaehoʻomalu, and the caves with their intensive carving, all seem to have some affinity to entrances or openings, or access to earth's underground and the power that resided therein. For a rationale, we may look to the idea of pō, the underworld and the opposite of ao, light. These correspond to Papa, mother earth, and Wakea, father sky, and are key to the understanding of religious concepts in Polynesia. Various stages of pō coincide with the development of a child from birth to the time when the light of reason dawns, and the person begins to act otherwise than from impulse. The idea of the birth of pre-human forms in the nether world of pō, up to the coming of man, the image (kiʻi) who ushers in the world of humans (ao), corresponds to the genealogical history of Hawaiʻi's line of chiefs (Beckwith 1970:312-313). Thus the use of natural openings in the earth's surface may have been an effort to summon the spirits from the underworld, pō, and access the power of that world. The lava arises from the depths and becomes land; the center of earth also was considered as a piko or navel. Perhaps these special places in the landscape reinforced legends in a concrete way, and enabled power to be extracted from them by means of petroglyphs.

In the case of rock art located on boulders, legends may provide the rationale behind their selection, for example, the Wailua site on Kauaʻi. The concept of humans being turned to stone by divinities is an old one with universal examples. Any unusually shaped rock or feature might make an impression, such as the ringing rock on Kahoʻolawe. The special properties of the rock would be interpreted as a supernatural or magical sign. Once something becomes part of an oral tradition, it would not be forgotten unless suppressed or it became so unimportant that it no longer was worthy of notice. Although few legends refer specifically to petroglyphs, petroglyphs do have connections to legends such as Kaupe the ghost dog, the bird monster of Lānaʻi, and the Wailua boulders.

VARIATION OF MOTIFS BY SITE

It has been noted that motifs vary according to site use. Trail sites have circles, cupules, and other geometric motifs. On the other hand, sites not associated with trails tend toward figurative motifs. The earlier the site, the more stick figures. Later sites have a preponderance of triangle torso anthropomorphs. Thus change in figure type is time-based, and variation of design type is related to site function.

On the Kona side of Hawaiʻi Island, large sites located within a few miles of each other show considerable variation in their universe of design elements. Kaʻūpūlehu's extraordinary designs have connections to royalty, status, and power. Puakō's main site at Kāeo 1 appears to be very early due to its focus on stick figures and figure density, suggesting the site had considerable supernatural power. The anthropomorphs at the cave at Kalaoa reflected ritual concerns. All these are very different from ʻAnaehoʻomalu, which is associated with a trail.

However, ʻAnaehoʻomalu and the site of Puʻuloa in the southern part of Hawaiʻi

Island have a comparative design inventory and these two stand apart. What they have in common is an ancient trail—and cracks (a collapsed lava tube in the case of 'Anaeho'omalu)—which suggests that the petroglyphs had some functional value that related to a trail, and the numerous cupules perhaps had a relation to the piko ceremony. With thousands of units functioning as piko receptacles (or symbols of the ceremony) at Pu'uloa and 'Anaeho'omalu, the concepts of kumu and piko, kapu and mana, are possibly the keys for understanding levels of meaning in Hawaiian rock art. The ritualistic care given the piko came, in part, from the knowledge that the cord connected the baby with a living ancestor who, after death, would be a directly linked 'aumakua. The ceremonies and the petroglyph making were a means for transmission of power and mana from 'aumakua, demi-gods, or gods to the infant.

Whether or not the piko was placed within the cupule or the cupule simply was a symbol that represented a deposition of an umbilical cord in a crevice remains to be determined. It appears that, due to the vertically-placed cupules in the cracks at Pu'uloa, cupules probably functioned as symbols.

VARIATION IN QUALITY OF PETROGLYPHS

Travelers may have made some of the petroglyphs along the trail sites. If this is so, it would explain the great variety of expertise we see in the petroglyphs. Some are beautifully made with deep grooves, fine pecking, and careful finishing. Others are crudely pecked, some half finished. It takes little skill to peck a cupule. Judging from the variety of images at Pu'uloa and its closest corollary, 'Anaeho'omalu, it seems probable that many carvers with varying motivations made them, and perhaps this accounts for the stylistic variations seen. Kahuna may have had dominion over most petroglyph making throughout the islands, but perhaps not so much control along trails which were open to many image-makers with imagination, independence of thought, and the tendency to personalize beyond acceptable traditional patterns.

DATING

The practice of carving petroglyphs surely disembarked in Hawai'i with the first settlers from the Marquesas. They brought with them, as a sort of cultural baggage, images from their homeland—stick figures, dogs, circles, and cupules. A comparison of Marquesan petroglyphs and those of Hawai'i leaves little doubt of their origin, as will be discussed in the following chapter. That the knowledge and tradition survived in Hawai'i suggests that some petroglyphs were made soon after arrival. According to Hunt and Holsen (1991:158), humans were living in Hawai'i as early as the first century AD. This view not shared by all; some scholars argue that settlement was as late as the 9th century AD (Graves and Addison 1995; Masse and Tuggle 1998). Whatever the time of arrival, some petroglyphs assuredly date from around the time of first settlement and continue up into historic times.

The dating efforts of the petroglyphs at Kaho'olawe, Puakō, and Pu'uloa demonstrate attempts to obtain dates by scientific methods (Appendix A). Those dates are the first for petroglyphs in Hawai'i, but surely will not be the last. If this methodology proves to be valid, then we are facing an entirely new view of petroglyph sites in the islands. However, stylistic approaches to dating should not be discarded in favor of scientific dating, particularly for Polynesian rock art which has, relatively speaking, little time depth (Lee 1998). Temporal information also can be obtained by determining evolution of style, changes in subject matter, associations with legendary events, oral histories, archaeological findings, known volcanic eruptions, and written records of the post-contact period. Relative sequences can be suggested by the overlapping of images, patination of units at a particular site, and by the small body of testimony from early informants.

HUMAN IMAGES

The major focus of Hawaiian petroglyphs is on human imagery in various forms: mainly stick figures and triangle torso figures. Furthermore, regardless of which island in Hawai'i is under consideration, it is apparent that similarity is the general rule. Although sites might have a different universe of designs (circles vs. anthropomorphs) there are neither "breaks" nor any evidence of intrusion.

It is clear to us that, over time, the stick figure anthropomorph developed into a triangle-bodied figure. What might have triggered this evolution? It may have been an attempt to show power and force, as if warriors, chiefs, or gods were to be depicted. It may have simply been an artistic development, to indicate form and bulk. Perhaps these figures were a reaction to the arrival of Spanish soldiers in armor at some early date. Whatever the impetus, it reflects a change of perception in the society, which we suggest occurred around AD 1500-1600, based on dates obtained from excavations.

THE DOG MOTIF

The Polynesian dog as depicted in rock art has been noted at some sites and islands, but not all. The island of Hawai'i includes few dogs in the rock art; none are reported from either Kaua'i or Moloka'i. They are common however, on Lāna'i, Maui, Kaho'olawe, and O'ahu. The dogs that arrived on Hawai'i with the Polynesians were small, of terrier size and type. Some were used as pets by women of high status, but they were not companions as we think of pets today. They were not trained; there were no animals to hunt. They never became feral. Dogs were, however, highly esteemed as a food resource and usually were saved for chiefs' use only. Dogs' teeth were used for decorative anklets worn in dances and for various other decorative purposes and, as offerings, dogs were appropriate for certain deities, usually feminine. They appear in legends: Māui is credited with creating the first dog and dogs play parts in some legends, such as warning people of danger. The most interesting tale concerns Kaupe, the cannibal 'ghost dog' which could appear as either a man or a dog. Another mythological dog is Ku'ilio-loa, a huge dog represented in god form. He was closely linked to man because of the Māui legend of forming Dog from his brother-in-law (Titcomb 1969:20-24).

Dog images in rock art may refer to 'aumakua, ancestral guardians, or protective spirits in animal form. Personal protection could be created by the deification of a deceased family member whose essence was released into an animal by a kahuna. At times we see dogs juxtaposed with human figures; it is possible that such images represent an individual and his 'aumakua. It is therefore not surprising to find images of dogs in the petroglyphs. What is unexplained is the distribution of this motif, for dogs themselves were not restricted to certain islands only. For some reason, dog-as-image was important on some islands, but not on others.

CIRCULAR MOTIFS

Circles and circular motifs, so prominent at Pu'uloa and 'Anaeho'omalu, have been described as symbols of travel around the island. We think that circles implied something more elemental: "For the Hawaiian the circle evokes a being closed in on itself because it is complete and self-sufficient. Accordingly, circular things and things capable of circular movement are often considered divine. . . such as the stars or the moon. . . . Even an arc of a circle, such as a rainbow, evokes the divine perfection." (Valeri 1985:89). Circles mirror natural patterns—not only of the heavenly bodies but also such things as drops of rain which produce circular waves in water. The circle and its variations probably served as metaphors and contained layers of meaning. Circles could have been symbols of the individual or, perhaps of the family, particularly when a circle enclosed a series of small cupules.

MEANING

We have only one example of good ethnographic evidence about petroglyph making. A beach site adjacent to the Keʻeku Heiau near Kailua-Kona recorded by Tuggle (1990) has a distinctive figure that, appears to commemorate a specific event—and one that was significant in the history of Hawaiʻi Island, the death of Kamalalawalu. Forbes' unpublished notes from the mid 1980s mention the event and Stoke's informant in the early 1900s described the chief's sacrifice and indicated that the petroglyphs were in remembrance of that event (Tuggle 1990). The figure is in low relief, a rare technique in Hawaiian rock art, and Tuggle suggests that the sculptural approach is a measure of the petroglyph's importance, being created with the ritual and attention associated with carving images of the gods. The site is submerged at high tide.

Cox and Stasack (1970:77) state, ". . . some prior knowledge of Hawaiian culture is necessary if we are to recognize the connotations intended by the makers." Consequently, expert knowledge of the language of Hawaiʻi is of vital importance to understanding petroglyphs, and the authors of this book make no such claim. For one thing, many petroglyphs surely contained multiple hidden meanings (kaona), understood by those initiated into a select group. We can state that petroglyph sites were wahi pana (legendary places), many are manifestations of belief and power, prayer and offering, made by ritual experts, kahuna, in the process of working magic and offering prayers. Mana may come from the gods, but potent speech and correct ritual actions are required for its successful transfer to man (Valeri 1985:101).

CONCLUSION

One of the central purposes of this book is to suggest a connection between the rock art of Hawaiʻi and some of the profound cultural and religious practices of the Hawaiians. While we cannot enter the minds of those long gone nor can we share the same psychological states of those who made the carvings, the fact that the practice of making petroglyphs continued for centuries indicates they were appreciated and, by implication, found to be useful. Just as other cultures have used writing, petroglyphs may have been used to keep records, or to mark boundaries, or to commemorate events. It appears that many were recording legends, or proclaiming domain or custodianship. Surely some documented births and perhaps deaths; battles won or lost; genealogical records; as focus for ritual and ceremonial activities; for sorcery; cues for story tellers; the deification of personal and family ʻaumakua; to seek mana and favor from the gods.

The petroglyphs have outlasted the cultural context in which they were created. If they mark a boundary, specifically or symbolically, the mark is certain. If they mark the existence of a person, an event, a concept, it is no less certain and, except for erosion, these are as durable as the rock upon which they were carved. This poses significant problems for those who would seek to change history by altering or vandalizing the petroglyphs.

The petroglyphs must be preserved as long as possible, not only for their intrinsic value but for their importance as indicators of the progressive development of Hawaiian heritage. We hope that this book will help increase the awareness of this need and assist in the understanding and recognition of the beautiful culture and tradition that produced the petroglyphs; and help to preserve the sites of Hawaiʻi nei by making them more understandable and comprehensible to the general public. Petroglyphs are irreplaceable; visitors should be made aware that walking on them, taking rubbings and moldings, or chalking them is detrimental.

Conservation is a major problem. On the island of Hawaiʻi, petroglyphs are usually pecked into pāhoehoe lava. These are endangered by disintegration of the rock or by encroaching lava flows. Not much can be done to halt natural processes such as these. However, the petroglyphs at nearly every site in Hawaiʻi also are being physically harmed by humans. Deterioration is evident, even at the relatively well managed and protected sites. Some can be considered lost as, for example, the site at Molokaʻi where carved graffiti covers the ancient designs. It is our perception that vandalism in its various forms stems, in part, from a lack of appreciation for the petroglyphs and a lack of understanding of their importance to the ancient society.

FOOTNOTES

[1] This is 'Ili'ili'opae, a massive stone structure said to be the oldest on the southeast coast. The main platform is 86 x 27 meters and rises 18 meters on the east end. Island legends say it formerly was much larger and was a 'stronghold' for powerful kahuna (Summers 1971:134).

[2] The narrator used the term 'crazy woman' (Summers 1971:43).

[3] This and the following estimates for sites and petroglyphs given by Cox and Stasack in 1970 generally are from secondary sources and are low in all instances. As they state (ibid.:7), ". . . merely a generalization, indicating concentration."

[4] One is at 'Anaeho'omalu; the other at Pu'uloa.

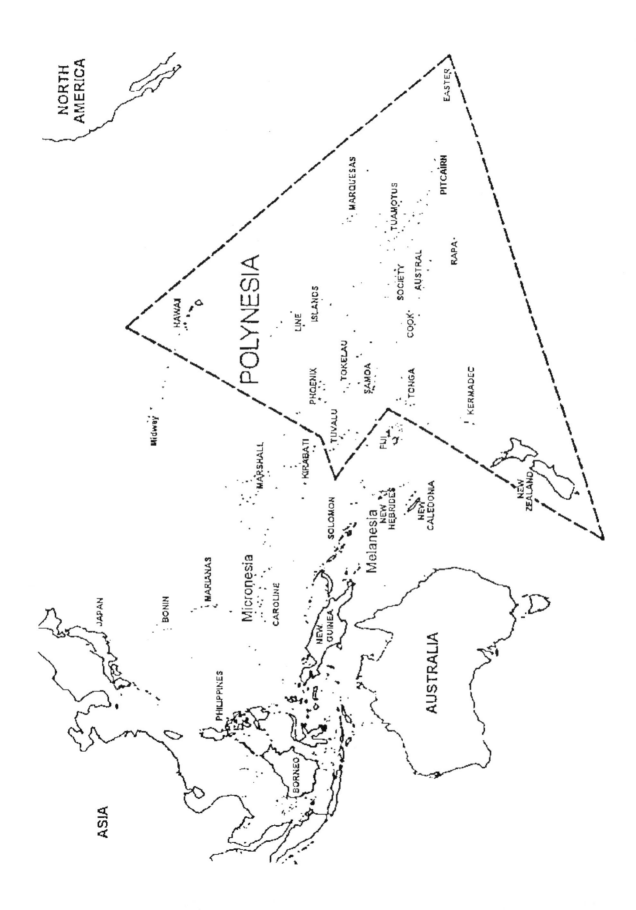

11

POLYNESIAN CONNECTIONS

Wherever human beings have been, they have made their mark upon the landscape. . . . With this mark, one declares that the place on which one stands is meaningful. In this way, humans show that they have a relationship with the world around them; a relationship whose sanction and purpose transcends the mere physical character of the place."

—S.D. Gill, *Beyond the Primitive: The Religions of Nonliterate People (1982)*

Polynesia's inter-connections are strong. As Kirch (1984:2-4) has pointed out, the fifty ethnographically known societies that comprise Polynesia were all derived from a single ancestral society. Problems of diffusion are reduced in isolated islands, enabling us to look to internal developments rather than search for influences arriving from outside Polynesia. Their socio-political structures—chiefdoms—are fascinating examples of society in that they display a range from very complex and highly stratified polities (as in Hawai'i) to those that remained relatively simple. Each Polynesian society possessed its own body of traditions.

As we shall see, each also took a slightly different direction in the arts— which are intimately connected to culture—although we can observe a certain 'Polynesian characteristic' in that there are more similarities than differences between island groups (Lee 1996). Hawaiian rock art is Polynesian in its general characteristics. Its closest affinity is with the Marquesas Islands and, to a lesser degree, Tahiti. It has least similarity with New Zealand and Easter Island, but the islands of Hawai'i are also great distances from both of those places (Figure 11.1).

A custom of carving on rock can be traced westward through eastern Polynesia, New Caledonia, and beyond into Southeast Asia—a study of origins that goes beyond the confines of this book. Some stylistic conformations are constant throughout this extensive area: the so-called bent-knee forms begin in Southeast Asia and appear in the arts across the Pacific. We can assume that each group did not travel with an object in hand that displayed that form. But it may have come along as a memory of artistic expression, or as an unconscious symbol (cf. Schuster and Carpenter 1996). The bent-knee posture may refer to dance (Teilhet 1973), flexed burial position (Feldman 1985:7) or the posture when presenting offerings to ancestors or worshipping the gods (Ch'i-lu 1972:409). The ramifications of this form will be discussed below.

In Polynesia, we look for petroglyphs on volcanic "high islands," because coral atolls lack proper surfaces. For some islands where we would expect to have petroglyphs, such as the Cooks and Mangareva, none have been reported. Perhaps the absence of petroglyphs may provide information. For example, Samoa is a puzzle; it was one of the 'stepping off' places for early migrations, yet it lacks any authenticated petroglyphs with the exception of a few crude designs located near Pago Pago. It is incongruous that the tradition of carving on rocks skipped one of the places through which it is thought the Polynesian dispersal took place. The fact that some naturally marked rocks in Samoa served as sacred places may be significant—perhaps they were sacred enough without the addition of other elements.

Although exceptions exist, when suitable surfaces were to be found in special and sacred places, aboriginal peoples tended to place petroglyphs or paintings on them. In any culture many activities of great significance have their origins in fortuitous circumstances, e.g., having a conveniently accessible and smooth boulder or lava flow and a ritual priest sympathetic to, or skilled in, carving images. The tradition of making petroglyphs undoubtedly came to the various islands along with the earliest settlers but its perpetuation required support from the custodians of mana, the religious leaders.

TAHITI

There are surprisingly few examples of rock art in the Societies although some petroglyphs are found on the islands of Tahiti, Bora Bora, Ra'iatea, Mo'orea, Huahine, Ra'ivavae, and Tubua'i. Perhaps the reason is due to a general focus on oratory, dance, and performance, considered to be the highest art forms of the culture.

Of those images that have been recorded, turtles are found on marae, either of stone or coral; these relate to the sacredness of turtles in the ancient society (Figure 11.2). Recent work on Mo'orea (Millerstrom 1998) has revealed three sites associated with marae. Motifs include turtles and human figures (Figure 11.3), as well as geometrics.

Double outlining of figures is fairly common at some sites in Tahiti. One, recorded at Tipaerui (Barrow 1972:109), appears to represent a double figure (see page 161). Other motifs recorded at Ra'iatea and Tahiti represent mourners' head-dresses (Emory 1979:212; Garanger 1980). Concentric rings and canoe motifs also have been noted.

A single bas relief carving has been noted on tiny Rapa Iti (Smith 1965:91). It is a human figure, carved on a tomb.

A recent discovery of bas relief petroglyphs from the island of Ra'ivavae is noteworthy. These designs are probably the most elaborate and well-carved in Tahiti Polynesia; they include faces, geometrics, and a sort of lizard-like creature with a fan tail (Lee 1991:51) (Figure 11.4a, b). Other petroglyphs recorded on Ra'ivavae are incised geometric designs on marae slabs, similar to what is found on nearby Tubua'i. The bas relief designs are very different, and they are an unusual find in

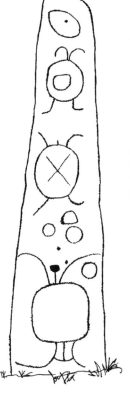

Figure 11.2. Turtle motifs from Mo'orea (Millerstrom 1998). The panel is 95 cm high.

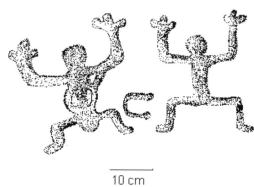

10 cm

Figure 11.3. Human figures from Mo'orea (Millerstrom 1998).

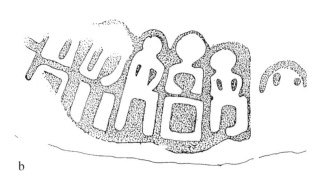

Figure 11.4 a). Ra'ivavae boulders showing bas relief figures. One motif resembles a lizard. b) Bas relief petroglyphs from Ra'ivavae, Austral Islands. These were discovered a few years ago. This site has the only known bas relief designs on the island.

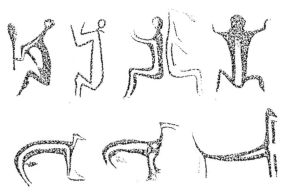

Figure 11.6. Human and animal figures from New Zealand. Note "bent knee" profile form and a stylistic open form that resembles the double outline seen elsewhere in Polynesia (after Trotter and McCulloch 1971).

Figure 11.7. Ahuriri Group, copied from a cave roof on the Ahuriri River. Site now submerged. This copy now in Canterbury Museum

the Societies in general. These petroglyphs deserve further study. Bas relief brings up the suggestion of a connection with Easter Island, noted for this type of rock carving.

The limited number of petroglyphs in Tahiti provides too small a base from which to generalize but there are similarities with Hawaiian and Marquesan forms, including a group of faces with headdresses carved on a boulder at Vaiote, Tahiti, one of which bears a resemblance to some headdresses in Hawaiian petroglyphs. An image from a drawing by Emory (1979: Figure 8.10-g) shows a face with two dots for eyes and a third dot centered below. Of the few faces depicted among Hawaiian petroglyphs the "three dot" type dominates.

NEW ZEALAND

Rock art in New Zealand includes paintings, charcoal or dry pigment drawings, and petroglyphs. All have Polynesian overtones and/or characteristics. Motifs include geometrics, dogs, fish, canoes, birds, footprints, and human or bird figures in squatting or bent-knee form. Bird-headed human figures have been recorded. Some of the paintings are very fluid and elaborately curvilinear, having much in common with intricate Maori wood carvings (L. Barrow 1998). 'Creature' forms and abstract patterns have been recorded and a few petroglyphs are carved in bas relief (Trotter and McCulloch 1971).

The early Archaic period (AD 800-1400) has certain stylistic features including chevron motifs and bold *taniwha* (sea monster) figures in an angular style. South Island drawings have much stylistic similarity but those located on North Island, which may date from a later period in time, are more individualized and most of these are engravings. An interesting site on North Island, Tongaporutu, has stylized foot prints, many with toes indicated. These bear a resemblance to some petroglyphs of feet recorded on Hawai'i Island at Puakō in that the toes are shown as a row of cupules across the top of the foot. Another well known carving (Figure 11.8) has bas relief-like figures.

Later period rock art on South Island features bold curvilinear paintings in red on cliff faces; these display the typical Maori curvilinear forms and spirals. Rock art studies are continuing in New Zealand; many newly discovered sites have been reported but so far remain unpublished.

Trotter and McCulloch (1971:73) find ". . . no more features . . . than one would reasonably expect to find in the art of peoples with such similar cultures." But they do not discuss a stylistic feature in figures of both humans and dogs that appears to resemble the double outline feature found in both Tahiti and the Marquesas carvings (Figures 11.6, 11.7).

Figure 11.8. A petroglyph panel from Waverly, Taranaki, from the east coast of North Island, New Zealand. Designs include a lizard, bird/human figures, spirals, and other forms. Some are deeply cut and portions border on bas relief. (Photograph courtesy of Wally McGalliard).

PITCAIRN

Pitcairn has one group of petroglyphs, carved ten feet above ground level on a cliff face. Sketches exist of these in various guides to Pitcairn Island, and also in other esoteric places (Brodie 1851), but they have not been systematically documented. The figures (Figure 11.9) are shown in double outline and one appears to be bas relief.[1] These figures and a possible canoe, resemble those from Tahiti and the Marquesas. Other motifs include circles with interior lines.

Figure 11.9. Petroglyphs from Pitcairn Island. These are drawn from photographs of chalked images, thus their accuracy cannot be verified. There may be features in the face of the central figure but the photo is not clear enough to confirm this.

MARQUESAS

Marquesan rock art motifs are very close in style to those of Hawai'i and include stick figures, dogs, tattoo designs, fish, lizards, turtles, human faces and geometrics. Both paintings and carvings have been recorded. Among the approximately 6000 units documented for the Marquesas (Millerstrom 1990), only 23% are anthropomorphic figures. However, the stick figure humans and dogs (Figure 11.10) are so similar to those in Hawai'i (see this book, pages xii, xiii and Figures 3.7, 3.8, 8.8, 8.12) that it is startling to compare them. Because they reflect common sources of inspiration, there is an inevitability of similarity between some human and dog images. Nevertheless, the correlation suggests a close connection. Marquesan anthropomorphic figures also are depicted in double outline (Figure 11.11) and a few are shown in profile (Figure 11.12).

At times, stick figures are shown with dots for heads, or dots associated with heads, a characteristic noted for Hawaiian stick anthropomorphs.

The major differences between the rock art of the Marquesas and Hawai'i is that the Marquesan sites contain a fair amount of human faces (Figure 11.13 a,b), including the 'eye-mask' face (similar to those seen on Easter Island) whereas these are rare in Hawai'i and, indeed, are problematical in that the "faces" may be fortuitously placed circles. The largest category of types in the Marquesas is geometric designs (Figure 11.14), accounting for over 66% of all petroglyphs documented (Millerstrom 1990).

Tattoo designs are found in the rock art, which is not surprising since tattooing was a highly developed art form in the Marquesan Islands.

The strong similarity between stick figure humans and dogs in these two island groups supports

Figure 11.10. Some typical anthropomorphs and dogs recorded in the Marquesas (Millerstrom 1990). Many of these would fit stylistically into Hawaiian sites.

Figure 11.11. Double outline figures from the Marquesas (Millerstrom 1990).

Figure 11.12. Profile figures from the Marquesas (Millestrom 1990). The figure on the left is virtually identical to one from the Kaua'i Wailua River site.

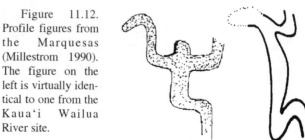

Figure 11.13a. Marquesan face motifs (Millerstrom 1990).

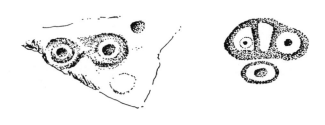

Figure 11.13b. Two possible faces from Hawai'i, at An-aeho'omalu. Because of their rarity, it may be that the placement of the elements forming faces is simply fortuitous.

the belief that the early migrations to Hawai'i originated in the Marquesas. Dogs are not mentioned in Marquesan legends and early on it was believed they had not made it to those islands. But images of dogs are in found the rock art, dog bones have been excavated from Ha'atuatua by Suggs (1961:181,195), and Sinoto (1966:291) found dog burials in Hane, Ua Pou. By historic times, dogs seemingly died out or became very rare.

EASTER ISLAND

When we compare the rock art of Easter Island to that of other Polynesian islands, we see differences in design, scale, and methods of carving. A few motifs appear to have a relation to those from the Marquesas and Hawai'i, but not as many as one might expect. Easter Island also has sophisticated paintings in red and white that decorate cave ceilings or interior house slabs.

Petroglyphs on Easter Island are carved on dense basalt boulders or hard lava flow, called papa. Some are in bas relief and a few are carved in intaglio. Double outlining is a common feature (Figure 11.15). Scale is significantly larger than is seen in the rest of Polynesia: designs may be in excess of three meters, and one great petroglyph of a double canoe at La Pérouse bay measures 12 meters long. There is a sculptural quality about many of the motifs, particularly bas relief carving that continues a motif around on several faces of a boulder. Relief carving is often fairly deep, resulting in a play of light and shadow. The carving techniques we see on Easter undoubtedly reflect the expertise of stone carving in general as is exemplified in the great *moai* (statues).

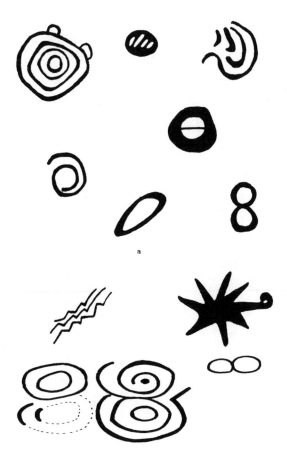

Figure 11.14. Geometric Marquesan motifs, the lower examples perhaps forming abstracted faces (Millerstrom 1990).

In contrast to the focus on the full human form in Hawai'i, Easter Island has only 24 anthropomorphic figures out of some 4000 design motifs (Lee 1992). No 'stick' figures are found. When compared to the Marquesas and Hawai'i, this is a major difference. It is possible that representations of the human face or the presence of some 1000 monolithic statues in the Easter Island landscape was sufficient, with the result that petroglyphs focused on animal imagery and items of material culture.

Excluding cupules, the most numerous motifs on Easter Island are faces (Figure 11.16 a, b ,c), both full face and "eye mask" with a total of 517; vulva forms or *komari* with 564 examples documented (Figure 11.17); and birdmen (usually carved in bas relief) with 499 examples (Figures 11.18 and 11.19). Other motifs that are abundant are fishhooks and fish of all kinds including shark, octopus, and turtle. Stylized canoe shapes are prevalent (Figures 11.15 and 11.21), and the presence of sea creatures are in contrast to Hawai'i where they are rarely shown in the rock art. Interesting design types seen in the rock art of Easter Island represent sea forms combined with human features (Figure 11.22) (Lee 1992).

Some motif types on Easter Island, such as the birdman, relate to changes in the socio-political situation; others refer to myths and are still so identified by islanders today. Certain designs surely are clan indicators and others appear to be related to status and kingship. No dog petroglyphs are found on Easter Island: if the original settlers started out with these animals, they did not survive the voyage.

The study of Easter Island's rock art was, like that of Hawai'i, analyzed with the help of a computerized data base. Upon completion, distribution patterns emerged that at first glance made little sense on this tiny island of about 170 sq. km. Fishhook motifs were concentrated in one section of the island only and birdmen motifs were localized at the southwest part of the island; canoe shapes with unusual end extensions were found in one area. However, when placed within ancient tribal boundaries, some distribution clusters fit into specific clan territories. Others, such as the birdman figure, clearly related to places in the landscape where rituals were conducted.

In regard to archaeological associations, Hawaiian sites are associated with trails, boundaries, religious or ritual sites, and locations of chiefs. Easter Island's sites seem to correlate with religious or ritual and chiefly sites. As for locales, Hawaiians were attracted to mounds, lava domes, lava slumps, cliff walls, caves and cracks. Easter Islanders also used caves

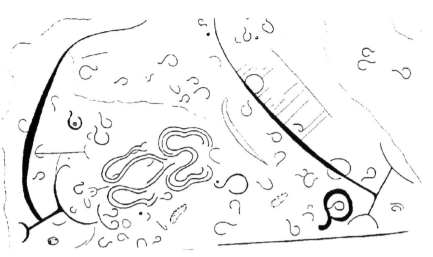

Figure 11.15. Double outlining from Easter Island is seen in this octopus figure (123 x 69 cm). Note the fishhooks and canoe shapes. This fine panel is from the La Pérouse bay area.

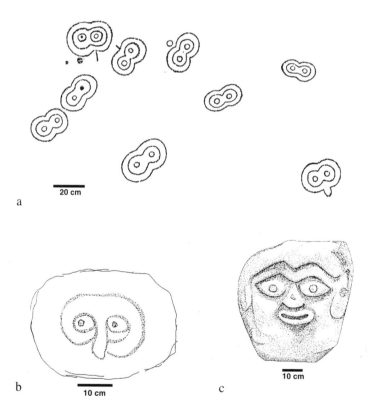

Figure 11.16. Examples of human faces in the rock art of Easter Island. a) "eye-mask" faces; b) the eyes/nose (Kilroy) face; and c) a bas relief "Makemake" face. Makemake was the creator god of the island. It has been suggested that the eye-mask faces were clan markers due to the distribution of this motif (Lee 1992).

and were attracted to volcanic craters. The choice of locale on Easter Island depended upon availability of surface: papa is found in limited areas. There are virtually no petroglyphs in the interior of Easter Island. There may have been other reasons for this but, in actuality, few suitable rock surfaces can be found in those areas. On Hawai'i Island, there was a wider choice, given the vast areas of pāhoehoe.

How did rock art function in the cultures that produced it? We have some ethnographic information about the use of cupules in Hawai'i, but otherwise the function of petroglyphs in that ancient society is poorly described. The situation in Easter Island is different where ethnographic information exists for an important part of the petroglyphs—the birdman carvings (Figures 11.18 and 11.19). The cult responsible for the birdman petroglyphs was still on-going in historic times so we have descriptions that help us understand the function of some petroglyphs. 'Orongo was the

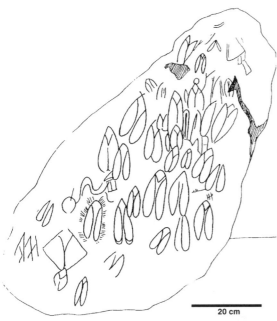

Figure 11.17. Numerous incised vulvae (*komari*) cluster on this boulder from Easter Island. Komari are the most frequently recorded motif in the island's rock art.

Figure 11.19. The elegantly carved boulders at 'Orongo, Easter Island are covered with birdman, faces, komari, and other designs. Most are carved in bas relief. The site perches above the ocean on the edge of 300 meter cliff.

site for ritual activities revolving around the cult of the birdman, an annual spring ceremony and contest (Lee 1992:15-19). According to McCoy, it likely had its basis in 'first fruits ceremonies' (McCoy 1978:198). The most sacred precinct, Mata Ngarau, is literally covered with petroglyphs, many superimposed (Figure 11.19). Motifs depicting a half man, half bird are carved deeply on basalt boulders, in bas relief. Other figures—faces, vulva forms, birds, and others crowd every surface. It is possible that each birdman represented a winner in the annual contest, as is suggested by Routledge (1919).[2] It is assumed that the petroglyphs were carved by experts who chanted and prayed for the success of the contest and who lived at the site during the competition. The designs relate to power and status, prayer and offering. To our knowledge, nothing similar exists in the rest of Polynesia. The closest parallel is Samoa where great pigeon hunting rituals were held (Williamson 1924, II:237).

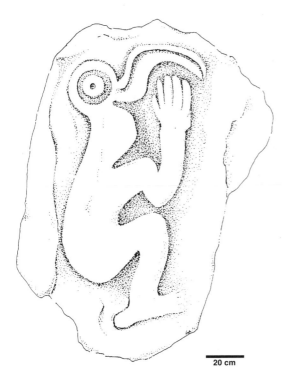

Figure 11.18. A typical birdman from Easter Island showing the bent-knee crouching pose of a human form with bird head and gular pouch. Carving is in deep bas relief.

The known function of cupules in Hawai'i was different from Easter Island. In Hawai'i they either held the piko of an infant (or symbolized it). On Easter Island, cupules outline large panels, like a border (Figure 11.20). Although Easter Islanders are familiar with the piko concept in that a newborn's umbilical cord was placed into a, natural, not man-made hole.

Comparison between two other sites in these islands should be made: Ka'ūpūlehu, on Hawai'i Island and a great panel at Ahu Ra'ai, La Pérouse Bay, on Easter Island. Both are noted for their fine quality of workmanship and unusual motifs, and both appear to have been connected to status and sailing concerns. Ka'ūpūlehu features sails, the La Pérouse panel features canoes (there are no sails depicted in the rock art of Easter Island). Instead of elegantly pecked muscled

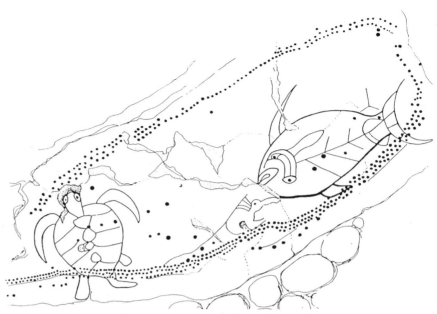

Figure 11.20. Cupules on Easter Island appear to have been used as parts of elaborate panels, and are too small to have contained anything. This differs from cupules in Hawai'i which were larger and probably intended to hold piko. This panel is from Tongariki and is one of several at this site. Note the turtle, and tuna fish with the bones indicated.

figures with headdresses and great curving sails, Ahu Ra'ai's site has fish, turtles, shark, and octopus, and canoe shapes with curved ends. Some canoes have an unknown appendage at one end which is in the form of an opposing line with curved elements at each end. This might have been intended to represent a fishing device. Running the length of the panel is a great double canoe pecked out in intaglio with tiny cupules inside the body of the curve and a line of them outside (Figure 11.21). It is tempting to suggest these represent individuals who sailed in the royal canoe of the

Figure 11.21. The great panel at La Pérouse Bay on Easter Island. This elegantly carved double canoe stretches 10 meters across the panel and is associated with numerous other smaller canoes. Note tiny cupules that line the major canoe. Other elements are fishhooks and turtles. Many man-made depressions are on the panel, perhaps the result of smoothing stone fishhooks, or were created to catch and hold rain water.

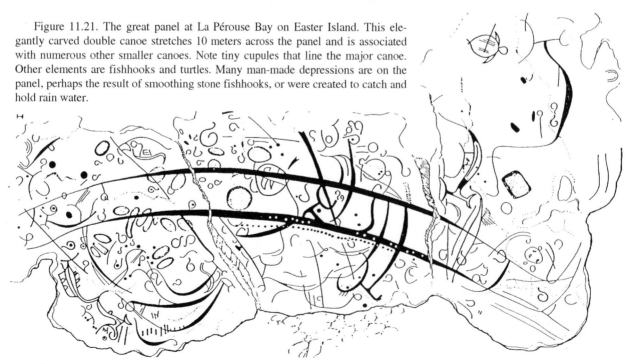

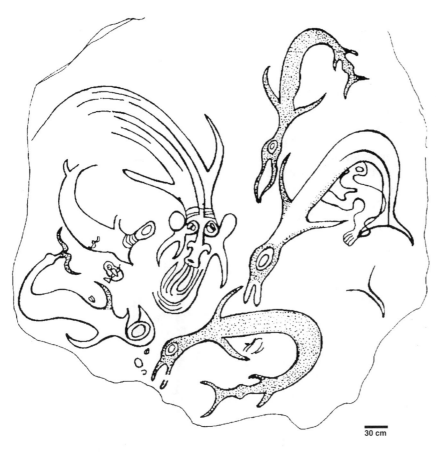

30 cm

Figure 11.22. Fish forms partially carved in relief and intaglio from Easter Island. The designs wrap around a huge basalt boulder over 5 meters in diameter. Note the sea creature with human face—surely a creation of myth or dream. This may be the finest example of rock art in Oceania.

founding ancestor. Unfortunately the ethnographic sources are silent about both these sites, but it can be said with confidence that they are status oriented, dealing with chiefs or kings.

Human figures were the focus in Hawai'i; Easter Island's sites contain birds and creatures from the sea, carved with enough detail to depict species. Perhaps these creatures were metaphors. Birds or fish combined with human attributes are particularly fascinating and are obviously mental conceptualizations, creatures of mind and dream. What was their symbolic value? Possibly to acquire the power of that animal, depicted as a spirit frozen in the process of transforming. Some sites with these fabulous creatures are associated with legends. In those, of which we have knowledge, sea creatures had a magical ability to swim or fly away, to come or go at will (Figure 11.22). No doubt these reflect the intense isolation of this lonely and confined island.

Figure 11.23. Fishhook from 'Anaeho'omalu, Hawai'i. This is a typical Polynesian fishhook, close in form to those found on Easter Island. Compare to fishhooks in Figure 11.12.

Other elements of similarity between Easter Island and Hawai'i are petroglyphs of fishhooks (Figure 11.23). These are so close in style and carving as to be virtually interchangeable; however, the numerical differences are striking: only 34 have been documented in all Hawai'i [3] whereas 380 have been documented on tiny Easter Island (Lee 1992) .

Let us return to the famous birdman figure of Easter Island—that of a crouching human in profile with the head and beak of a bird (Figures 11.18, 11.19). We have seen a corollary for this motif in Hawaiian rock art (Figure 11.24), as well as in the bent-knee profile drawings from New Zealand. Whether this position referred to prayer, dance, offering, death, or fertility is unknown; the fact that this posture is found in art motifs throughout such a wide area suggests that it is of great antiquity. If we can base an understanding of this motif on what we see in Easter Island's birdman cult—intimately linked to the bird-man figure—we see elements of death and rebirth, descent into the ocean, hiding in caves (the womb), the sacred egg, human sacrifice, confinement and seclusion (symbolic death), and finally a return to society (rebirth).

a

FOOTNOTES

[1] Photographs show the double-outlining and the bas relief, but in Brodie's 1851 sketch they are drawn as simple lines.

[2] The contest itself is an oddity in Polynesia; it involved competitors who descended 'Orongo's sheer 300 meter cliff, swam to a tiny islet some 3 km offshore, and hid in caves until the annual arrival of the flocks of seabirds. The first to acquire an egg swam back and presented it to his sponsor who was then declared birdman of the year, a high (but temporary) position and one of the few ways a man not born into chiefly rank could acquire status. The birdman designated some unfortunate to be sacrificed for the good of his reign (and his selection generally resulted in yet another round of warfare); he shaved his head and went into seclusion for a year, serving as a sort of oracle. At the end of the year, he rejoined society but retained status for his lifetime.

[3] Puako has 12 fishhooks; Pu'uloa has 10; Ka'ūpūlehu has 10; the island of Lāna'i has one; Kaho'olawe has one. Several have been noted at 'Anaeho'omalu but the full extent of their numbers at that site is unknown.

b

Figure 11.24. Two bent knee figures from Hawai'i: a) is from Puakō and has a bird head; b) is from Pu'uloa.

12

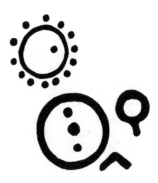

RECORDING, TYPOLOGY AND STATISTICS

METHODS OF RECORDING

Our goal was to make a record that would stand despite what the future might bring to the sites. Volcanic activity on Hawaii Island has destroyed many petroglyph sites before they could be documented, and this activity continues, leaving the future in doubt for sites in that part of the island. Sadly, vandalism is a fact in the Hawaiian Islands and it occurs despite many efforts to safeguard sites. Our study recorded the theft of entire panels from the Paniau area of Puakō after we had recorded them. In this instance we know what the petroglyphs looked like should they reappear at some time in the future. It is unfortunate that some sites were not recorded prior to vandalism, such as the one on Nanaoa Hill, Molokai. When we arrived at the site, virtually all of the petroglyphs were completely obscured by names and dates carved into the boulders. Thus the petroglyphs once existing at this site will never be known. For these reasons, we decided to record each individual petroglyph and its location in such a way that the entire site could be reconstructed to scale if desired.

Figure 12.1. Recording a panel using a string grid and 10/10 grid paper. The procedure provides the maximum amount of information.

A deficiency in many earlier petroglyph recording projects was the method used for documentation, if indeed a method was employed. Many researchers have relied and do rely on photography alone; some have used rubbings or other methods of obtaining a copy. Early efforts at Puakō and Puʻuloa (Bishop Museum Survey) attempted documentation by taking photographs and then drawing or tracing the images onto paper. In some instances, this resulted in fairly good representations of the petroglyphs. However, when superposition is present, it is difficult to sort out the individual elements from photographs alone and to locate them accurately in the site. Although our method is tedious, we think the results justify the effort.

Once a site was located, a datum was established and its location on a USGS map was determined using a global positioning system. A map was drawn of the site locale, showing location and relationship of boulders or pāhoehoe. No excavation was attempted at any of the sites.

Measuring from the datum, the site (if of sufficient size) was divided into a 10 meter grid, oriented NS-EW. Each square of the grid (referred to as a section) was numbered. Within the section, a panel of petroglyphs was covered with a string grid

(Figure 12.1), assigned a panel number, and located with respect to the ten-meter grid. In this way the location and orientation of each petroglyph was established within the overall site. Petroglyphs were drawn to scale on cross-section paper using the gridlines as guides. All motifs within a panel were recorded in their entirety, noting relationships, overlapping, method of production, and information on orientation, rock type, and archaeological association. In rare instances, panels were traced on mylar. A few mylar tracings were rendered on incised panels at Kahoʻolawe that were composed of a mass of tiny lines and some panels in caves were traced on mylar where gridding was not feasible due to dampness, fragility of surface, or undulating walls. The tracings were subsequently photographed and slides projected onto sheets of paper and

traced. Photographs and 35 mm slides were used for supplementary information and site context.

Our recording method relies heavily on scale drawings. Although photography is the single best way to document the appearance of a site and is a vital component of any documentation project, scale drawings are superior for details, for the human eye and the fingers can detect such things as faint traces beneath other motifs and subtle variations in line that are difficult to retrieve from a photograph. Thus, the making of a drawing forces the recorder to study a petroglyph in detail. Also, because the motifs are drawn with a grid, a finished scale drawing lacks the distortion that frequently occurs in panels which are sketched or photographed as can be seen in Figure 12.2. Compare also the photograph in Figure 7.35, a large motif that cannot be photographed without some distortion due to its size.

Upon returning from the field, drawings were reviewed against slides and corrected, and then re-drawn in India ink. The final step in the recording process consisted of entering the attributes of each petroglyph into a computerized data base.

It should be noted that this documentation process utilizes neither chalking nor rubbings, nor application of any substance to the petroglyph itself.

When the Hawaiian project began, no typology existed to help systematize the data and provide for the organization of distribution patterns. It took two field seasons before we felt confident enough to initiate such a project, and the original typology has been evolving since that time as new categories have been encountered.

Figure 12.2. An example of how photography may distort a petroglyph image. Compare this photograph with the scale drawing of the same panel in Figure 3.6. The long central figure is foreshortened in the photograph and the density of pecked images plus superposition makes it difficult to see the images clearly. Photography in addition to scale drawings provides the best record.

Typology

The typology created for Hawaiian petroglyphs represents a concept of grouping that should be considered as a framework for the classification of design types and to help sort out patterns of distribution. The numbering system was selected to allow for efficient computerization and for maximum flexibility. As different types are identified, they can be inserted into the typology.

The data base includes detailed information about the site, the panel, and the petroglyph. This information is stored in a standard relational data base computer program from which it can be retrieved, manipulated, and analyzed. To simplify the storage of data, the branching "data tree' was divided at the level of 'panel' into a site data set and a motif data set. The site record contains information about the site, and refers to one or more contiguous petroglyph loci. The motif record contains information about each individual design or motif. (These terms designate the individual figures of artistic work and are used interchangeably). The two data sets are related by a panel number that indicates the site name and number, and panel. In the case of anthropomorphic figures, additional information on body parts and objects related to the figure is included.

Anthropomorphs, Types 1100 to 1700

The major focus of Hawaiian petroglyphs is on human imagery in various forms, thus it was necessary to provide many separate categories and sub-categories. Basically, three major figure types are found: stick figures (including T figures); triangle torso forms (including muscled figures); and the 'other body shape' category. The remainder includes a small percentage of naturalistic or profile figures.

T Figure: a line for torso and cross line for arms. May or may not have a head. The arms may be up or down; digits are rare. Originally thought to be unfinished stick figure but so many examples were encountered, it was decided to create a category when it became apparent that something specific was intended.

Stick Figure: characterized as a line representing a torso, a head, lines for arms, and legs; may have a penis. A few have a dot in the crotch area that may refer to a female figure; however, some have been recorded with a vulva. Feet and hands may be indicated by an opposing short line (shelf-like) and digits may be present. An object may be in hand or held overhead by both hands. Action or posture is frequently indicated and many stick figures are quite lively. May be interacting with or connected to adjoining figures.

Triangle Torso Figure: wedge-shaped torso, arms and legs and head; may have penis. Some are fully pecked in the torso as opposed to outline. Feet and hands may be indicated by an opposing short line (shelf-like) and digits may be present. Legs can vary but figures are apt to be static and solid. An object may be in hand or held overhead by both hands. Some triangle figures have open bases. These variations may indicate female.

Muscled Figure: a variation on the triangle form. Legs with muscles are more common but many have both arms and legs showing muscles. In a few instances, the muscles are carried across the chest. May have object in hand or held overhead by both hands, and may be phallic. These figures as a group tend to be static; however, the bird-like forms from Lāna'i are exceptions as are those figures that may be paddle dancers, warriors, or runners in action.

Special Body: anthropomorphic figures with square, round or rectangle bodies that do not fit into either the stick or triangle form catagory. In the same manner there is a category for naturalistic figures, and profile forms.

Connected Figures: these caught our attention and thus a category was created in order to select out such examples. However, in the major bar-charts, all stick figures are counted as individuals regardless of connection, their arm and leg position, sex indication, and other variations. This is because we begin with the basic figure type. In the same way, all triangle bodied forms are counted as individuals regardless of their specific attributes (connected or not, etc.). Due to the nature of the data base it is possible to select out variations for study; for example, one can pick out all figures with arms up, or arms opposed, with headdresses, or digits, and so on.

DISCONNECTED BODY PARTS, INCLUDING FOOTPRINTS, TYPES 2100 TO 2300
Images of footprints are the most frequent body parts documented, with 332 examples. Footprints may or may not have toes indicated and sizes range from greatly over-sized adult to tiny baby footprints.

PREHISTORIC FAUNA, TYPES 3100 TO 3600
Of the eight categories of fauna, only the dog is significant, with 128 examples. Many are shown with curly tails, and may have two or four legs. Some appear to be barking.

SEA FORMS, TYPES 4100 TO 4500
Of the four varieties of sea life, only turtle (17 examples) and fish (12 examples) are represented with more than two examples. In fact, 4400, octopus, may be missidentified as that particular petroglyph also could be interpreted as wavy lines.

MATERIAL CULTURE, TYPES 5100-5621
This category includes functional as well as ceremonial objects of material culture. Included are sails, canoes, fishhooks, paddles, capes, kāhili (feather standards) and kapu sticks.

HISTORIC, TYPES 6100 TO 6700
Ships and anchors, introduced animals such as goats and horses, and historic lettering are in this category with nine types. Lettering appears most often, with 59 examples. The most frequently depicted introduced animal is the goat with 17 examples, most of which are found on Kahoʻolawe.

GEOMETRIC, TYPES 7100 TO 7710
The geometric category was one of the most difficult to define. So many variations on basic shapes led to a proliferation of types. This group started out fairly small as our first documentation efforts were on Lānaʻi and at Puakō where geometric motifs are a minority. As the categories expanded, we had problems of description: is a cupule with a circle around it recorded as two items, or is it a 'cup and ring' motif? When does a circle become an oval? Are two cupules joined by a line called by their individual components or do we name it what it looks like, a barbell? The final decision was to create many categories and to combine them later if necessary.

The cupule is the most numerous type in this category. Randomly placed cupules were distinguished from those that form patterns such as long lines or circles since this information may be of interest in the future and would be difficult to retrieve otherwise. By adding cupules to cupule patterns we have a total of 19,667. However, if the number of cupules that have tails (237), crossbars (19), radiating lines (20), barbells (454) (each barbell has two cupules), and cup and ring motifs, the total is increased by another thousand.

Cupules per se are distinguished from papamū (game boards pecked in stone). Although composed of tiny cupules, papamū had a specific function and are counted as separate motifs.

Circles and variations thereof also posed a problem; if all the variations (linked circles, circle clusters, tailed circles, circles with interior divisions or designs, semicircles, open circles, concentric circles, and cup and rings) are added together, this becomes a substantial category. Spiral (Type 7240) was not recorded by us, but is included because this form has been found on Kaua'i by Kikuchi.

UNIDENTIFIED, TYPE 8000
Petroglyphs which defied categorization or which were too eroded and faint to describe fell into this category, for a total of 898. Some of these were faint traces beneath other petroglyphs.

MODERN FAKES, TYPE 8010
Our final category, 8010, is for fakes, 18 of which were recognized. Surely there are more of these but when rapid patination occurs, the only remaining means for identification is stylistic aberration or traces of modern tools. A few petroglyphs appeared to be reworked ancient motifs; although we noted our suspicions during the recording processes, these were not included into the 8010 category.

HAWAIIAN ROCK ART TYPOLOGY

Anthropomorph, Type 1100 to 1700

1100 simple T-shaped stick figure, no legs

1101 simple T-shaped stick figures, compound/connected

1110 simple T-shaped stick figure, horizontal line in torso

1120 simple T-shaped, arms curve to form loops

1200 anthropomorph, simple stick figure

1201 anthropomorphs connected

1202 anthropomorph, extra legs/arms

1203 anthropomorphs, extra limbs/connected

1204 anthropomorph, partial (head/shoulders or legs only)

1210 anthropomorph, circle in torso

1220 anthropomorph, legs end in circle

1221 anthropomorphs, legs end in circle/connected

1230 anthropomorph, horizontal line in torso

1231 anthropomorphs, horizontal line in torso, connected

1240 scene: 2 or more figures in action pose

1300 anthropomorph, special torso treatment; (closed square, round, or rectangle torso)

1301 anthropomorphs, rectangle or other special torso type, / connected

1310 anthropomorph, special torso treatment: (open body)

1311 anthropomorphs, open torso, connected

1400 anthropomorph, triangular torso

1401 anthropomorphs, triangular torso, connected

1410 anthropomorph, triangular, open base

1411 anthropomorphs, triangular open base, connected

1420 anthropomorph, triangular torso with muscles

1421 anthropomorphs, triangular w/muscles, connected

1422 anthropomorph, open base/ muscled

1430 anthropomorph, triangular torso with circle legs

1431 anthropomorphs, triangular torso w/circle legs, connected.

1500 anthropomorph, naturalistic

1600 profile or squatting human figure

1601 profile figures/connected

1602 two profile figures back to back (or splayed figure)

1700 other anthropomorph

Anthropomorphic features for figure typology

Head

    A: absent

    L: line over head

    H: hook shaped head

    D: headdress

    B: birdlike

    T: dots for head, or dots associated with head

    P: open circle

    R: regular

    F: face (eyes, mouth indicated)

    O: other

Arms

    U: up

    D: down

    O: opposed

    B: object in hand

    I: wing-like

    G: digits

    T: out

    M: muscled

    W: wavy

Legs

    A: action

    M: muscled

W: wavy

C: curved

R: regular

G: digits

N: no

Gender

    M: male

    F: female

    N: no indication

Disconnected body parts, Types 2100 to 2300

   2100 eyes

   2200 footprints

   2210 arm

   2300 vulva

Prehistoric Fauna, Types 3100 to 3600

   3100 dog

   3200 pig

   3300 chicken

   3400 bird

   3410 bird tracks

   3420 owl

   3500 lizard

   3600 unidentified zoomorph/bug-like figure

Sea Forms, Types 4100 to 4500

   4100 turtle

   4200 fish

   4300 whale

   4400 octopus

   4500 fabulous sea creature, unidentified

Material Culture, Types 5100 to 5621

   5100 canoe

   5110 double canoe

5120 canoe with sail

5130 sail only

5200 fish hook

5210 fish trap

5300 paddle

5400 poi pounder

5500 adze

5510 kite

5600 ceremonial regalia: fan

5610 ceremonial regalia: cape

5620 ceremonial regalia: kapu sticks

5621 ceremonial regalia: kāhili

Historic, Types 6100 to 6700

   6100 historic ship

   6200 anchor

   6300 church

   6400 gun

   6500 horse

   6510 horse with rider

   6515 goat

   6520 other historic motifs

   6600 lettering

   6610 script

   6700 historic anthropomorph

Geometric, Types 7100 to 7710

7100 parallel straight lines

7110 rectangle

7111 rectangle segmented

7115 zigzag

7120 straight line(s), random

7121 curved line(s)

7122 combination straight/curved line

7125 enclosure

7200 circle

7202 linked circles

7203 circle clusters

7204 circles, tailed

7210 circle with interior divisions

7211 circle with interior design

7220 semi-circle

7221 double semicircle

7222 open circle

7230 concentric circles

7231 open concentric rings

7240 spiral

7310 cupule with tail

7311 cupule with cross bars

7312 bar bells

7400 cupules, random

7401 cup and ring

7402 cup with more than one ring

7403 cup and ring with tail

7410 cupules, patterned (not pāpamu)

7420 pāpamu

7500 oval

7510 oval with cup inside

7600 straight lines with circle ends

7610 circles with lines
 (including possible comets)

7612 circles with cup plus extending lines

7614 cupule with radiating lines

7620 edge notching

7630 raised knob

7700 other geometric

7710 polissoir

Unidentified, Type 8

8000 unidentified motif

8010 modern fake

STATISTICAL DATA

Information about each site was stored in a Site Data Set (Figure 12.3). Information about each motif was stored in a Motif Data Set (Figure 12.4), based upon the typology for Hawaiian petroglyphs. The two data sets are related through the Panel Numbers and constitute the database for an island or large site.

PANEL	SITE NAME	STATE NUMBER	LOCUS	AHUU-PUAA	OUTCROP SIZE	OUTCROP TYPE	PANEL SIZE	CUPULES	ARCHAEO. ASSOCIATION	COMMENTS	RECORDER	DATE
KAH121G-01	AHUPUIKI	50-20-97-121G			170X190 cm	BOULDERS	60X62 cm	NO	HABITATION	MUCH VANDALISM	STASACK	2/1/93
KAH110AP-01	LOA'A	50-20-97-110	1,2,3 A			BOULDER	70X80 cm	NO	TEMPORARY CAMP	LARGE BOULDER CLUSTER, INLAND	LEE/STASACK	3/30/93

Figure 12.3. Example of two entries in the Site Data Set for Kahoʻolawe Island

PANEL	PETRO	PETRO-SIZE cm	MOTIF TYPE	MOTIF NAME	HEAD	ARMS	LEGS	GENDER	TECHNIQUE	VANDALS	SUPERPOSITION	COMMENTS
KAH121G-01	01	17X20	6515	GOAT					PECKED, FAINT		NO	BACKWARD FEET, LONG EARS, TAIL OUT & UP; 1 OF 3+ THIS PANEL.
KAH121G-01	02	18X20	6515	GOAT					PECKED BODY, FAINT; LEGS INCISED	NO	NO	3 LEGS, INCISED. TAIL OBSCURE.
KAH121G-01	03	8X17	8000	UNIDENT					PECKED	YES	NO	PROB. BODY OF GOAT, BULLET IN CENTER. NO LEGS, HEAD, ETC. UNCLEAR.
KAH110AP-01	01A-1	16X20	1200	STICK FIG. ANTHRO	R	O	R	N	PECKED, FINE	NO	NO	SHELF FEET, ARMS MORE CURVED THAN LEGS. HOMMON SAW 7 FIGS HERE, WE FOUND ONLY 2.

Figure 12.4. Example of four entries in the Motif Data Set for Kahoʻolawe Island

Information extracted from the Kahoʻolawe Data Set is shown in Figure 12.5 spreadsheet for the individual sites around the island (see map Figure 9.1)

DISTRIBUTION OF MOTIF TYPES ON KAHOʻOLAWE

SITE NAME	SITE NUMBER	1100	1120	1200	1201	1202	1204	1230	1300	1310	1400	1401	3100	5200	6100	6515	6520	6600	7100	7120	7121	7400	7410	7700	8000	TOTAL
Hakioawa	480I	2		1										1							1				1	6
	481N			5																						5
	482J			1																						1
	485	3		4	4		5	1	1		6	3									1				4	32
	486			9		1	1		1		6		2							1						21
Kaulana	444										1															1
Kuheia	128			1							16	1	2					3							1	24
Ahupū NE	113																	1								1
Ahupū Bay	673																	2								2
Ahupū Ridge	123			3	4				2		2									4		1				16
Ahupū Iki	121		1	19	5		1	1	3		25	5	6			13			1	6	1			3	4	94
Ahupū Iki West	669			4		1				1	1															7
Kaukaukapapa	135	7		38	1	1	10		6	2	36	1	2				2			3			1	3	6	119
Kealaiha Iki Point	137										1									1						2
	142										1															1
Loa'a	110	2		28	2	4	2	1		1	6	1						5		1	1		32	2	3	91
TOTAL		14	1	113	16	7	19	3	11	4	101	11	12	1	2	13	2	11	1	16	4	1	33	8	19	423

Figure 12.5. Spreadsheet, taken from the database, summarizes the distribution of motif types found in the sites of Kahoʻolawe.

DISTRIBUTION OF MOTIF TYPES ON LĀNA'I

Motif type numbers are read vertically (MOTIF / TYPE / NUMBER) at the head of each column.

Site Name	Site Number	1100	1101	1120	1200	1201	1202	1203	1204	1210	1230	1300	1301	1310	1400	1401	1410	1420	1421	1430	1500	1700
Kahe'a	294				6	8			2							1						
Kaunolu	169	1	1		45	12	4	1	5			14			86	38	1	13		3		
Luahiwa	177	20	1	1	126	21	7	2	19	1		21	3	1	90	35	6	3	3		2	16
Māmaki	173						1					1			6	2						
Palaoa	172				6				1			2			5	1						
Kukui Point	205	2			20	4	2		4	1	1	24	4		92	4	2			2		2
Total		23	2	1	203	45	14	3	31	2	1	62	7	1	279	81	9	16	3	5	2	18

Site Name	2200	3100	3200	3300	3400	3500	4100	5120	5200	6500	6510	6515	6600	7120	7121	7200	7400	7420	7500	7620	7700	8000	8010	Total
Kahe'a		7	1																			3		28
Kaunolu		9			7								2		4			5		1	3	21		276
Luahiwa	2	68			2	2	2	1	1	1	9	1	1	1		2	18		1		3	75		568
Māmaki							1									1						1		13
Palaoa		2																				3		20
Kukui Point		19		3	1										5		28					24	2	246
Total	2	105	1	3	10	2	3	1	1	1	9	3	3	1	9	3	46	5	1	1	6	127	2	1151

Figure 12.6. Spreadsheet, taken from the database, summarizes the data for the motif types found on Lāna'i.

MOTIF TYPES AT PUAKŌ: KĀEO 1

MOTIF	1	1	1	1	1	1	1	1	1	1	1	1	1	1	1	1	1	1	1	1	1	1	1	1	1	1	1	2	2	2
TYPE	1	1	1	1	2	2	2	2	2	2	2	2	2	3	3	3	4	4	4	4	4	4	5	6	6	6	7	1	2	2
NUMBER	0	0	1	2	0	0	0	0	0	1	2	3	3	0	0	1	0	0	1	1	2	3	0	0	0	0	0	0	0	1
	0	1	0	0	0	1	2	3	4	0	0	0	1	0	1	0	0	1	0	1	1	1	0	0	1	2	0	0	0	0
SECTION																														
1	7				26	4	1		1								1							3					1	
2	12	5	1		24	14					1						1							1	1				2	
3	1				10	3										1														
4	3				21	2								2					1											
5	31	3			63	32	3							1	1	1	7	6	1	1	4			1					1	1
6	14			1	30	4	1																							
7	5				12	1	1									1	1							1					3	
8	11				1																									
9	3				18	2										2								1		1				
10	20	3			39	12	1		1							1	1									1			13	
11	23	3			47	22	3									1	1							1	2				1	
12					3			1																						
13	4				6																									
14	5	2			9																									
15	22	2			58	23	1				2	1					1							1	1				2	
16	45	4			127	51	7	5		1		1	3				1							1	1				15	
17	26	8			76	103	1	5									1							1					51	
18	1				15																									
19	18	11			72	55	1	1		1							1							4	1				10	
20	8	1			9	1	1									1		1												
21	10				25	3	1	1									2													
22	6	2			30	7	1	1									2	1											6	
23	10	3			24	14	1	1	1	1		2		2				1						1		1				
24	3	3			13	7	1		1			1		1	1													1	16	
25	5				10																								1	
26	12				19	13							1																	
27	18	6			64	33	4	2	10		1		2			2	1							1			1		16	1
28	12	6			40	12	4		9			2				1	1								1		1		11	2
MOTIF TOTAL	335	62	1	1	891	418	33	17	21	4	4	8	7	3	2	8	22	9	2	1	4	1	6	16	4	2	2	1	149	4

Figure 12.7. Spreadsheet, taken from the database, summarizes the distribution of motif types found in the 28 sections of site Kāeo 1.

2	3	3	3	3	3	4	4	4	5	5	5	5	5	6	7	7	7	7	7	7	7	7	7	7	7	7	7	7	7	7	8	8	
3	1	4	4	5	6	1	4	5	1	1	2	5	5	6	1	1	1	1	1	2	2	2	4	4	4	5	6	6	7	7	0	0	
0	0	0	2	0	0	0	0	0	2	3	0	0	1	0	1	2	2	2	2	0	2	2	0	0	1	0	0	1	0	1	0	1	
0	0	0	0	0	0	0	0	0	0	0	0	0	0	0	0	5	0	1	2	5	0	0	2	0	1	0	0	0	0	0	0	0	**section total**
						2									1																2	6		55
			1						1							2	5			1	1		1						1	2	7		85
																														3	1		19
			1													1														1	8		40
																1	2			1	1		42	1	10		1		2		21		240
											1						1										1				12		65
																															5		31
																																	12
																															6		33
																														3	12		106
1																					2									2	11	1	120
																															1		5
							1							1																			12
			1								1					2				2	2										17		140
2	1																1			1			82					1	2	1	41		395
																3				5			13	2	2	5			6	8	46		361
		1														4				1						1					9		32
				1												3				1			5		2				2		24		212
																1															4		27
																										1					4		46
																										1					6		63
1																							3								6		70
								1																2	4						4		60
																															4		20
1				1												1							2								3		53
	2		1			4					2	2	1			15	8	1	3	1	1	2	28			1				1			234
					1											5	10			1			33						2	1	9		164
5	3	1	3	2	1	6	1	1	1	1	4	2	1	1	1	38	27	1	3	16	7	2	209	5	18	9	1	2	17	21	269	1	2718

Figure 12.7 continued.

MOTIF TYPES FOUND AT PUAKŌ BOUNDARY SITES INCLUDING KĀEO 1

MOTIF	1	1	1	1	1	1	1	1	1	1	1	1	1	1	1	1	1	1	1	1	1	1	1	1	1	1	1	1	1	1	1	2	2	2	2	3	3	3	3	3	3	4
TYPE	1	1	1	1	2	2	2	2	2	2	2	2	2	3	3	3	3	4	4	4	4	4	4	4	4	4	5	6	6	6	7	1	2	2	3	1	3	4	4	5	6	1
NUMBER	0	0	1	2	0	0	0	0	0	1	2	3	3	0	0	1	1	0	0	1	1	2	2	2	3	3	0	0	0	0	0	0	1	0	0	0	0	2	0	0	0	0
	0	1	0	0	0	1	2	3	4	0	0	0	1	0	1	0	1	0	1	0	1	0	1	2	0	1	0	0	1	2	0	0	0	0	0	0	0	0	0	0	0	0
KĀEO LOCUS																																										
1	335	62	1	1	891	418	33	17	21	4	4	8	7	3	2	8		22	9	2	1			4		1	6	16	4	2	2	1	149	4	5	3		1	3	2	1	6
2	2				3																																					
3	1	1			6	1																											2									
4	9				58	11	2	1						2				5	1	1		1			1		1						2			3						
5					2																																					
6	5				7	1										1																										
7	1	3			21	11												3		1								1					1									
8	1				4																												2									
9	5				12											1		1		1		2			1		1	1					4									
10	4	1		1	20	1								3		1		9	3	1					1			1														
11	1				3											1		3																								
12					14																								1													
13																																										
14	4	1			14	5	2							4				3										1					5									
15	2				1													2																								
16					2																																					
17	2				3												1	5	2	2							1															
18	2			1	13	2								1		1		12	2	1	1	1	3				1						4			1	2	1				
19	4	1		1	12	6												10	5	2	2	4						1					24		1	2	1	1				
20	2				5	2	1													1													1									
21																																										
22																													1													
23																													1													
24	3	1			7	4												4	1														1									
25	1				7	1										1		2					1		1		1				1											
26	2				5													2	1																							
27	7				10																															1	1					
28					2													1															1									
29																		1																								
30	1				1	1																																				
31	1				1													1															2									
32	1				1																												2									
33					1																												1									
34					1																																					
35	1				9													3					1																			
36	1				5	2																																				
37					2																																					
38																		1																								
39																																							1			
TOTAL	398	70	1	4	1143	465	40	18	21	4	4	8	7	10	2	13	1	93	23	13	4	10	5	4	2	3	8	21	5	2	5	1	201	4	7	10	3	2	3	2	1	6

Figure 12.8. Spreadsheet, taken from the database, summarizes the distribution of motif types found along the boundary sites (Nos. 1-39) at Puakō.

4400	4500	5100	5120	5130	5200	5500	5510	5620	6100	6600	7100	7110	7125	7120	7121	7122	7205	7210	7220	7220	7232	7400	7400	7411	7500	7510	7600	7610	7700	7710	8000	8010	TOTAL
1	1		1	1	4	2	1			1		1	38	27	1	3	16		7	2		209	5	18	9		1	2	17	20	269	1	2717
																														2	1	1	9
																						1									3		15
					1									1					1		1		2				1		1		9	2	118
																															1		3
													3									1	1		1						4		24
					1									1	2		1		2			8					1		1		8		68
																																	7
								1								1	1										1				3		36
														1			1	1				2									6		57
														1			4														1		14
																															1		16
																														3			3
																	2					2			1				1		5		50
																	1						1								4		11
																							3	11									16
								1													1	1									2		21
														1			1		2	1		1			1				2		9		68
			2	5	2									1			6	2				9	1	6	8	2			6		18		144
														1			1														2		16
								1																									1
																															1		2
																																	1
				2	1	1							1						1			1									7		35
													1				2					3	1						3		4		28
																													1		1		12
																	1												1		3		24
																	1																5
																															1		1
	1																						1								1		6
				3													1														3		12
																															1		5
			1																												3		3
																																	1
			2														3								1						2		22
																																	8
																																	2
																																	1
				3																											3		7
1	1	1	3	11	15	3	1	1	1	6	2	1	54	31	3	3	46	2	10	2	3	238	10	38	14	3	2	2	33	25	372	4	3589

Figure 12.8 continued.

MOTIF TYPES FOUND AT RECORDED SITES ON HAWAI'I ISLAND

MOTIF	1	1	1	1	1	1	1	1	1	1	1	1	1	1	1	1	1	1	1	1	1	1	1	1	1	1	1	1	1	1	1	1	1
TYPE	1	1	1	1	2	2	2	2	2	2	2	2	2	2	2	3	3	3	3	4	4	4	4	4	4	4	4	4	5	6	6	6	7
NUMBER	0	0	1	2	0	0	0	0	0	1	2	2	3	3	4	0	0	1	1	0	0	1	1	2	2	2	3	3	0	0	0	0	0
	0	1	0	0	0	1	2	3	4	0	0	1	0	1	0	0	1	0	1	0	1	0	1	0	1	2	0	1	0	0	1	2	0
LOCATION																																	
'Anaeho'omalu	14			1	40	1	1		10		1					1				40	2	11					2		1				
Kalaoa	4				26	14										1	2			21	13	3							1				
Ka'ūpūlehu	14			3	31	3			4						1	9	2	6		80	13	4		4									2
Pu'uloa	17				32		3	1	22	1						23		2		267	21	47	1				7		1	2			4
Puakō	393	71	2	4	1288	473	40	18	21	4	4	1	8	7		15	2	13	1	140	28	18	4	11	5	4	3	3	8	22	5	2	6
MOTIF TOTAL	442	71	2	8	1417	491	44	19	57	5	5	1	8	7	1	49	6	21	1	548	77	83	5	15	5	4	12	3	11	24	5	2	12

MOTIF	2	2	2	2	3	3	3	3	3	3	4	4	4	4	5	5	5	5	5	5	5	5	5	5	5	6	6	6	6	6	6	6	7	7	7	7	7	7	7	7
TYPE	1	2	2	3	1	3	4	4	5	6	1	2	4	5	1	1	1	2	2	3	5	5	6	6	6	1	2	5	5	6	6	7	1	1	1	1	1	1	1	1
NUMBER	0	0	1	0	0	0	0	2	0	0	0	0	0	0	0	2	3	0	1	0	0	1	1	2	2	0	0	1	2	0	1	0	0	1	1	1	2	2	2	2
	0	0	0	0	0	0	0	0	0	0	0	0	0	0	0	0	0	0	0	0	0	0	0	0	1	0	0	5	0	0	0	0	0	0	1	5	0	1	2	5
LOCATION																																								
'Anaeho'omalu	2	109													1	1		4					1				1		1	8			3	1		4	34	12	3	6
Kalaoa																																								
Ka'ūpūlehu		3				1			1		4	12					109	10	5	1		2			2	1				9							9	9		
Pu'uloa		19		5	1				1		4			1		7	12	10					4	6		3		1		21	12		25	45	6	17	495	313	33	38
Puakō	1	201	4	7	10	3	2	3	2	1	6		1	1	1	3	12	15			3	1		1		1				7		1	2			1	54	31	3	3
MOTIF TOTAL	3	332	4	12	11	4	2	3	4	1	14	12	1	2	2	11	133	39	5	1	3	3	5	7	2	5	1	1	1	45	12	1	30	46	6	22	592	365	39	47

MOTIF	7	7	7	7	7	7	7	7	7	7	7	7	7	7	7	7	7	7	7	7	7	7	7	7	7	7	7	7	7	7	7	8	8	
TYPE	2	2	2	2	2	2	2	2	2	2	2	2	3	3	3	4	4	4	4	4	4	5	5	6	6	6	6	6	6	7	7	0	0	
NUMBER	0	0	0	0	1	1	2	2	2	3	3	4	1	1	1	0	0	0	0	1	2	0	1	0	1	1	1	2	3	0	1	0	1	
	0	2	3	4	0	1	0	1	2	0	1	0	0	1	2	0	1	2	3	0	0	0	0	0	0	2	4	0	0	0	0	0	0	
LOCATION																																		TOTAL
'Anaeho'omalu	265		1	11	5	42	67	3	20	51		1	5	2	2	745	130	25	1	310		36	4	1	5	1	1			15		59	2	2126
Kalaoa																10																15		110
Ka'ūpūlehu	4	1					1									7	2			5	18	2								6		35		435
Pu'uloa	786	27	5	41	24	37	266	8	99	63	10	1	232	17	225	16602	814	42	34	1657		399	101	4	6	3	19	85	33	74	43	269	10	23566
Puakō	46				2		10		2	3						260	11			40	1	14	4	2	2					34	6	383	4	3829
MOTIF TOTAL	1101	28	6	52	31	79	344	11	121	117	10	2	237	19	227	17624	957	67	35	2012	19	451	109	7	13	4	20	85	33	129	49	761	16	30066

Figure 12.9. Spreadsheet, taken from the database, summarizes the distribution of motif types recorded at Sites on Hawai'i Island.

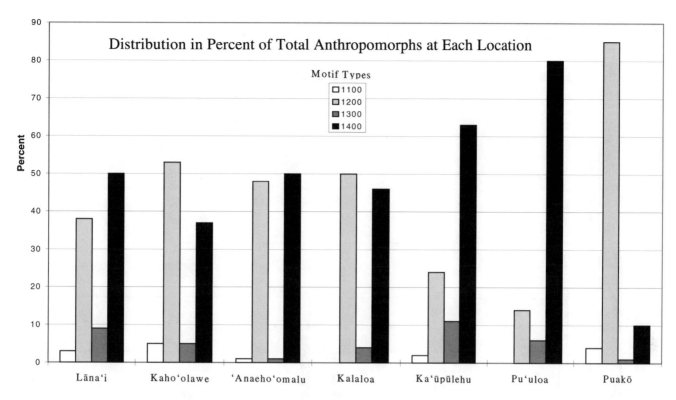

Figure 12.10. Distribution of anthropomorph types for the locations recorded in percent of total anthropomorphs at each location.

It is argued that anthropomorph design changes over time from the 1100 types (stick figures) to the 1400 types (triangle torso figures). Since the majority of figures were either the 1200 or the 1400 types, these predominate for all locations and are about equal for Lānaʻi, Kahoʻolawe, ʻAnaehoʻomalu, and Kalaoa as can be seen in Figure 12.10. However one finds a significant difference between Kaʻūpūlehu and Puʻuloa where the 1400 types predominate, and Puakō where the 1200 types predominate. The distribution of motifs at these locations suggests that Puakō predates Kaʻūpūlehu and Puʻuloa in the production of petroglyphs and, perhaps, the other four locations as well. The preponderance of 1200 types at Puakō may be related to the persistence of tradition at that site. also suggests that the most recent production of petroglyphs occurred at Kaʻūpūlehu and Puʻuloa.

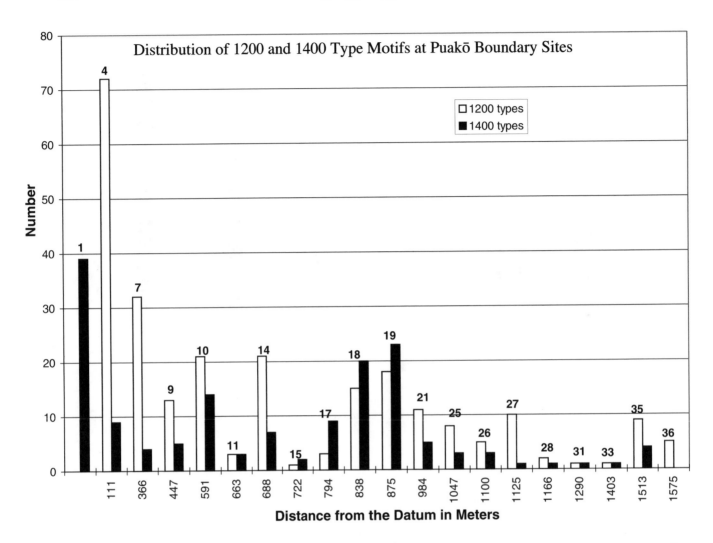

Figure 12.11. Comparison of the numbers of all 1200 and 1400 motif types in relation to distance from the datum at Kāeo 1 (for those Puakō boundary sites which had a significant number of these motifs). The 1200 types number (1403) for Kāeo 1 is omitted because it is disproportionately large. There were no 1400 types at Site 36. Site numbers are indicated at the top of the bars.

During recording of the boundary sites at Puakō it appeared that the number of triangle torso figures increased relative to the number of stick figures as one moved further from Kāeo 1. Because triangle torso figures are thought to be more recent than stick figures, it was assumed that the boundary sites were extended—over time—beyond the original focus of the site, Kāeo 1. The results shown in Figure 12.11 suggest that this was not so. The earlier figure type predominates at most of the sites, and all the way to site 36—1575 meters from Kāeo 1. This may indicate that all boundary sites were carved over the same time period. The presence of Type 1400 suggests the production of that type of petroglyph continued on all sites over time. However, Sites 17, 18 and 19 have a relatively large number of triangular torso figures. Why these sites were chosen for this carving activity is not clear.

It should be mentioned that the boundary sites were confined to a very narrow region while hundreds of square meters of pāhoehoe remained untouched on both sides. Beyond Site 39, the last boundary site, the pāhoehoe disappeared.

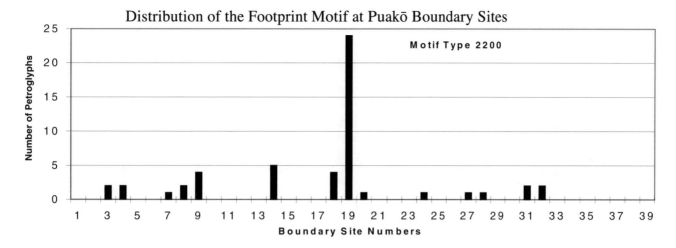

Figure 12.12. Distribution of the footprint motif Type 2200 among the boundary sites of Puakō. The bar for Kāeo 1 (149 footprints) has been omitted for clarity.

Puakō has 201 carvings of footprints, an unusually large number. Only 'Anaeho'omalu comes close to this with 109. Moloka'i was said to have had nearly 500 at one site (Stokes 1910) but we located only 50 there during a brief visit in 1996. The distribution of footprints along the Puakō boundary is interesting. There are 24 prints at Site 19, the most numerous single motif type. Why the relatively large number at this location, a distance of 875 meters from Kāeo 1? Perhaps this is related to the unusual level of activity suggested at this site by the production of triangular torso figures (Figure 12.11) and to the presence of five sails, half of the number of sails at Puakō.

Percentages of the Most Frequent Head Formations for All Locations						
Type	Head Absent	Headdress	Open Circle	Regular	Other	Total
1200	9	1	2	65	22	96
1400	11	2	2	64	18	93

Figure 12.13. Percentages of the most frequent head formations are summarized for the 1200 and the 1400 anthropomorph types.

The preponderance of head shapes is "Regular," that is, having a round cupule-like head. As can be seen in the Typology for anthropomorphic features, there are many variations for heads, although not in large numbers. The category "Other" is too large to be left unexamined. Future investigation of the data for this category may require additions to the list for head types.

MOTIF TYPE NUMBER	1200			1400	
	Male	Female		Male	Female
Kahoʻolawe	17	2		6	0
Lānaʻi	47	6		20	4
ʻAnaehoʻomalu	6	0		2	1
Kaʻūpūlehu	9	1		6	1
Puʻuloa	3	0		2	6
Puakō	363	25		7	2
Total	445	34		43	14
% of anthropomorphs	25.7	2.0		4.6	1.5

Figure 12.14. Distribution of figures in which gender is indicated.

Gender is indicated on many anthropomorphs. A count of this occurrence is shown in Figure 12.14. Since Polynesian society was male dominated, it is not surprising that there are more males indicated than females. Females have a slight edge in triangle torso types at Puʻuloa, however, a location where birth seemed to be emphasized. The much larger number for which male gender is indicated in Type 1200 may simply be that it is easier, and perhaps inadvertent, to extend the trunk of a stick figure.

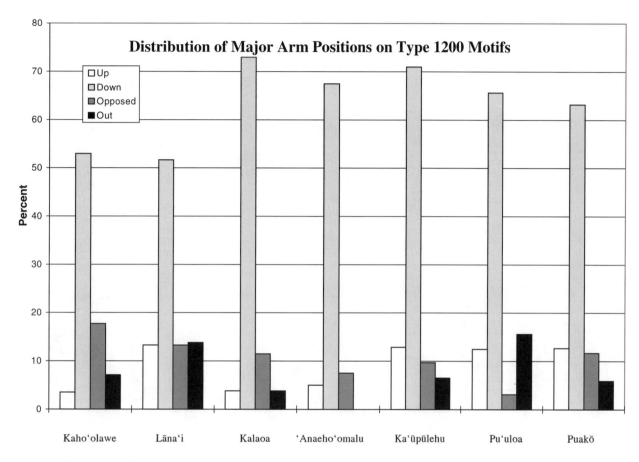

Figure 12.15. Distribution of Up, Down, Opposed, and Out arm positions shown in percent of the total motif Type 1200 at each location.

It was thought that some significance might exist in the position of the arms, particularly on stick figures (Type 1200) which are capable of a considerable degree of expression. Arm positions were recorded in 93% of all Type 1200 anthropomorphs (Figure 12.15) and in 66% of all Type 1400 anthropomorphs (Figure 12.16). A summary of arm positions for all locations is shown in Figure 12.17. The ordinary human stance with both arms Down predominates and amounts to two thirds of the positions for Type 1200 and Type 1400. The arm position of Up and Opposed are more prominent on Type 1200 while the arm position Out is more numerous on Type 1400. There does not seem to be any significant preference for a specific arm position at any location.

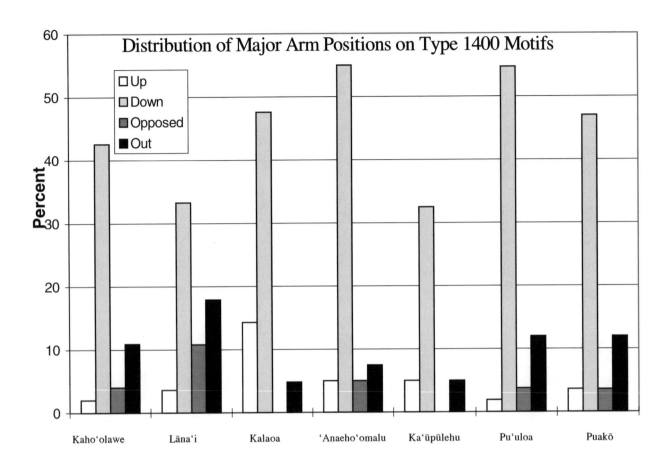

Figure 12.16. Distribution of Up, Down, Opposed, and Out arm positions in percent of the total of motif Type 1400 at each location.

Major Arm Positions in Percent for All Locations					
Type	Up	Down	Opposed	Out	Total
1200	12	62	12	7	93
1400	3	44	6	13	66

Figure 12.17. A summary of arm positions at all locations for the motif types 1200 and 1400 as percent of total motif type.

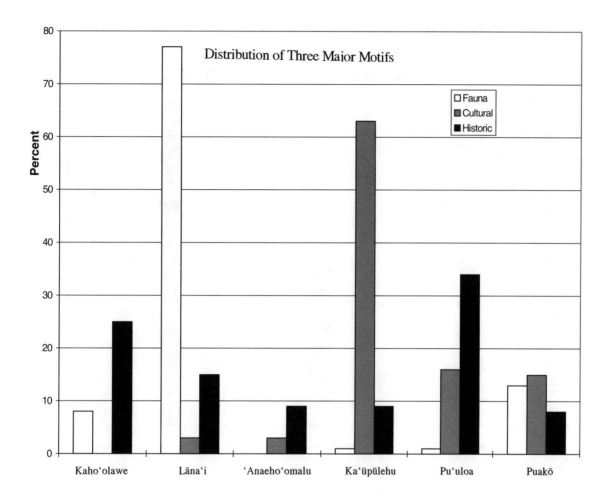

Figure 12.18. A comparison of how the motifs of fauna, cultural artifacts (including papamū), and historic elements are distributed among two islands and the Hawaiʻi sites. (Data taken from the spreadsheets and calculated as percent of the total for all locations of a given motif type).

Lānaʻi has the majority of fauna petroglyphs, specifically dogs (Figure 12.18). Why this is so is unknown. Kaʻūpūlehu has the majority of cultural petroglyphs (sails and papamū). The high relative numbers of Type 1400 motifs and the unusually high quality of the petroglyphs, suggest that Kaʻūpūlehu was a high-status site. Puʻuloa has the largest percent of historic petroglyphs (lettering and script). Kahoʻolawe is next in number of historic petroglyphs, both goats and lettering, which indicates that petroglyph production continued at these two locations well into historic times.

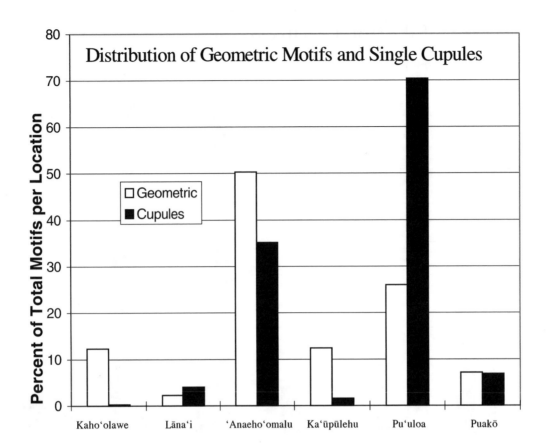

Figure 12.19. Comparison of the distribution of geometrics and cupules in percent of the total motifs for a location. Geometric motifs (Types 7100-7710 excepting Type 7400) and all Type 7400 cupules are included. This chart shows the emphasis on geometrics at 'Anaeho'omalu, and on cupules at Pu'uloa which also has a large share of geometric motifs.

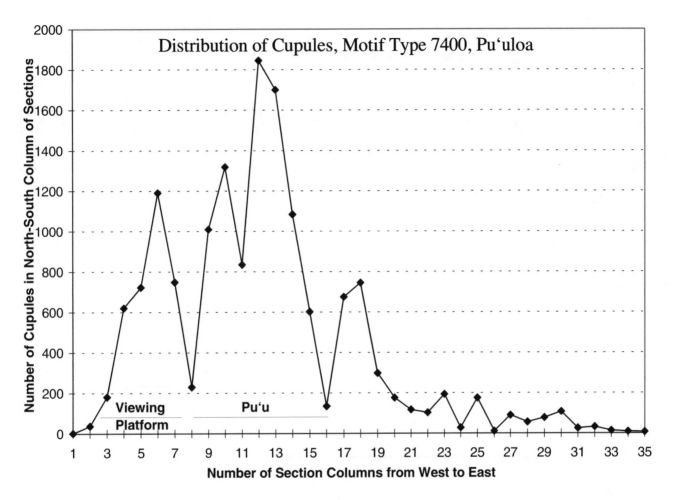

Figure 12.20. Distribution of cupules at Pu'uloa. The number of cupules is taken as the sum of cupules in each north-south column of sections (see Figure 7.7 for section arrangement). The sum is plotted for each section column (every 10 meters) in the west to east direction. The locations of the viewing platform and the pu'u are indicated. The plot begins west of the viewing platform and continues eastward for 350 meters.

Because cupules (poho) are the dominant motif at Pu'uloa (of a total 23566 petroglyphs, 16602 cupules were documented) it is interesting to consider Figure 12.20 which shows the distribution of cupules in the vicinity of the pu'u. Cupule numbers increase rapidly as the pu'u is approached from the west and decrease to the east. The low numbers at columns 8, 16, and 24 are due to gaps in the lava. Flat areas of lava occur around the viewing platform and just east of the pu'u; this partially accounts for the high concentration of petroglyphs found in these sections. This chart also shows the distribution of cupules as one proceeds along the trail from west to east over a distance of 350 meters.

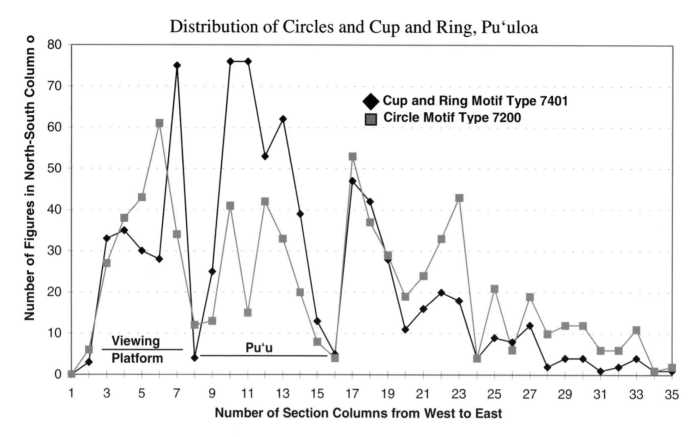

Figure 12.21. Distribution of cup and ring (Type 7401) and circle (Type 7200) motifs in the vicinity of the puʻu. These counts were determined in the same way as were cupules in Figure 12.20.

Cup and ring and circle motifs also occur frequently around the puʻu as demonstrated in Figure 12.21. This chart was created to determine if these motifs had a relation to the puʻu in the same way as do the cupules. Their distribution is very similar to cupules, but they occur in smaller numbers: the total is 814 cup and ring and 786 circles, one twentieth of the cupule total.

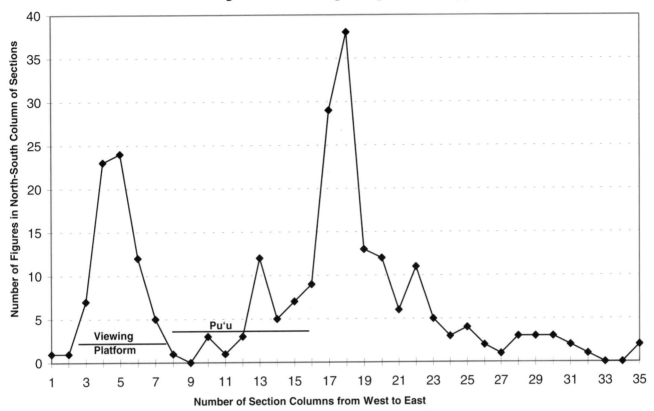

Figure 12.22. Distribution of triangle torso anthropomorphs in the vicinity of the puʻu. These counts were determined in the same way as were cupules in Figure 12.20.

As can be seen in Figure 12.10, triangle torso anthropomorphs are relatively prominent at Puʻuloa. Figure 12.22 shows that this motif is concentrated at locations near the viewing platform and just east of the puʻu where flat areas of lava are to be found. The low concentration of this motif on the puʻu indicates that the importance of this motif is not associated with the puʻu itself, as are the motifs shown in Figures 12.20 and 12.21. However, the concentration of motif Type 1400 decreases at about the same rate as does that of the other motifs as one proceeds eastward along the trail going away from the puʻu. Perhaps anthropomorphs postdated the poho.

EPILOGUE

First of all, I would like to thank Georgia Lee for giving me the privilege of writing a short epilogue to this truly remarkable and much-needed study of Hawaiian petroglyphs. My first encounter with the amazing rock art of Hawai'i was in 1975. I had just arrived from the mainland and was beginning a new life in the islands. It was at this time that I discovered the mysterious carvings in stone.

The Queen Ka'ahumanu Highway had just opened, providing a unique gateway to the discoveries I was about to encounter. This was a remarkable time, for the newly constructed highway exposed the Kona-Kohala coast to the public, connecting the sleepy fishing village of Kailua-Kona with the port of Kawaiihae, nearly thirty miles distant. Parking my car along the road, I would scarcely see another vehicle for hours at time—unlike today with its constant stream of traffic shuttling back and forth between the big Kohala resorts.

My friends, Fred Cabalis and Calvin Pacheco, now deceased, were the first to take me on the many long hikes along this historic coastline. I was amazed by the richness of the archaeological sites in the area, particularly 'Anaeho'omalu and Kīholo[1] bays. We would hike for hours, Fred on the lookout for goats or Calvin for the perfect spot to cast his net.

The Kings Trail was still mostly intact at that time. The remarkable Trail had been built around 1800 and stretched for miles. I would walk along the trail and find areas of petroglyphs, often spending hours at a time looking at the motifs in the stone and contemplating what the ancient Hawaiians were trying to say. I was particularly drawn to one area near the present-day Kona Village resort, Ka'ūpūlehu, where there are some of the most remarkable petroglyphs I have ever seen.[2] Aside from the well-known sail motifs, I found a small field with 'fighting warriors' and the most remarkable of all, a dancer with a feathered headdress—to my eyes a direct link to the Marquesas and Tahiti.

At that time, the Kona-Kohala coast was basically undeveloped, with the Kona Village Resort and the Mauna Kea being the only resorts on the coastline. This area was an archaeologist's dream, with both minor and major sites everywhere. For the most part, they have been lost to the developers' bulldozers. Although permits were obtained, only limited archaeological surveys were done. Projects were always grounded in the "good of the people," offering jobs and prosperity for all—only to have the bubble burst in the early 1990s. Resort developments usually included a token "Hawaiian" element, making minor attempts to appease the locals when, in reality, they needlessly destroyed archaeological sites with their golf courses, hotels, and luxury residences.

A friend of mine was recently walking around one of the newest hotels when he was asked to not stray from the path because it was a sensitive area to Hawaiians. This is the same hotel that constructed a golf course over petroglyph sites, habitation caves, and burials—areas where I used to walk.[3]

Hawai'i's economy is in shambles today due, in part, to what I believe is the disregard of the 'āina (land). Newspapers report massive layoffs at major banks and well-known retailers. Major hotels built on speculative Asian money during the boom period of the 1980s now suffer from low occupancy and foreclosures. These are the same hotels responsible for destroying the many sites that provided an important link to Hawai'i's past.

The current depressed economic situation has led to social and economic problems that range from domestic violence and drug abuse to an exodus of Hawaiians for "work" destinations at Las Vegas, Los Angeles, and Seattle. In my opinion, the future for Hawai'i lies—not in designer handbags and luxury goods—but diversified agriculture and eco-tourism. Petroglyphs are an important part of eco-tourism, nonrenewable assets of historical importance, both spiritually and physically.

The petroglyph sites, along with all major cultural sites, should be protected once and for all, with proper conservation and preservation efforts. This is the true future for the islands—a future lying in the past, a gift from Hawaiians of old, mana manifesting itself in its true sense.

Mark Blackburn, Hilo, Hawai'i

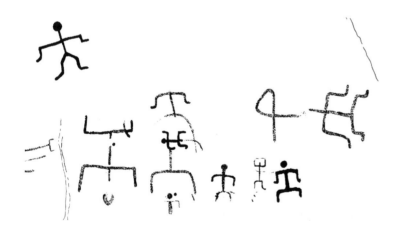

[1] Kīholo bay is an oasis with fresh water springs and fishponds. It is sad to note that several luxury residences have been built on this historic site by a few very wealthy people with total disregard for the local environment.

[2] On the drawing boards today are massive housing developments slated for this site. Local opposition may prevent such development, but in reality it may be poor economic times that will ultimately spare it.

[3] This hotel, with total disregard for the environment, blew up the reef at night, causing severe ecological damage. Subsequently, swimmers reported all sorts of strange rashes and lesions. The Sierra Club intervened; litigation is in process.

APPENDIX A: DATING

DATING THE PETROGLYPHS

Petroglyphs are notoriously difficult to date. At times there are elements in a design that provide clues: an historic ship, or a human figure holding a gun, etc. But for absolute dates, much research still needs to be done. Techniques are being developed and there is not only progress, but some genuine expectation of providing absolute dates in the future. The attempts at dating petroglyphs in Hawai‘i thus far by Ronald Dorn, furnish us with dates that are well within the time-frame for occupation.

In general, dating efforts for rock art must be viewed with caution. As noted by Dorn (1996), there are problems discriminating between the carbon being dated, and that which comes from prior organic weathering episodes. Basalt flows in particular present difficulties in this regard. Petroglyph samples could have experienced multiple prior episodes of organic weathering. A considerable amount of research concerning the dating of rock art is now underway at various sites around the world. Much of this research involves attempts to date organic components of rock paintings.

Rosenfeld and Smith (1997) point out that a recent trend questions the value of "style" as a device for dealing with rock art dating because "it is too imprecise." However, the study of style should not be discarded; such analyses can be undertaken in a rigorous manner through the use of stylistic sequences (ibid.:407). Style may vary with the social contexts of its production, for it is unlikely that any one culture will have only one single representative style but probably will have a range of styles for both the individual and the group. Patterning may vary according to age, gender, or social factors. Thus differences in style may not relate to time or space but could have a connection to social contexts; " . . . the challenge will be to differentiate those traits which are due to temporal or geographic factors from those due to the influences of social context" (ibid.:408). An excellent summary of the uses of style in archaeology can be seen in Conkey and Hastorf (1990).

While we have relied heavily upon style as a key element in our study of Hawaiian petroglyphs, some of our observations have come from a careful study of superposition of design elements, and the physical location of varying styles of figure type. The archaeological work by Cleghorn (1980) at Hilina Pali and of Hammatt and Folk (1980) at Kalaoa O‘oma provides firm stratigraphic evidence for the evolution of figure types in Hawai‘i. With that in mind, it is interesting to compare the results of the 1996 dating project from Kaho‘olawe Island.

As part of the documentation of Kaho‘olawe Island's petroglyphs, provisional dates were obtained by Dorn using radiocarbon analyses from accelerator mass spectrometry (AMS).[1] These were the first petroglyphs from Hawai‘i to be dated by this or any other analytical method (Stasack, Dorn and Lee 1996).

The approach to dating is to obtain a minimum age for the petroglyph by collecting carbon that accumulated after the petroglyph was made. (Charcoal was located from a stratigraphic position on top of the rock, and it postdated the petroglyph). Organic matter was also found in weathering rinds, deposited by organisms that have grown and left remains after petroglyph manufacture. In both cases, a coating of silica (cf. Curtiss et al. 1985) had been deposited over the organic matter, encapsulating it. Examples of organic matter encapsulated in the same manner at other sites can be found in Dorn et al. (1992); Nobbs and Dorn (1993), and Dorn (1994).

Petroglyphs were sampled in such a way as to mimic natural erosion patterns. Pieces of basalt

(~1-2 mm diameter) were chipped from each sampled petroglyph, taken from microspots where the rock coating would most likely start to grow. Fragments of these samples were then examined with light and electron microscopes to assess the microstratigraphic context of the organic matter. If the organic matter appeared to be in an appropriately layered context, it was processed further.

For samples that showed evidence of charcoal, the upper layers of silica were removed with a tungsten-carbide needle. Then the charcoal was scraped and collected. Those samples with organic substances in weathering rinds had the underlying rind scraped and collected. These were then subjected to chemical pretreatment with hydrofluoric acid, hydrochloric acid, and sodium hydroxide and vigorous washing with deionized water between treatments. These organic residues were then submitted to an accelerator facility in New Zealand for radiocarbon analysis.

Samples examined for layering were mounted in epoxy and polished for examination by electron microscopy and wavelength dispersive electron microprobe analysis. The samples were scanned from end-to-end and the development of the coating was characterized by microchemical analysis, as well as backscatter electron microscopy. The microstratigraphy was examined carefully for unconformities that would indicate past erosional events.

Samples were taken from Hakioawa (7); the Ahupū Iki area (13); Kaukaukapapa, (6); and Loaʻa (13). Petroglyphs chosen were those that may provide information on periods of occupation, historical and cultural clues, and the emergence of the triangle torso figures. Motif types were selected (stick figures, dogs, triangle figures) that might span the widest time period up to the obviously historical motifs such as goats, names, and inscriptions.

Five other samples were examined by electron microscopy to assess the relative development of the rock coating. In two cases, there was a visual difference. One image had three components with different degrees of coating suggesting that the motif was re-pecked at different times in the past.

All of the dates listed (in order of age) below are the calendar ages assigned to the 'best estimate' of the radiocarbon age, measured for each petroglyph (Figure A.1).

K23, a stick figure (site 485D, panel 2-2), AMS age, AD 983-1168. This stick figure, K23, is the earliest date obtained. This unit was an obvious selection due to its heavy patination which rendered it nearly invisible.
K33, stick figure (site 135D, panel 9-2), AMS age, AD 992-1168.
K22, a fishhook (site 480I, panel 2), AMS age, AD 1230-1290.
K12, stick figure (site 110AP, Panel 5A-2), AMS age, AD 1282-1404.
K11, stick figure (site 110AP, panel 3B-1), AMS age, AD 1290-1400.
K30, dog (site 135C, panel 9-3), AMS age, AD 1286-1416.
K28, stick figure (site 135E, panel 1-1), AMS age, AD 1037-1272.
K16a, stick figure (site 121G, panel 2-1), AMS age, AD 1301-1438.
K16b, triangle torso figure (site 121 G, panel 2-2), AMS age, AD 1432-1634.
K15a, a stick figure (site 121G, panel 1), AMS age, AD 1320-1440.
K26, stick figure (site 486N, panel 6-3), AMS age, AD 1460-1640.
K10, stick figure (site 110AP, Panel 4A-1-1), AMS age, AD 1660-1950.
K19, triangle figure (site 121G, panel 8), AMS age, AD 1650-1950.

A triangle torso figure from the gulch west of Ahupū Iki (K16b) provided a date of AD 1301-1434. (This age estimate was older than expected and may be due to contamination by an ancient organic material). If verified in the future, this age determination contradicts the hypothesis that the triangle torso style emerged around AD 1600.

Aside from this one result, the dates obtained by these experiments are consistent with the archaeological findings on Kahoʻolawe. Further dating efforts should clarify these preliminary conclusions and help identify the periods more exactly, although it should be kept in mind that there is not a great time-depth in the islands of Hawaiʻi.

[1] The Kahoʻolawe Conveyance Commission provided support for the collection of 39 samples from four petroglyph sites. Primary support for dating 13 of the samples was granted by the Spoehr Foundation, Honolulu, with supplemental support from the University of Hawaiʻi Committee for the Preservation and Study of Hawaiian Language, Art and Culture which funded approximately one-half of the second group of samples. In Phase I, dates were obtained for six petroglyphs and for an additional seven in Phase II.

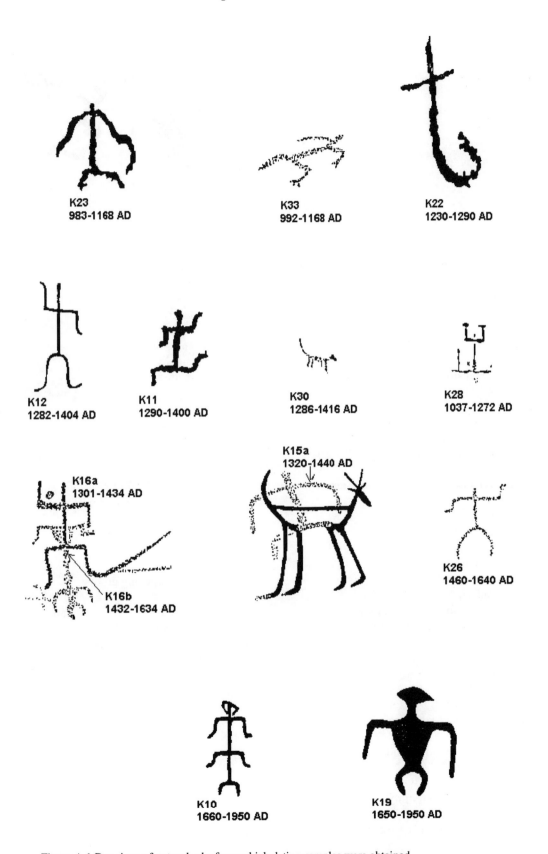

Figure A.1 Drawings of petroglyphs from which dating samples were obtained.

GLOSSARY

'a'ā: lava flow, rough
'ahā: four times
ahupua'a: land division
'āina: land, earth
akua: god
ali'i: chief or chiefly class
'anā'anā: evil sorcery
ao: light, day
'aumakua: ancestral spirit guides
'elepaio: bird, flycatcher
hā: four; to breathe
hala: error, sin
hale: house
Hawaii nei: this [beloved] Hawaii
heiau: religious shrine
'ie'ie: woody climber (*Freycinetia arborea*)
'ili: land section
kāhili: ceremonial regalia, feathered standards
kahuna: priest
kahuna 'anā'anā: sorcerer
kahuna kālai: carving expert
kālai: to carve, cut
kanaka: man, Hawaiian
kaona: secret meaning
kapu: forbidden (taboo)
ka'upu: bird, probably an albatross
keia manawa: this time, this turn
keikei: child
ke'i pōhaku: image in rock
kiwa'a: pilot bird
ko'a: fish shrine
kōkua: help, assist
kōnane: game played on papamū game boards
kūkini: runners
kumu: source, heredity, foundation
kupua: demi-god
lena: to stretch out, bend
Lono: god of rain and fertility
lua iki: small hole
luakini: heiau where human sacrifices were made

lupe: kite
maka'āinana: people in general, populace
makani: wind
makahiki: spring festival
mālama: to preserve
mana: supernatural power, force
manu hakerere: kite (Easter Island)
mauka: inland
menehune: legendary "little people"
moku: district
mo'o: mythical lizard
mu'umu'u: a woman's loose gown
'ohana: kin group
'ōhi'a: a type of tree
pā: fence
pāhoehoe: smooth and ropy lava flow
palena: boundary
papamū: game board for playing kōnane
piko: the umbilical stump of a newborn or the place to put it
pō: underworld, darkness
pōhaku: rock, stone
poho: cupule
polissoir: sharpening groove
puka: hole
pū'olo: container, to tie in a bundle
pu'u: protuberance, bulge
ti: ki, a woody plant in the lily family [*Cordyline terminalis*]
ulua: fish, jack crevalle
wahi pana: legendary place
wāwae: foot

BIBLIOGRAPHY

Aitken, R. T. 1930. *Ethnology of Tubuai*. Bishop Museum Bulletin 70. B. P. Bishop Museum, Department of Anthropology.

Baker, Albert S. 1918. More Petroglyphs. *Thrum's Hawaiian Annual for 1918*:131-135.

    1923. Still More Petroglyphs. *Thrum's Hawaiian Annual for 1920*:49-52.

    1931. Puna Petroglyphs. *Thrum's Hawaiian Annual for 1931*:62-67.

Barrera, W., Jr. 1971. Anaehoomalu: A Hawaiian Oasis. *Pacific Anthropological Records* 15.

    1971. A Reconstruction of its History, Appendix. In *Pacific Anthropological Records*, edited by W. Barrera, Jr., pp. 109-113. B. P. Bishop Museum, Honolulu.

    1977. National Register of Historic Places Inventory, Nomination Form. United States Department of the Interior.

Barrera, W., Jr. 1984. Kahoʻolawe Archaeology: An Overview. *Hawaiian Archaeology* 1:31-43.

Barrow, L. 1998. The Birdman in Art and Mythology in Marginal Polynesia—Easter Island, Hawaiʻi, and New Zealand. *Easter Island in Pacific Context: South Seas Symposium*. C. M. Stevenson, G. Lee and F. J. Morin, eds. Easter Island Foundation, Los Osos, California.

Barrow, T. 1967. Material evidence of the bird-man concept in Polynesia. *Polynesian Culture History: Essays in honor of Kenneth P. Emory*. B. P. Bishop Museum Special Publication 56:191-214.

    1972. *Art and Life in Polynesia*. C. E. Tuttle, Vermont.

    1984. *An Illustrated Guide to Maori Art*. University of Hawaii Press, Honolulu.

Beaglehole, J. C. 1967. *The Exploration of the Pacific*. Stanford University Press, Stanford.

Beckwith, Martha. 1970. *Hawaiian Mythology*. University of Hawaii Press, Honolulu.

Beckwith, Martha. n.d. Field Notes. Department of Anthropology, Hawaiian Sources Collection, pp. 384-397. B. P. Bishop Museum, Honolulu.

Bennett, W. C. 1976. *Archaeology of Kauai*. Krauss, New York.

Bidault, J. 1945. *Piroques et Pagaies*, Paris.

Bonk, W. J. 1965. Site HV-225. In *The Archaeological Resources of Hawaii Volcanoes National Park, Part 3*, edited by K. P. Emory, E. J. Ladd, and L. J. Soehren. B. P. Bishop Museum, Honolulu.

Brigham, W. T. 1906. Old Hawaiian Carvings. *B. P. Bishop Museum Memoir* 2.

Brodie, Walter. 1851. *Pitcairn's Island and the Islanders in 1850 . . . Reports of all Commanders of H M Ships Arriving There . . . Since 1800*. Whittaker, London.

Brown, J. M. 1927. *Peoples and Problems of the Pacific*. J. M. Sears Publication, Honolulu.

Buck, Peter H. 1938. *Vikings of the Sunrise*. University of Chicago Press, Chicago.

    1957. *Arts and Crafts of Hawaii*. B. P. Bishop Museum, Honolulu.

    1968. *Polynesian Migrations. Ancient Hawaiian Civilizations*. Charles E. Tuttle Co., Vermont.

Burley, D. V. 1994. As a prescription to rule: The royal tomb of Malaʻe Lahi and the 19th-century Tongan kingship. *Antiquity* 68:504-517.

Bushnell, O. A. 1979. *The Return of Lono*. University Press of Hawaii, Honolulu.

Candelot, J-L. 1980. Note préliminaire sur les pierres gravées de Tubuai. *Journal de la Société de Océanistes* 66-67, Tome XXXVI:133-139.

Carter, L. A. and G. F. Somers. 1990. *Here today lava tomorrow: Archaeological work in Hawaii Volcanos National Park, 1987-1989*. National Park Service, Pacific Area Office, Honolulu.

Ch'i-Lu, Ch'en 1972. Early Chinese Art and its possible Influence in the Pacific Basin. In *The Aboriginal Art of Taiwan, Vol. 2, Asia*, edited by Noel Barnard, pp. 395-430. Intercultural Arts Press, New York.

Charlot, Jean 1979. The hula in Hawaiian life and thought. In *Honolulu Magazine*.

Cleghorn, P. L. and D. W. Cox. [1976]. Phase 1 Archaeological Survey of the Hilina Pali Petroglyph Cave (Site HV-383) and Associated Sites, Hawaii Volcanoes National Park. Department of Anthropology, Report, B. P. Bishop Museum.

Cleghorn, P. L. 1980. *The Hilina Pali Petroglyph Cave, Hawai'i Island.* B. P. Bishop Museum
Report.

Conkey, M. W. and C.A. Hastorf, eds. 1990. *The Uses of Style in Archaeology.* Cambridge University Press, Cambridge.

Cook, J. and J. King. 1784. *A voyage to the Pacific Ocean . . . on His Majesty's Ships Resolution
and Discovery.* G. Nicol and T. Cadell, London.

Corney, B.G., ed. 1915. *The Quest and Occupation of Tahiti by Emissaries of Spain during the
Years 1722-1776,* London.

Cox, D. W. [1974]. Fieldwork Report on Mapping of Puuloa Petroglyph Field-Puna Site HA-
HV-225. Report, Hawaii Volcanoes National Park.

Cox, J. H. [1961]. Petroglyphs at Pohue Bay. Manuscript, Department of Anthropology, B. P.
Bishop Museum.

Cox, J. H. 1971. Appendix B: Results of a Preliminary Investigation of the Anaehoomalu Petroglyphs. In *Anaehoomalu: A Hawaiian Oasis. Pacific Anthropological Records,* pp. 114-126.
B. P. Bishop Museum, Honolulu.

Cox, J. H. and W. H. Davenport. 1974. *Hawaiian Sculpture.* B. P. Bishop Museum Press, Honolulu.

Cox, J. H. n.d. Corrections and additions to Bonk [1965]. B. P. Bishop Museum, Department of
Anthropology.

Cox, J. H. and E. Stasack. 1970. *Hawaiian Petroglyphs.* B. P. Bishop Museum, Honolulu.

Curtiss, B., J. B. Adams and M. S. Ghiorso. 1985. Origin, development and chemistry of silica-
alumina rock coatings from the semiarid regions of the island of Hawaii. *Geochemica et
Cosmochimica Acta* 49:49-56.

Daws, G. 1980. *A Dream of Islands.* W.W. Norton and Co., New York.

Daws, G. 1994. *Shoal of Time: A History of the Hawaiian Islands.* University Press of Hawaii,
Honolulu.

Dening, G. 1980. *Islands and Beaches. Discourse on a silent land: Marquesas 1774-1880.* The
University of Press of Hawaii, Honolulu.

Did Gaetano or Cook Discover the Sandwich Islands. 1967. In *American Activities in the Central
Pacific 1790-1870,* edited by R. G. Ward, pp. 187-188. The Gregg Press, Ridgewood, New
Jersey.

Dixon, B., A. Carpenter, F. Eble, C. Mitchell and M. Major. 1995. Community Growth and Heiau Construction: Possible Evidence of Political Hegemony at the Site of Kaunolu, Lana'i,
Hawai'i. *Asian Perspectives* 34:229-255.

Dorn, R. I., P. B. Clarkson, M. F. Nobbs, L. L. Loendorf and D.S. Whitley. 1992. New approach
to the radiocarbon dating of rock varnish, with examples from dry lands. *Annals of the Association of American Geographers* 82:136-151.

Dorn, R. I. 1994. Dating petroglyphs with a 3-tier rock varnish approach. In *New Light on Old
Art: Advances in Hunterer-Gatherer Rock Art Research,* edited by D.S. Whitley and L. Loendorf, pp. 12-36. UCLA Institute for Archaeology Monograph Series, Los Angeles.
1996. A change of perception. *La Pintura* 23:10-11.

Dunbar, H. R. 1987. Kaunolu Village National Historic Landmark. National Register of Historic
Places Inventory, Nomination Form. United States Department of the Interior.

Edwards, E. and S. Millerstrom. 1995. Peintures rupestres de la vallée de Eiaone à Hiva Oa. *Bulletin de la Société des Etudes Oceaniénnes* 267:5-17.

Ellis, W. 1782 *An Authentic Narrative of a Voyage Performed by Captain Cook and Captain
Clerke, in His Majesty's Ships Resolution and Discovery During the Years 1776, 1777,
1778, 1779 and 1780.* Robinson, Sewell, and Debrett, London.
1823. Narrative of a tour through Hawaii. In *Hawaiian Gazette,* Honolulu.
1979. *Journal of William Ellis.* Charles E. Tuttle Co., Vermont.

Emerson, J. 1893. The Long Voyages of the Ancient Hawaiians. *Papers of the Hawaiian Historical Society* 5.

Emory, K. P. 1922. *Rock carvings and paintings of Kaupo, Maui.* B. P. Bishop Museum.
1924. *The Island of Lanai.* B. P. Bishop Museum Bulletin 12.
1951. Ancient carving is discovered on Kauai. In *Honolulu Advertiser,* p.1, Honolulu.
1955. Oahu's fascinating petroglyphs. In *Paradise of the Pacific,* pp. 9-11, 26.
1956. Acres of petroglyphs. In *Honolulu Advertiser,* p. 3, Honolulu.

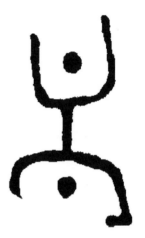

Emory, K. P. 1961. Le rocher des petroglyphes de Tipaerui (Tahiti). *Bulletin de la Société de Etudes Océaniennes* 135:281-287.

Emory, K. P. 1979. The Societies. *The Prehistory of Polynesia*. Jesse D. Jennings, ed. Harvard University Press.

Emory, K. P., J. H. Cox, W. J. Bonk, Y. H. Sinoto and D. B. Barrere. [1959]. Natural and cultural history report on the Kalapana extension of the Hawaii National Park. Report, B. P. Bishop Museum.

Emory, K. P. and L. J. Soehren. [1961]. Archaeological and historical survey of Honokohau Area, North Kona, Hawaii. Report.

Emory, K. P., E. J. Ladd and L. J. Soehren. [1965]. Additional sites, test excavations and petroglyphs. The Archaeological Resources of Hawaii Volcanoes National Park. Report, B. P. Bishop Museum.

Farley, J. K. 1898. The pictured ledge of Kauai. *Thrum's Hawaiian Annual for 1898*:119-125.

Feher, J. 1969. *Hawai'i A Pictorial History*. B. P. Bishop Museum Press, Honolulu.

Feldman, J. 1985. Ban Chiang and its importance to the art of the Pacific. *Ban Chiang: Discovery of a lost Bronze Age*, pp. 6-7. Hawaiian Committee for the Humanities.

Finney, B. R. 1997. Voyaging canoes and the settlement of Polynesia. *Science* 196:1277-1285.

Forbes, Rev. A. O. 1883. The Decrease of the Hawaiian People and the Causes Assigned for it. *Hawaiian Gazette*, 10 January. [An Essay read before the Honolulu Social Science Association, January 2, 1883].

Fornander, A. 1880. *An account of the Polynesian race: Its origins and migrations and the ancient history of the Hawaiian people to the times of Kamehamaha I.* Trubner, London.

Garanger, J. 1980. Prospections archéologiques de l'îlot Fenuano et des vallees Aiurua et Vaiote a Tahiti. *Journal de la Société des Océanistes* 66-67:77-104.

Geologic Map of the Island of Hawaii. 1996. USGS.

Gifford, E. W. 1929. *Tongan Society*. B. P. Bishop Museum Bulletin 61.

Gill, S. D. 1982. *Beyond the primitive: The religions of nonliterate peoples*. Prentice-Hall, New Jersey.

Gillett, R. 1987. *Traditional Tuna Fishing: A Study at Satawal, Central Caroline Islands*. B. P. Bishop Museum Bulletins in Anthropology 1.

Glidden, C. 1995. Lines of Descent: Of Umbilical Cords, Ancestors and Ahupua'a. *Rapa Nui Journal* 9:39-46.

Gosser, D. and B. Dixon. 1998.An organizational analysis of Kaunolu, Lana'i, Hawai'i. In *Easter Island in Pacific Context: South Seas Symposium*. C. M. Stevenson, G. Lee and F. J. Morin, eds. Pp. 253-258. Easter Island Foundation, Los Osos, California.

Graves, M. W. and C. Erkelens. 1991. Who's in control? Method and Theory in Hawaiian Archaeology. *Asian Perspectives* 30:1-17.

Graves, M. W. and D. J. Addison. 1995. The Polynesian settlement of the Hawaiian archipelago: Integrating models and method in archaeological interpretation. *World Archaeology* 26:380-399.

Guiot, H. 1995. Protohistoric rafts of the Society Islands. *Rapa Nui Journal* 9:21-23.

Haddon, A. C. and J. Hornell. 1975. *Canoes of Oceania*. B. P. Bishop Museum Press, Honolulu.

Hammatt, H. H. and W. H. Folk. [1980]. Archaeological excavations within the proposed Keohole Agricultural Park, Kalaoa-O'oma, Kona, Hawaii Island. Report: State of Hawaii, Dept. of Agriculture.

Handy, E. S. C. 1927. *Polynesian Religion*. B. P. Bishop Museum Bulletin 34.
    1940. Perspectives in Polynesian religion. *Journal of the Polynesian Society* 49:309-327.
    1943. Two unique petroglyphs in the Marquesas which point to Easter Island and Malaysia. *Studies in the Anthropology of Oceania and Asia*. Papers of the Peabody Museum of American Anthropology and Ethnology 20:22-31.

Handy, E. S. C. and E. Handy. 1972. *Native Planters in Old Hawaii: Their Life, Lore, and Environment*. B. P. Bishop Museum Bulletin 233.

Hanson, F. A. 1982. Female Pollution in Polynesia? *Journal of the Polynesian Society* 91:335-381.

Henry, L. L. 1998. Kites in Polynesia: Replicative experiments and Hawaiian petroglyphs. *Rapa Nui Journal* 12:45-47.

Hino, L. [1989]. An interpretative and management plan. Puako Petroglyph Archaeological Park, Hawai'i. Mauna Lani Resorts.

Ho, J. M. 1988. The Quest for Kahikoleihonua: A Comparative Analysis of Three Major Petroglyph Sites on the Island of Hawaii. Thesis, University of Hawaii at Manoa, Honolulu.

Holcomb, R. T. 1987. Eruptive history and long-term behavior of Kilauea Volcano. In *Volcanism*

in Hawaii, edited by R. W. Decker, T. L. Wright and P. H. Stauffer. U.S. Geological Survey, Washington D.C.

Holmes, T. 1981. *The Hawaiian Canoe*. Editions Ltd. Press, Honolulu.

Holt, J. D. 1985. *The Art of Featherwork in Old Hawaii*. Topgallant Publications, Honolulu.

Hommon, R. J. [1980a]. Multiple Resources Nomination Form for Kahoʻolawe Archaeological Sites. National Register of Historic Places, Washington D.C.

[1980b]. Kahoʻolawe: Final report on the Archaeological Survey. Report, Hawaiʻi Marine Research, Inc. U.S. Navy, Pacific Division.

[1982]. Kahoʻolawe Archaeological Excavations 1981. Report, Science Management Inc. US Navy, Pacific Division.

1986. Social evolution in ancient Hawaiʻi. In *New Directions in Archaeology. Island Societies: Archaeological Approaches to Evolution and Transformation.*, edited by Patrick Kirch. Cambridge University Press, Cambridge.

Hornell, J. 1936. *The canoes of Polynesia, Fiji, and Micronesia*. B. P. Bishop Museum Special Publication 27.

Hunt, T. and R. M. Holsen. 1991. An early radiocarbon chronology for the Hawaiian Islands: A preliminary analysis. *Asian Perspectives* 30:148-161.

Jackson, D. D. 1985. Around the world in 1,392 days with the Navy's Wilkes-and his 'scientifics'. *Smithsonian* 18:4--64.

Johnson, R. K. [1983]. Information Transfer and Technology (In Ancient Hawaii). Paper presented at Triconference, Hawaii-Alaska Librarians.

Judd, A. F. 1904. Rock carvings of Hawaii: Some possible tracing of prehistoric Hawaiian. *Thrum's Hawaiian Annual for 1904*:179-194.

Kahananui, D. M. 1962. *Music of ancient Hawaiʻi*, Honolulu.

Kamakau, S. M. 1870. *"Moolelo Hawaii" Ke Au Okoa, 1869-1871*. B. P. Bishop Museum.

1964. *Ka Poʻe Kahiko: The people of old*. B. P. Bishop Museum Special Publication, Honolulu.

Kanehele, G. 1986. *Ku Kanaka*. University of Hawaiʻi Press, Honolulu.

Kelly, M. and D. Barrere. 1980. *Background history of the Kona Area, Island of Hawaiʻi*. Department of Anthropology, B. P. Bishop Museum.

Kepelino, S. 1931. *Traditions of Hawaiʻi*. B. P. Bishop Museum Bulletin, Honolulu.

Kikuchi, W. K. [1963]. Archaeological survey and excavations on the island of Kauai, Kona District, Hawaiian Islands. Typescript, Committee for the preservation of Hawaiian Culture.

1994. Ka pae kiʻi mahu o wailua: The petroglyphs of Wailua, Distict of Lihuʻe, Island of Kauaʻi. *Rapa Nui Journal* 8:27-32.

King, J. n.d. Maritime History of Hawaiʻi. Hamilton Library, Microfilm, University of Hawaiʻi, Honolulu.

Kirch, P. V. [1973]. Archaeological Reconnaissance Survey of Kalahuipuaʻa and portions of Wailoloa, Lalamilo, and Aneaehoʻomalu, South Kohala, Hawaiʻi Island. Report, Dept. of Anthropology, B. P. Bishop Museum.

1979. Marine exploitation in prehistoric Hawaiʻi: Archaeological excavations at Kakanuipuaʻa, Hawaii Island. *Anthropological Records* 29.

1984. *The Evolution of the Polynesian Chiefdoms*. Cambridge University Press, Cambridge.

1985. *Feathered Gods and Fishhooks. An Introduction to Hawaiian Archaeology and Prehistory*. University of Hawaii Press, Honolulu.

Knipe, R. 1989. *The Water of Life*. University of Hawaii Press, Honolulu.

Knudsen, E. 1945. *Hawaiian Tales*. Coca Cola Bottling Company, Honolulu.

1946. *Teller of Hawaiian Tales*. Mutual Publishing Co., Honolulu.

Krauss, B. 1988. *Keneti: South Seas Adventures of Kenneth Emory*. University of Hawaii Press, Honolulu.

Kreuzer, G. and M. Dunn. 1982. *Die Felsbilder Neuseelands*. Franz Steiner Verlag, Weisbaden.

Kuykendall, R. S. 1938. *The Hawaiian Kingdom 1778-1854*. University of Hawaii Press, Honolulu.

Kwaitkowski, P. F. 1991. *Na Kiʻi Pohaku: A Hawaiian Petroglyph Primer*. Ku Paʻa, Honolulu.

Ladefoged, T., G. F. Somers and M. M. Lane-Hamasaki. [1987]. Settlement Pattern Analysis of a Portion of Hawaii Volcanoes National Park. Report, Western Archaeological and Conservation Center, U.S. Department of the Interior.

Lawrence, D. H. 1964. *Studies in classic American literature*. Heinemann, London.

Lee, G. 1989. The petroglyphs of Puakō, Hawaii. *Rapa Nui Journal* 3:4-6.

1991. Lost Islands Cruise. *Rapa Nui Journal* 5:51-55.

1992. *The Rock Art of Easter Island: Symbols of Power, Prayers to the Gods*. Institute of Archaeology, UCLA, Los Angeles.

1995. Wahi Pana o Hawai'i Nei: Sacred sites in Hawai'i. *Rapa Nui Journal* 9:47-54.

1996. Rock Art of Polynesia. In *Rock Art Studies, News of the World I*, edited by P. G. Bahn and A. Fossati, pp. 163-172. Oxbow Monograph, Oxford.

1997. Petroglyph motif distribution in East Polynesia. *Rapa Nui Journal* 11:5-9.

1998. Function and Form: A study of petroglyphs at Pu'uloa, Hawai'i. In *Easter Island in Pacific Context: South Seas Symposium.*. C. M. Stevenson, G. Lee and F. J. Morin, eds. Pp. 240-245. Easter Island Foundation, Los Osos, California.

[1988]. The petroglyphs of Lanai, Hawaii. Report, Castle and Cooke.

[1989] .The petroglyphs of Puakō, Hawaii. Report, Historic Sites Section, Department of Land and Natural Resources, State of Hawaii.

[1990]. The Kāeo Trail petroglyphs, Puakō Hawaii. Report, Historic Sites Section, Department of Land and Natural Resources, State of Hawai'i.

[1993]. The petroglyphs of Pu'uloa (HV-225) Hawai'i Volcanoes National Park. Report, National Park Service, Hawaii Volcanoes National Park and Historic Sites Section, Department of Land and Natural Resources, State of Hawai'i.

[1997]. The Petroglyph Sites at Puakō, South Kohala, Island of Hawai'i. Report, Mauna Lani Resorts; Historic Sites Section, Dept. Of Land and Natural Resources; and County Planning Dept., Hawai'i Island.

[Lee, G.] 1996. Vandalism report, Hawai'i Island. *Rapa Nui Journal* 10:62.

Lyman, C. S. 1924. *Around the Horn to the Sandwich Islands and California-1945-1850*, New Haven.

Maguire, E. D. 1966. *Kona Legends*. Petroglyph Press, Hilo.

Malo, D. 1951. *Hawaiian Antiquities*. B. P. Bishop Museum Special Publication 2.

Marshack, A. 1972. *The Roots of Civilization*. McGraw-Hill, New York.

Masse, W. B. and H. D. Tuggle. 1998. The date of Hawaiian colonization. In *Easter Island in Pacific Context: South Seas Symposium.*. C. M. Stevenson, G. Lee and F. J. Morin, eds. Pp. 229-235. Easter Island Foundation, Los Osos, California.

McAllister, J. G. 1933a. *Archaeology of Oahu*. B. P. Bishop Museum Special Publication 104.

1933b *Archaeology of Kaho'olawe*. B. P. Bishop Museum Bulletin 115.

McBride, L. R. 1969. *Petroglyphs of Hawaii*. Petroglyph Press, Hilo.

McCoy, P. C. 1978. The Place of Near-Shore Islets in Easter Island Prehistory. *Journal of the Polynesian Society* 87:193-214.

Menzies, A. 1920. *Hawaii nei 128 years ago*. The New Freedom Press, Honolulu.

Métraux, A. 1971. *Ethnology of Easter Island*. B. P. Bishop Museum Special Publication 160.

Millerstrom, S. 1990. Rock art of Marquesas Islands, French Polynesia: A case study of Hatiheu Valley, Nuku Hiva. Masters Thesis, San Francisco State University.

1998. Archaeological art on Mo'orea, French Polynesia: An Overview. *Rapa Nui Journal* 12:35-39.

[1985] Project in Marquesas Islands. Report, Dept. of Archaeology, Tahiti.

[1994] Carved rock images: A source for studying long-distance and inter-island voyaging. Paper presented at The Chacmool Conference, Dept. of Archaeology, University of Calgary, Canada, 10-13 November, 1994.

Nobbs, M. F. and R. I. Dorn. 1993. New surface exposure ages for petroglyphs from the Olary Province, South Australia. *Archaeology in Oceania* 18:18-39.

Pacific Anthropological Records, 15. 1971. B. P. Bishop Museum

Poignant, R. 1967. *Oceanic Mythology*. Paul Hamlyn, London.

Pukui, M. K. 1942. *Hawaiian beliefs and customs during birth, infancy, and childhood*. B.P. Bishop Museum Occasional Paper 16:356-381.

1951. *How the Gods Made People. The Water Of Kane*. Kamehameha School Press, Honolulu.

1972. *Nana i Ke Kuma*, Vol. 1. Hui Hanai. Queen Lilikokalani Children's Center.

1979. *Nana i Ke Kuma*, Vol. 2. Hui Hanai. Queen Lilikokalani Children's Center.

Pukui, M. K. 1983. *'Olelo no'eau (Hawaiian proverbs and poetical sayings)*. B. P. Bishop Museum Special Publication 71.

Pukui, M. K., E.W. Haertig and C.A. Lee. 1983. *Nana i ke Kumu (Look to the Source)*. Hui Hanai, Honolulu.

Pukui, M. K., and S. H. Elbert. 1986. *Hawaiian-English Dictionary*. University of Hawaii Press, Honolulu.

Reeve, R. [1992] Na Wahi Pana o Kaho'olawe. Report, Kaho'olawe Conveyance Commission.

Report of the Puako Petroglyph Field in the Proposed State Historic Petroglyph Park, Puako, South Kohala. 1964. Manuscript, Bernice P. Bishop Museum, Honolulu.

Rolett, B. 1986. Turtles, priests, and the afterworld: A study in the iconographic interpretation of Polynesian petroglyphs. In *Island Societies*, P. V. Kirch, ed. Pp. 78-87. Cambridge University Press, London.

Rose, R., S. Conant and E. P. Kjellgren. 1993. Hawaiian standing kahili in the Bishop Musuem: an ethnological and biological analysis. *Journal of the Polynesian Society* 102:273-304.

Rosenfeld, A. and C. Smith. 1997. Recent developments in radiocarbon and stylistic methods of dating rock-art. *Antiquity* 71:405-411.

Routledge, K. 1919. *The Mystery of Easter Island*. Hazel, Watson and Viney, London.

Schuster, C. and E. Carpenter. 1996. *Patterns that Connect. Social Symbolism in Ancient and Tribal Art*. Harry N. Abrams, Inc., New York.

Sinoto, Y. 1966. A tentative prehistoric cultural sequence in the Northern Marquesas Islands, French Polynesia. *Journal of the Polynesian Society* 75:286-303.

Smart, C. D. [1964]. A report of excavations on Site H22, Puako, Hawaii Island. B. P. Bishop Museum Library.

[1965]. The Archaeological resources of the Hawaii Volcanoes National Park, Part 1: An archaeological survey of parts of Hawaii Volcanoes National Park, Hawaii. Report, B. P. Bishop Museum.

Smith, C. S. 1965. The burial complex on the island of Rapa Iti. In *Reports of the Norwegian Archaeologucal Expedition to Easter Island and the East Pacific*, T. Heyerdahl and E. N. Ferdon Jr., eds. Pp. 89-96. Allen and Unwin, London.

Soehren, L. J. [1963]. Archaeology and history in Kaupulehu and Makalawena, Kona, Hawaii. Typescript, B. P. Bishop Museum.

Soehren, L. J. and T. S. Newman. [1968]. Archaeology of Kealakekua Bay. Report, Department of Anthropology, B. P. Bishop Museum.

Stasack, E. and G. Lee. 1992. The Ka'upulehu Petroglyph Site, Hawai'i. *Rapa Nui Journal* 6:82-87.

[1993]. Petroglyphs of Kaho'olawe. Report, Kaho'olawe Conveyance Commission.

Stasack, E., R. I. Dorn and G. Lee. 1996. First Direct 14 C Ages on Hawaiian Petroglyphs. *Asian Perspectives* 35:51-72.

Stasack, E. and D. S. Stasack [1997] Petroglyph Recording Project, Cave HV-76 (State Site No. 50-10-62-750). Keahou, Puna-Ka'u Historic District. Report: Hawai'i Volcanoes National Park, Hawai'i.

Stearns, H. T. 1940. Geology and ground water resources of the islands of Lana'i and Kaho'olawe, Hawaii. *Division of Hydrography Bulletin* 6.

Steinbring, J. and G. Granzberg. 1986. Ideological and cosmological inferences from North American rock art: an exploratory discussion. *Rock Art Papers* 3:207-220.

Stokes, J. F. G. 1908. Stone sculpturing in relief from the Hawaiian Islands. *B. P. Bishop Museum Occasional Paper* 4:121-132.

1910. Notes on Hawaiian petroglyphs. *B. P. Bishop Museum Occasional Paper* 4:31-42.

1991. *Heiau of the Island of Hawaii: An Historical Survey of Native Hawaiian Temple Sites*. B. P. Bishop Museum Press, Honolulu.

Streck, C. F., Jr. [1980]. Kaho'olawe Site 669, National Register of Historic Places Inventory/Nomination Form.

Stuiver, M. and P. J. Reimer. 1993. Extended ^{14}C data base and revised calib 3.0 ^{14}C age calibration program. *Radiocarbon* 35:215-230.

Suggs, R. C. 1961. *The Archaeology of Nuku Hiva, Marquesas Islands, French Polynesia*. American Museum of Natural History, Anthropological Papers 49.

Summers, K. 1971. Molokai: a site survey. *Pacific Anthropological Records*. B. P. Bishop Museum, Honolulu.

Taylor, A. P. 1926. *Under Hawaiian Skies*. Advertiser Publishing Co., Honolulu.

Teilhet, J., ed. 1973. *Dimensions of Polynesia*. Fine Arts Gallery, San Diego.

Thrum, T. G. 1900. Interesting Hawaiian discoveries, more picture rocks. *Thrum's Hawaiian Annual for 1900* :126-128.

1923. More Hawaiian Folk Tales. *Thrum's Hawaiian Annual*.

Titcomb, M. 1969. *Dog and man in the ancient Pacific.* B. P. Bishop Museum Special Publication 59.

Tomonari-Tuggle, M. J. [1982]. An archaeological reconnaissance survey of a parcel adjoining the Puako petroglyph fields, Puako, Hawaii. Report, Waimea Hawaiian Civic Club and Mauna Lani Resort.

Tomonari-Tuggle, M. J. and L. A. Carter [1984]. Archaeological Mapping of the Kuhe'eia Bay Ranch Site, Kaho'olawe Island. State of Hawai'i, Historic Sites Section, Department of Land and Natural Resources, State of Hawai'i.

Trotter, M. and B. McCulloch. 1971. *Prehistoric rock art of New Zealand.* A.H. and A. W. Reed, Wellington.

Tuggle, H. D. [1962]. National Register of Historic Places Nomination Form. Puako, Hawaii.

[1990] Azubu Kona Resort: Historic Preservation Mitigation, Phase 1 Archaeological Investigations. Report Prepared for Belt Collins Associates. International Archaeological Research Institute, Inc. State of Hawai'i Historic Preservation Division.

Valeri, V. 1985. *Kingship and Sacrifice: Ritual Society in Ancient Hawaii.* University of Chicago Press, Chicago.

Vancouver, G. 1798. *A voyage of Discovery to the North Pacific Ocean and Round the World . . . performed in the years 1790-95.* G. G. & J. Robinson, London.

Walker, A. T. and P. H. Rosendahl. [1989] Archaeological Inventory Survey, Pu'uhonua Subdivision Development Parcel, Land of Kalaoa 5th, North Kona District, Island of Hawaii. Haseko (Hawaii), Inc.

Welch, D. J. [1984]. Archaeological reconnaissance of the area south of the Puako petroglyph archaeological district, South Kohala, Hawaii. Mauna Lani Resorts.

Westervelt, W. D. 1906. Picture rocks of Naalehu. *Thrum's Hawaiian Annual for 1906* :164-169.

1910. Legends of Maui-a demi god of Polynesia and of his mother Hina. In *Hawaiian Gazette*, Honolulu.

1915. *Legends of old Hawaii.* Ellis Press, Honolulu.

1963. Maui Stories. *Paradise of the Pacific* 75.

Whitney, S. 1994. Capturing the Ka'ai. *Honolulu Magazine*, November :68-71; 120-124.

Wilkes, C. 1861. *U.S. Exploring Expedition*, Philadelphia.

Williamson, R. W. 1924. *The Social and Political Systems of Central Polynesia.* Cambridge University Press, Cambridge.

Wise, J. H. 1965. The history of land ownership in Hawaii. In *Ancient Hawaiian Civilization*, E. S. C. Handy, ed. Pp. 81-93. Charles E. Tuttle Co., Vermont.

Wise, J. H. and H. P. Judd. 1968. The Hawaiian language. In *Ancient Hawaiian Civilization*, E. S. C. Handy, ed. Charles E. Tuttle Co., Vermont.